A Guide to Microsoft Excel 2002 for Business and Management

A Guide to Microsoft Excel 2002 for Business and Management

Second edition

Bernard V. Liengme

St. Francis Xavier University
Nova Scotia, Canada

BUTTERWORTH HEINEMANN

OXFORD AMSTERDAM BOSTON LONDON NEW YORK PARIS
SAN DIEGO SAN FRANCISCO SINGAPORE SYDNEY TOKYO

Butterworth-Heinemann
An imprint of Elsevier Science
Linacre House, Jordan Hill, Oxford OX2 8DP
225 Wildwood Avenue, Woburn, MA 01801-2041

First published 2000
Second edition 2002

British Library Cataloguing in Publication Data
A catalogue record for this book is available from the British Library

Library of Congress Cataloguing in Publication Data
A catalogue record for this book is available from the Library of Congress

ISBN 0 7506 5614 X

For information on all Butterworth-Heinemann publications
visit our website at www.bh.com

Printed and bound in Great Britain

Contents

Preface

It is arguable that the spreadsheet is the most widely used microcomputer application. Today the industry standard for spreadsheets is Microsoft Excel. This book is designed to show you how easy it is to take advantage of this important tool. It is written for the complete novice or the reader who has only a passing familiarity with Excel. Once you have mastered this *Guide* you will be able to make constructive use of Microsoft Excel in your workplace — be it your office or study room.

The approach is a series of step-by-step instructions leading to the required result. No assumptions about previous knowledge of Microsoft Excel or of business terminology are made. However, it is assumed that you have some familiarity with Windows or the Macintosh operating system. While this book shows screen captures from Microsoft's latest version, Excel 2002, users of Excel 2000 and Excel 97 should have no problems following the text and diagrams.

It is recommended that you start at the beginning and work through the book. Do not jump material even if you think you already understand the topic because there could be something new to you in the exercise. Please try the problems at the end of each chapter. Using the Microsoft Excel Help feature while tackling the problems is not considered cheating! Answers to the starred problems are given at the back of the book to encourage this process.

The *Guide* may be used either as a textbook or for independent study and it is hoped that even professionals will find that their knowledge of Excel will increase to such an extent that they will be able to solve one-off problems with ease.

A few topics are not covered in this book. While there is a chapter on working with lists, the database functions are not introduced. Likewise the application of Excel to statistical problems is not explored. These subjects are covered in more advanced books. We do not look at Visual Basic for Applications since this is an advanced topic.

I recommend that the information available on the Internet for Excel be fully explored. There are a number of useful websites maintained by Microsoft Excel experts. Newsgroups and list servers can be used in two ways: you can simply read the messages and learn from others' questions and answers, or you can submit your own questions. Visit my website to see an up-to-date list of addresses for these resources.

The first edition of this book was published by Arnold and I remain indebted to Nicki Dennis and Matthew Flynn, who were most helpful to me. My most sincere thanks go to Ms Rachel Hudson of Butterworth-Heinemann for her invaluable assistance. My wife, Pauline, has been a tower of strength and a wonderful support. To her: many thanks and all my love.

We have tried to ensure that this book is as error-free as we can make it, but you can be sure that some, hopefully minor, will have crept in. If you do find any, please let me know by e-mail and I will post a correction on my web page.

I hope you will enjoy learning Microsoft Excel.

Bernard V. Liengme — e-mail: bliengme@stfx.ca
January 2002 — www.stfx.ca/people/bliengme

Conventions used in this book

Information boxes in the left margin are used to convey additional information, tips, shortcuts, etc.

Information box: Boxes like this contain additional information, shortcuts, etc.

Data which the user is expect to type is displayed in a monospaced font. This avoids the problems of using quotes. For example: in cell A1 enter the text Office budget.

Non-printing keys are shown as graphics. For example, rather than asking the reader to press the Control and Home keys, we use text such as: press Ctrl+Home. When two keys are shown separated by +, the user must hold down the first key while tapping the second.

The Save tool

New to Excel 2002

Generally when a new reference is made to a button on a toolbar, a graphic of the icon is shown in the left column. New features in Microsoft Excel 2002 are flagged with an Excel icon in the left margin.

Website: www.bh.com/companions/075065614X

In the Problems section of each chapter, an asterisk against a problem number indicates that it is answered in Appendix B. Excel files for answered problems and additional files may be found at: www.bh.com/companions/075065614X.

1
The Microsoft® Excel Window

Objectives

Upon conclusion of this chapter, you will:

- be familiar with the parts of a Microsoft Excel screen;
- know how to make cell entries;
- be able to edit cell entries;
- make use of the Help facility.

What is Excel?

The first really successful application for personal computers was a spreadsheet program called Visicalc which evolved into Lotus 1-2-3. Later Microsoft introduced Excel which has become the *de facto* industry standard.

The electronic spreadsheet was designed to replace the green ruled ledger sheets once beloved by accountants and bookkeepers. The idea was to replace the drudgery of keeping such things up to date. Over the years the spreadsheet has taken on a life of its own and become an indispensable application for anyone who works with numbers in the business world.

Versions of Excel

In recent years Microsoft has released a number of upgrades to its Office suite of business applications. The latest of these is called Microsoft Office XP. The spreadsheet component of Office XP is called Excel 2002.

This book refers to the newest version but most of the information is applicable to the last three versions: Excel 97, 2000 and 2002. Users of Excel 95 should be able to follow the text but will find their screens somewhat different from those shown here; the Chart Wizard in particular is quite different. It should be noted that the file formats are the same for Excel 97, 2000 and 2002 and that these versions can open files in older Excel formats.

Exercise 1: Anatomy of the Workspace

When we approach a new task, we need to become familiar with our surroundings. So we will look at the Microsoft Excel window and learn some terminology. Begin by starting Excel. If you are using Excel 2002, your screen will look similar to that in Figure

1.1. It may not be identical because the user can customize the toolbars. The screens in other versions are slightly different but the concepts introduced here are common to all versions.

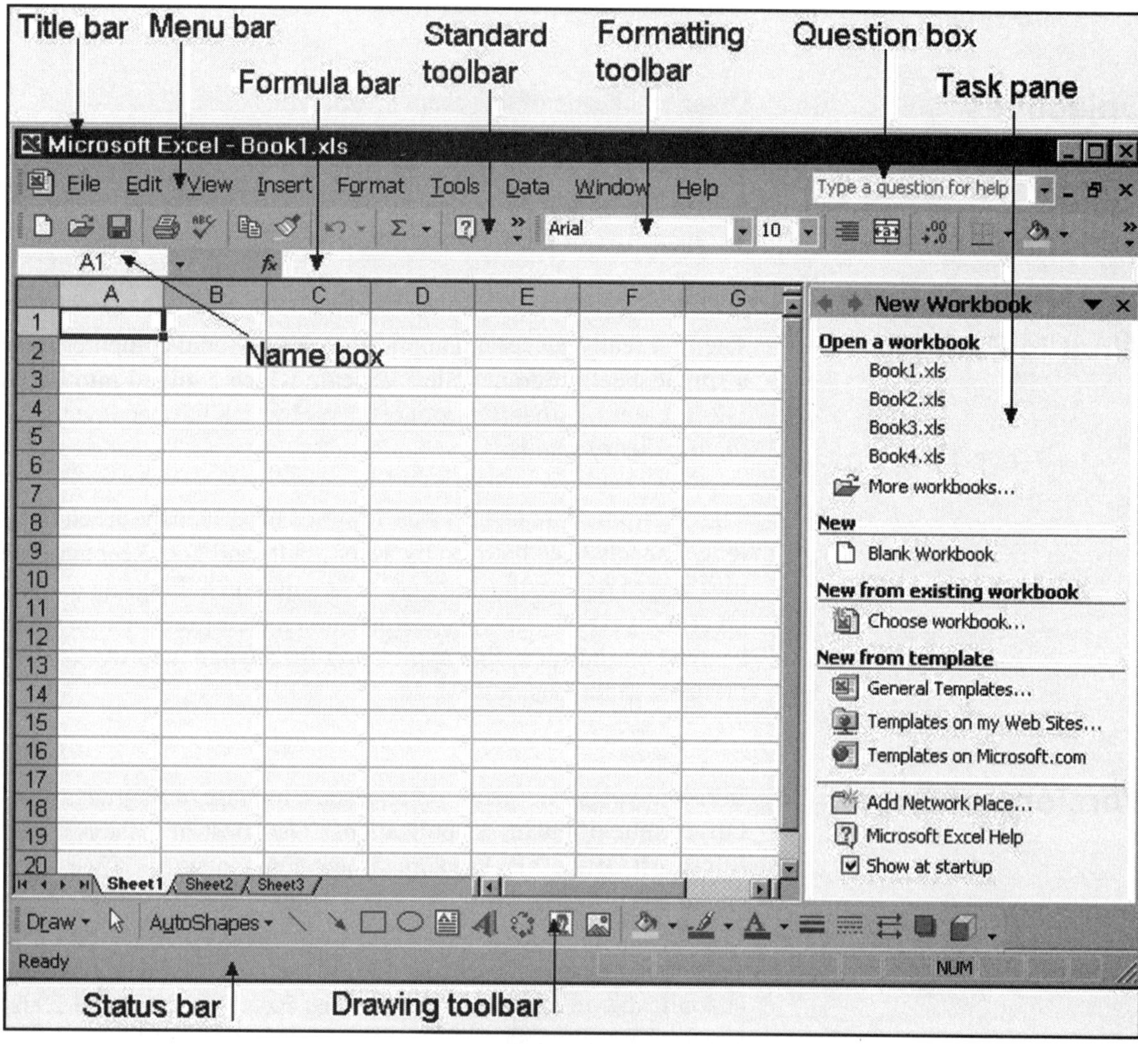

Figure 1.1

It is convenient to divide the screen into these main parts: title bar, menu bar, toolbars, formula bar, worksheet window, status bar and task pane. You should be familiar with the first three areas from using other applications, so they will be described only briefly.

Title bar

On starting Excel, we have opened a new *workbook*. Because we have not yet saved our work, Excel has given this the default name of *Book1* or, with a Macintosh, *Workbook1*. To the far right of the title bar you will see three tools that minimize, restore/maximize and close the Excel application. If these are new to you, you may wish to experiment. The same tools are available by clicking the Excel icon on the left of the title bar.

Menu bar

The menu bar provides the user with one way to access the Microsoft Excel *commands*. Commands are actions you perform on your worksheet. Examples are: saving your work to a file, printing a worksheet, changing the appearance of some text, etc.

New to Excel 2002

To the right of the menu items is a new Excel 2002 feature called the *Ask a Question Box* which we explore in Exercise 5. To the far right are the three tools to minimize, restore/maximize, or close a workbook. Note that the same tools on the title bar operate on the Excel application while those on the menu bar operate on a single workbook. With this in mind, you should be able to predict the purpose of the Excel icon at the far left of the menu bar.

Toolbars

Toolbars are another, more intuitive and quicker method of accessing commands. Excel has a number of toolbars. The complete list can be seen by click the View item on the menu and selecting Toolbars for the subsequent menu. The menu can be used to select which toolbars are to be permanently displayed. Most people configure Excel to display at least the Standard and the Formatting toolbars when the application is first started. These can be on either a single row (as in Figure 1.1) or as two separate rows — see Exercise 5.

Shortcuts: The shortcut letters of menu items are shown underlined as in *View*.

The Excel from which Figure 1.1 was made had been customized to show the Drawing toolbar at the bottom of the window. This is very useful for annotating worksheets. Windows often provides more than one way to accomplish a task. Another way to change which toolbars are on display is to right click on any toolbar.

In Exercise 5 we see how to become familiar with the purpose of the various toolbar buttons.

Formula bar

We will examine this more closely in a later chapter. For now, click the mouse in several places within the worksheet window and watch the information change in the *Name box* or *Reference box* which is the lefthand part of the formula bar.

Worksheet window

This is the central part of your work. It is here that you will type data and perform calculations. Note how the main part of the space is ruled horizontally and vertically by *gridlines*, dividing the space into *rows* and *columns*. The smallest unit of space, where a row and a column intersect, is called a *cell*. At the top of the worksheet are the 256 *column headings* starting with A and ending with IV. To the left are the *row headings* numbered 1 to 65,536. How many cells are there on a single worksheet?

Note: It is unlikely that your PC has sufficient memory to allow you to fill every cell in a single worksheet.

Figure 1.1 shows only part of one of the *worksheets* which makes up your *workbook*. To the far right, and at the bottom of the workspace, you will see the vertical and horizontal *scroll bars*. You can use these bars and their associated navigation arrows to *view* other parts of the worksheet. At any given time, one cell in the worksheet is the *active cell* — this is the cell which will accept any data you type on the keyboard. When a new workbook is opened the top lefthand cell (it is referred to as A1) is the active cell. To select a new active cell you can: (a) use the keyboard arrow keys ↑, ↓, ← or →; (b) use the Tab key or the combination of Shift+Tab; or (c) simply click the mouse on the required cell. You are encouraged to experiment with these methods. There is a handy, quick way to return to cell A1: use the combination Ctrl+Home. Other shortcuts are introduced later.

Keyboard shortcuts: To execute a command such as Ctrl+Home, hold down the first key and tap the second one before releasing the first.

At the bottom of the window are the *sheet tabs* which give you access to the other worksheets. By default, Excel 5 and 95 open new workbooks with 16 worksheets while later versions start with three. It is possible that your copy of Excel has been configured to give fewer and hence save memory. We may delete or add extra worksheets to a maximum of 255 — if your computer has sufficient memory. Later on we will see another type of sheet, the *chart sheet.*

We can switch from one sheet to another by clicking on a sheet tab. Click on the Sheet2 tab to make Sheet2 the active sheet. Here are some experiments for you to try: right click on the Sheet2 tab and learn how to change its name. Drag your newly named tab to the left so that it becomes the first worksheet. Right click on any sheet tab and use *Insert|Worksheet* or use the Menu command Insert Worksheet to add a new worksheet to your workbook.

Status bar

The status bar provides information. To the left is the *message area.* If your mouse pointer is within the workbook area, this should be showing the word *Ready*. To the right are some sculptured boxes called the *Keyboard indicators*. Press the CapsLock key a few times and watch the text 'CAPS' appear and disappear. In Exercise 6 we look at the AutoCalculate feature on the status bar.

Finally, we will close the workbook. The quickest way is to click on the top, right hand close icon (✕). This closes all open workbooks and then closes Microsoft Excel. You will be presented with a dialog box asking if you wish to save the workbook. We have not created anything worth saving, so click on the No button.

New to Excel 2002

Task pane
This is a new feature in Excel 2002. It provides no new functionality but is designed to give the user quick access to frequently performed operations. Some users may find it helpful, others will think it takes up valuable worksheet space. To the right of the task pane title bar is the symbol ✕ which may be used to close the pane. To redisplay it, right click on the menu or toolbar and click *Task pane* to put a check mark beside its name.

Exercise 2: Making Cell Entries

Note: Cell *reference* is the correct term to use when speaking about, for example, A1 or G20. You may find books that use the term cell *address*. However, this is a term that is never used in Microsoft documentation. It was used by Lotus 1-2-3, a spreadsheet application that preceded Microsoft Excel. Surprisingly, Excel does have a worksheet function called ADDRESS that returns a cell reference! Do not use the term *name* in place of *reference*; in Chapter 3 we will learn that this term has a very specific use in Excel.

Clearly, we need a way to refer to a specific cell on the worksheet. We have seen that a cell occurs at the intersection of a column and a row. To refer to a specific cell we use a *cell reference.* This is a combination of the column heading and the row number. The cell at the top left, which is at the intersection of column A and row 1, has a cell address of A1. The cell below is A2 while the cell to the right is B1. This method of naming cells using the column letter is called the A1 method. There is another method in which the column letter is converted to a number; this is called the R1C1 method since the top left cell has the address R1C1 using this method. We shall not explore this topic.

As we will see later, a workbook may have more than one worksheet. Sometimes we need to refer to a cell in another sheet. Suppose that within Sheet1 we wish to refer to the cell M5 in Sheet2. We can do this by combining the sheet name and the cell address separated by an exclamation mark. In the example, we would use Sheet2!M5 as the cell address.

In this exercise you will learn how to make and edit cell entries. We will meet different types of entries including *numbers*, *text* and *formulas.* At the end of this budgeting exercise, your worksheet should resemble that in Figure 1.2.

(a) Open Microsoft Excel to begin this exercise on a new workbook.

(b) We wish to enter some data into cell A1 so this needs to be the *active cell*. The active cell has a box, called the *cell selector*, around it. Note how the shading of the A column heading and the 1 row heading now stands out from the other headings — the exact effect will depend on your Windows screen settings. Furthermore, the Name box of the formula bar (it is just above the A column heading, see Figure 1.3) displays the address of the active cell. If A1 is not the active cell, the quickest way to make it so is to press Ctrl+Home.

	A	B	C	D
1	Office furniture calculation			
2	Item	Cost	Quantity	Extension
3	Desk	234.56	2	469.12
4	Chair	75.43	6	452.58
5	Coat rack	45.67	1	45.67
6	Total			967.37

Figure 1.2

(c) With A1 as the active cell, type Office Furniture calculation and then press the Enter key to complete the entry. Pressing Enter moves the cell selector down one row so the active cell becomes A2. If you make a typing error, continue, as we will see how to make corrections later. Enter the word Item in A2 and press Enter once more to move to A3.

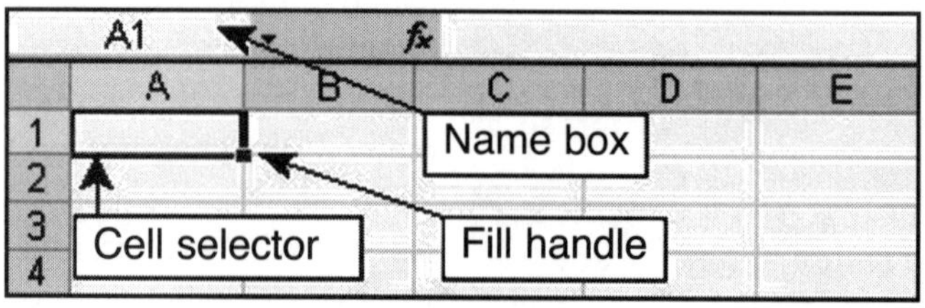

Figure 1.3

(d) Enter the text in the rest of column A in the same way.

(e) Use the keys ↑ and → to make B2 the active cell. In B2 type Cost and press the → to complete the entry. This demonstrates a second method of completing an entry — using an arrow key. In this case we used the right arrow to take us to C2.

(f) Type Quantity in C2 and complete the entry by pressing [Tab]. This third method of completing an entry makes the new active cell one to the right of the current one. So we are now in D2 where we need to type Extension.

(g) Now that you know how to navigate the workspace, enter the numeric values shown in the range B3:C5. A *range* is a rectangular block of cells. Hopefully your PC is set up to allow you to use the numeric keypad to enter numbers. Check that the message area of the status bar displays NUM. If not, press the [NumLock] key which is generally at the top of the numeric keypad.

(h) We are now ready to enter a *formula* in D3. We need the product of the unit cost and the number of items. A formula begins with the = symbol. In D3 enter =B3*C3 where the asterisk is the multiplication operator. As you type the formula note how Excel places coloured boxes (*range finders*) around the cells referred to in your formula and how the cell references in the formula are correspondingly coloured. This is illustrated in Figure 1.4. We have much more to say about formulas in later chapters. Note how the status bar displays *Enter* until you complete the formula.

Keyboard: To enter an asterisk, it is more convenient to use the [*] key on the numeric keypad rather than [Shift] [8]. All the arithmetic operators can be found in this one location.

Complete the entry by clicking on the Entry button (green check mark ✓) in the formula bar. This method of completing a cell entry does not alter the position of the active cell. You can see that the cell selector has remained around D3. Once the entry is complete, the cell displays the value 469.12 while the formula bar shows the formula =B3*C3. The cell contains the formula but displays the result.

Note: A formula can be entered with lower case letters for the cell references (as in Figure 1.4); Excel will automatically convert it to upper case when the entry is completed.

(i) Rather than typing formulas in D4 and D5, we shall copy the formula in D3 to D4 and D5. However, the process we shall use is not the normal Windows Copy and Paste but is an Excel feature called *AutoFill.*

In step (a) we learnt that the box around the active cell is called the cell selector. The lower right corner of the cell selector is the *fill handle* — see Figure 1.3. Move the mouse until the pointer is over the fill handle. The pointer will change from a hollow cross to a solid cross. Now depress the left mouse button and drag until the range D3:D5 is selected. Release the mouse button. Click on cell D4 and note how the formula has been automatically adjusted to =B4*C4.

The Spell tool

(j) To calculate the total in D6, enter the formula =D3+D4+D5 and click on ✓in the formula bar. Later we shall learn how to use the AutoSum tool for summing ranges.

The Save tool

(k) You may wish to check the spelling in the worksheet. The quickest way is to click the Spell tool. You may also wish to locate the menu command Tools|Spelling or use the shortcut F7.

(l) Using either the Save tool (picture of a disk) or the menu command File|Save, save this workbook as CHAP1.XLS. You may find it convenient to create a new folder to hold the files you make when working with this book. It is suggested that you use the name CHAP1.XLS for this file.

Your worksheet should now be similar to that in Figure 1.2. Make B3 the active cell and type another value for the cost of a desk. Note how the values shown in cells D3 and D6 immediately change once you have completed the entry. Recall that a cell entry is completed when you (i) move to another cell by pressing Enter↵, Tab⭾ or any of the arrow keys →, ←, ↑ or ↓ or (ii) click the Enter icon (✓) on the formula bar. Do not get into the habit of clicking another cell to complete a cell entry; this can play havoc when you are entering or editing formulas!

We have entered three types of data: text, numbers and formulas. Note how text is left justified while numbers are displayed right justified. Later we will see how to change this justification.

We have learnt how to move around the worksheet using the mouse and the arrow keys. Before completing this exercise, take some time to explore how the scroll bars work and find what happens when you press PageDown and Page Up. Compare the effects with pressing these keys when the Alt key is held down. Remember that Ctrl+Home (for Macintosh users: ⌘+ home) will always return you to A1. With cell A1 as the active cell, see what Ctrl + ↓ does. Now try starting from A3 and then from A6. Return to A1 and find the effect of Ctrl + End. You may also wish to try Go To — either from the Edit menu or by using either F5 or Ctrl+G as a shortcut. Do not save the workbook if you make any changes.

Other ways of completing a range
In step (i) we dragged the fill handle to copy the formula from D3 to the two cells below it. We will now experiment with two other ways of completing a range.
1. Select the two cells D4:D5 and use [Delete] to clear the entries. Make D3 the active cell. We are now back to the start of step (i). This time double click on the fill handle. Excel fills the empty cells. This method works (i) with a empty column of cells that has data in a column immediately to the left or right of it, or (ii) to replace existing data in a column.
2. Delete the formulas in the three cells D3:D5. With the range still selected type =B3*C3 (this will be entered into D3). Complete the entries by holding down [Ctrl]+[Enter↵].

Exercise 3: Editing

In this exercise we learn a variety of ways to edit existing cell entries. We shall change row 2 of the worksheet created in the previous exercise so that it looks like Figure 1.5.

	A	B	C	D
1	Office furniture calculation			
2	Item	Unit cost	Number	Cost
3	Desk	234.56	2	469.12
4	Chair	75.43	6	452.58
5	Coat rack	45.67	1	45.67
6	Total			967.37

Figure 1.5

The File Open tool

(a) If you had a break after completing Exercise 2 you will need to open the file CHAP1.XLS using one of these techniques: click on the File| Open tool, use the menu command File|Open, open the File menu and select the file from the list of most recently used files or select the file name from the list of recently opened files in the task pane. The last two methods work only if you have not opened too many Excel files since you last used CHAP1.XLS.

The Undo tool

(b) We start by making a deliberate mistake. With cell A2 as the active cell, type Unit cost and press [Enter↵]. Oh dear! This was supposed to go in B2 not A2. Click the Undo tool and the original text is returned to A2.

Escape key: You can use [Esc] at any time when you say to yourself 'I wish I had not started this.'

(c) In step (b) we realized the error after we had completed the entry. In this step we see how to correct things when the error is recognized in midstream. Go back to A2 and type Unit but do not complete the entry. Now imagine you had done this in error and realized the mistake after typing the 't'. Simply press [Esc] and the new typing is removed. An alternative way of terminating an entry and leaving the cell in its original state is to click the Cancel button (✕) on the formula bar.

(d) Double click on B2. Notice how the bottom right corner of the cell selector is no longer a small square (the fill handle) but an inverted 'L'. You are now in edit mode; this is confirmed by the word *Edit* on the status bar. Within the cell there is a flashing I-beam shape known as the *insertion point*. Move the insertion point to the front of the 'C' and edit the cell content to read Unit cost. Complete the entry by pressing [Tab] which will move the active cell to C2.

(e) Make C2 the active cell and press [F2]. This is an alternative way to go from Ready mode to Edit mode. This time we will do the editing in the formula bar. Click the mouse inside the formula bar and select the word *Quantity* and type Number. When you type after selecting, the selected material is deleted.

(f) Next we will change the text in D2 from Extension to Cost. Make D2 the active cell and press [Delete]. Type Cost in the cell.

The File Save tool

(g) Save the workbook by clicking the Save tool.

Exercise 4: Select from the Menu

In this exercise we learn to find our way around the menu bar; we are introduced to terms such as *submenu* (or *cascading menu*) and *dialog box*; and we find that the [Esc] key really does let us escape.

Starting with Excel 2000, Microsoft introduced 'learning' menus and toolbars. When you first use Excel the menus and toolbars display only the most commonly used items. But Excel learns what commands you use most frequently and adjusts the menus and toolbars correspondingly. Read on to learn more.

(a) You may be wondering why some letters in the names of menu items are underlined. You can open a menu using this letter in association with the [Alt] key in place of clicking the mouse. To open the Edit menu, hold down [Alt] and press the [E] key. You can use either upper or lower case for shortcuts.

The menu will resemble that in Figure 1.6. There are a number of features to explain but most will be familiar from other Windows programs.

If you keep the menu open for about five seconds, it will display menu items that you use infrequently. Close the menu. The quickest way to exit a menu (or dialog box) that has been opened in error is press [Esc] — try it now.

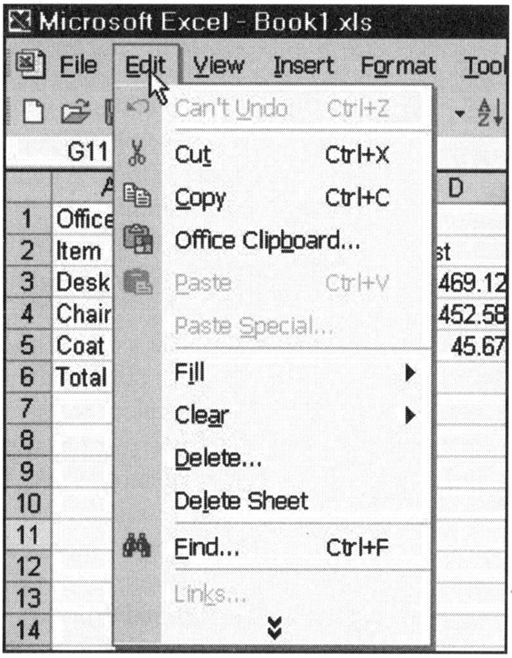

Figure 1.6

(b) Reopen the menu and note the downward pointing chevrons at the bottom. Click on this to more quickly display the full menu.

(c) In Figure 1.6 the first item *Can't Undo* is greyed out. This is because the user has performed no action since the file was last saved that can be undone. Any menu item that is greyed out is unavailable to use at that time.

(d) To the right of some items are icons. These are the toolbar shortcuts for the equivalent operation. Note, however, that not every icon on the menu is necessarily displayed on your currently used toolbars. As you use Excel more, you will find these keyboard shortcuts very convenient.

Some useful shortcuts:
Copy [Ctrl] + C
Cut [Ctrl] + X
Paste [Ctrl] + V

 Click this to expand a menu

(e) Note the triangle symbol (▸) to the right of, for example, the Fill and Clear items. When you open an item with this symbol, a *submenu* appears. Click on Clear to observe this. Use Esc to close the submenu.

(f) The word Find on the menu ends with an ellipse (three dots ...). A menu item with this always leads to a *dialog box*. Open the Find item and fill in the dialog box to locate the cell with the word 'coat'.

Exercise 5: Know Your Tools

In this exercise we will learn how to work with the toolbars. As with the menu, you will find the toolbars very similar to those in other Windows applications. Starting with Microsoft Office 2000, the Standard and Formatting toolbars are by default displayed on one row but this can be changed. We will also see how to adjust the space each toolbar uses when one row is used.

 The What's This tool

(a) The icons on the toolbars were chosen to be self-explanatory but some may initially be confusing. If you let the mouse pointer hover over an icon for a few seconds, a small information label (a Screen Tip) is displayed. To see this, place the mouse over the icon depicting a disk and pause; a Screen Tip reading 'Save' is displayed. Should the Screen Tip be too cryptic, more help is available. Press ⇧Shift+F1 to change the cursor to an arrow with a question mark. With this cursor showing, click the disk icon. This time a more detailed Screen Tip is displayed. The Help cursor then disappears; it must be called up again if you wish to check another tool.

 Click this to Expand a toolbar

(b) With two toolbars displayed on one row it is not possible for every tool to be visible. You may prefer to have the toolbars on separate rows. Locate the Toolbar Options icon; look for a right pointing chevron with a downward pointing triangle just to the left of the font name which is most likely Arial. Remember to let the cursor linger over things so that the Screen Tips display. Click on the icon to open the Toolbar Options menu and select Show Button on Two Rows.

When the toolbars are on separate rows, the Toolbar Options icon is the downward pointing triangle at the far right of each. Use this to open a menu from which to reset Excel to display the toolbars on one row.

(c) When the toolbars are sharing a row, you can open the Toolbar Options menu to display more buttons. Click on any one of these previously hidden buttons (you can always use [Esc] to end any operation this may start); e.g. the Cut tool (pair of scissors), if it is one of the previously hidden buttons. Note that the tool is now one of the unhidden buttons.

(d) Finally, with the toolbars sharing a row, again locate the Toolbar Options icon. Just to its right is a set of small horizontal lines. Drag this left and right to change how the two toolbars share the row.

Exercise 6: Getting Help

No matter how competent you become with Excel, there will be times when you ask yourself 'How do I ... ?' Often the quickest way to get the answer is using the Microsoft Excel on-line help facility. For this exercise we will find the answer to the question 'How do I put a box around one or more cells?'

The Help tool

(a) Click on the Help item on the menu bar or on the toolbar. The dialog box that pops up has three or four tabs. If a so-called assistant (a comic figure) appears, click on the Option button and in the resulting dialog box uncheck the first item: Use Office Assistant. This creature is totally unnecessary in Excel 2002. Now use the Help menu or toolbar item again. The Help facility should open up and resemble Figure 1.7.

(b) If only one pane is visible, click the second tool (Show/Hide) under the Help title bar. If it is not already open, click on the Answer Wizard tab. Type in the 'What would you like to do box' *How do I draw a box around a cell.* Either press [Enter ↵] or use the Search button to complete the question.

In this case there is only one item in the *Select topics* area. When there are more results use the mouse to make a selection.

(c) In the right pane your question is answered. From this we learn that Excel speaks about *borders* not boxes — these are items made with the Drawing toolbar.

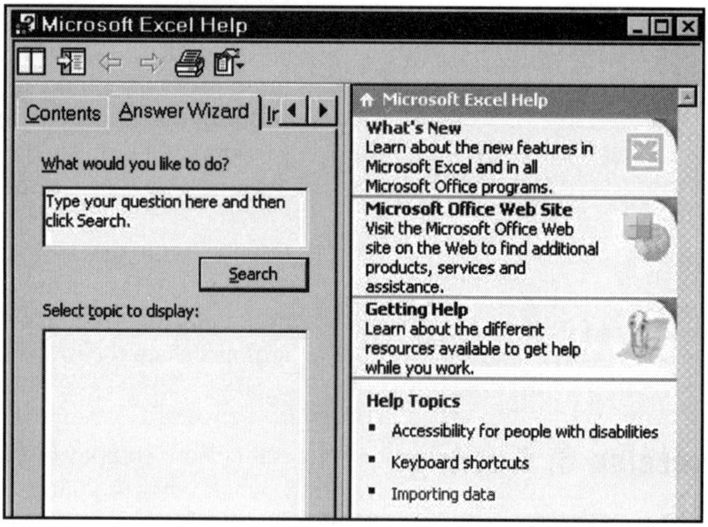

Figure 1.7

(d) Open the Contents tab to become familiar with what it offers you. Later you may wish to use the Index tab when searching for help but generally the Answer Wizard is best. Close the Help facility by clicking the X in its title bar.

(e) With Excel 2002 there is a shortcut to getting the Answer Wizard — type the question in the Ask a Question box on the menu bar! Before you rush to try this think how the Answer Wizard must work. It cannot understand the question; it must use key words. So let us phrase our question with what we think are the keywords. If you type *draw box* in the Ask a Question box and press Enter, Excel displays a list of possible topics. Most of these relate to the Drawing tool but one of them is *Apply or remove cell borders.*

Exercise 7: The AutoCalculate Feature

Sometimes you need to know a property of a set of numbers (for example: the sum, how many, what is the largest, etc.) in a hurry but do not need the value to appear on the worksheet. The AutoCalculate feature was designed for just such an occasion.

(a) Open CHAP1.XLS using the File menu. If you recently saved this file, its name will appear in the Most Recently Used List (MRL) at the bottom of the menu. Otherwise, you will need to use the Open command.

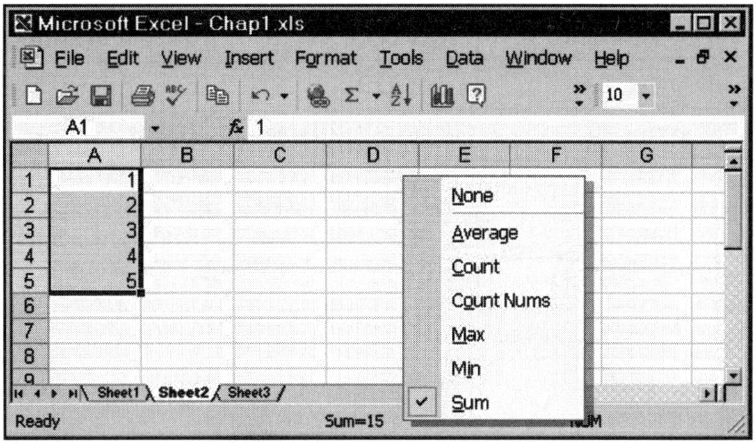

Figure 1.8

(b) Open Sheet2 by clicking on its tab and type the series 1, 2, 3, 4, 5 in column A. Using the mouse, select the range A1:A5.

(c) On the status bar you will see *Sum = 15*. Microsoft Excel has summed the selected range.

(d) Right click anywhere on the status bar to bring up the menu (see Figure 1.8) from which you may select other quantities such as Max, Min or Count.

(e) Replace one of the numbers in A1:A5 with some text. Experiment to find the difference between AutoCalculate's Count and Count Nums.

Summary

The material in this chapter lays the foundation for the rest of the book. The reader is encouraged to read through it a second time if the material was new. It is important that you feel comfortable with the Microsoft Excel interface. Do not hesitate to experiment; you will not damage the PC if you make a mistake!

The concepts of *cell range* and *cell address* should now be familiar to you. You should understand instructions such as 'Make D5 the active cell', 'Select the range A1:C4' and 'Click on the Bold tool'.

There are a number of ways of moving around or *navigating* the worksheet: clicking the mouse, using the scroll bars, and using keystrokes. Figure 1.9 lists the navigational keystrokes.

Target location	Keystroke	Target location	Keystroke
Cell to the right	→ or Tab	Lower right of active area	Ctrl+End
Cell to the left	← or Shift+Tab	Down one screen	PageDown
Cell below	↓ or Enter	Up one screen	PgUp
Cell above	↑ or Shift+Enter	Right one screen	Alt+PageDown
Top left cell (A1)	Ctrl+Home	Left one screen	Alt+PgUp
Bottom cell in a range	End+↓	Top cell in a range	End+↑
Far right cell in a range	End+→	Far left cell in a range	End+←

Figure 1.9

Data is entered into the *active* cell. We can change existing data. Typing in a cell will replace any existing data. Pressing Delete will delete the contents of the active cell or of a selected range. The last change made in a worksheet (over typing an existing entry, deleting the content of a cell, etc.) can usually be undone with either the menu command Edit|Undo or the Undo tool. The Esc key will terminate the current activity — if we are midway through typing in a cell and wish we had not started, this key will return us to the status quo, or if we mistakenly open a menu, it will close it.

There are a number of help facilities. The most elementary are the Screen Tips. The menu command Help gives us access to an on-line manual which has an index. In addition, there is the Answer Wizard or the Assistant for a user-friendly solution. We can also get help from the Web.

Problems

1. Use the Help command to find how to hide a worksheet.

2. Open the workbook you saved in Exercise 2. Can you make the table look more interesting? Some suggestions: display the items in row 2 in italic; right align the text in B2:D2; put a border under row 5; and display D6 in a different colour.

3 In C7 of the worksheet of Exercise 2, enter Tax and in D7 enter the formula =0.1*D6 to compute the sales tax at 10%. In row 8 add entries for a grand total. Oh dear, D7 displays 96.737. Select D7:D8 and see if you can find a tool that will cause the values to be displayed rounded to two decimal places.

4. Design a worksheet in which you list all your fixed monthly expenses (food, travel, rent/mortgage, phone, etc.) and total these. In another cell enter your after-tax monthly income. Finally compute your discretionary income. Hint: suppose you spend 3.25 a day on travel; you can enter =3.25*28 to compute the total travel expenses for 28 working days.

5. Did you spell everything correctly in Problem 4? Find two ways to have Microsoft Excel spell-check a worksheet.

2
Formulas and Formats

Objectives

Upon completion of this chapter you will:

- be able to construct formulas using the arithmetic operators: +, −, *, / and ^;
- understand the concept of operator hierarchy and the use of parentheses;
- understand what is meant by the *order of precedence* of operators;
- change the way a number value is displayed (i.e. formatting);
- be familiar with the Microsoft Excel error values;
- be familiar with Excel 2002's formula checking features;
- enhance the appearance of a worksheet using fonts, colours and borders.

Exercise 1: Filling in a Series of Numbers

For Exercises 1 to 3 we shall develop a worksheet based on this scenario: your company sells a product by the square metre but some of your customers are more comfortable working in square yards. You wish to print a quick conversion table. On completion, the worksheet will resemble that in Figure 2.1. We will take three exercises to complete this rather simple task. The pace will quicken after that.

	A	B
1	Conversion Table	
2	$/sq m	$/sq yd
3	10	8.36
4	11	9.20
5	12	10.03
6	13	10.87
7	14	11.70
8	15	12.54
9	16	13.38
10	17	14.21
11	18	15.05
12	19	15.88
13	20	16.72

Figure 2.1

The Center Align tool

(a) Open a new workbook. Type the text in cells A1:B2 as in Figure 2.1 using the currency symbol of your choice. Note that the text will be left justified after you have entered it and how the text in A1 overflows into the next cell. Select A2:B2 and click the Center Align icon on the Formatting toolbar. If your toolbars are sharing a row you may need to expand the toolbar to locate this tool.

(b) Enter the numbers 10 and 11 in A3 and A4, respectively. Select A3:A4 and capture the fill handle — see Figure 1.3. The pointer will assume a solid + shape. Drag the fill handle down to A13. The range A3:A13 will now have the values shown in Figure 2.1 but they will be right aligned.

(c) Save the workbook as CHAP2.XLS.

AutoFill

In step (b) we have made use of the AutoFill feature. We selected two values 10 and 11 (difference of 1) and Excel generated a list 10, 11, 12, 13, etc. Note the constant difference between successive cells. Had the values in A3 and A4 been 10 and 15 then successive values in A3:A13 would have differed by 5.

Try this experiment in a new worksheet: in A1 enter Week 1, select A1 and pull the fill handle down to A6. The values will be Week 1, Week 2, Week 3, etc. Excel displays the value in a Screen Tip as you drag the mouse. The same behaviour results when you copy any text which ends with a digit. AutoFill also works with days of the week and month names. To see this enter Jan (or January) in B1 and drag the fill handle to M1. Using Tools|Options|Custom Lists, you can add your own list. A possible example is a list of your company's departments: Sales, Shipping, etc.

Shortcut

Since we wish to have a series in which the terms differ by 1, we may use an Excel shortcut in step (b). Enter just the number 10 in A3 and, while holding down Ctrl, drag the fill handle down to A13. The required series is produced automatically.

New Excel 2002 feature

Excel 2002

When you use the AutoFill feature in Excel 2002, an AutoFill|Option *smart tag* appears near the new entry. This will remain until another change is made to the worksheet. When the mouse hovers over the smart tag, a downward pointing arrow is added to the icon and clicking the smart tag opens a menu —

Figure 2.2. This feature may be used when we want to fill a range with values but do not wish to use the formatting from the source cell.

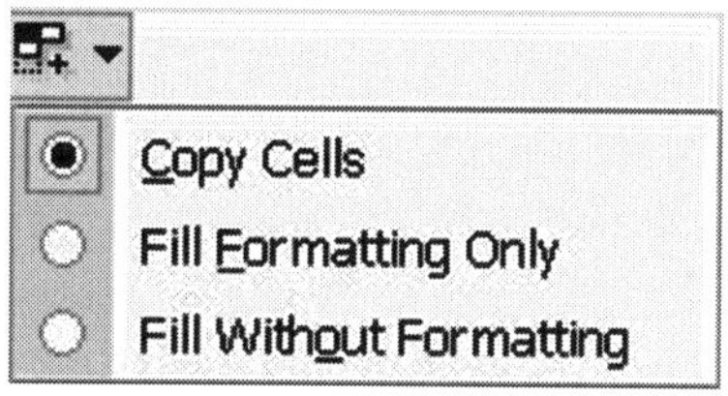

Figure 2.2

Exercise 2: Entering and Copying a Formula

A formula is an expression telling Excel to perform an operation. For the time being we will limit ourselves to arithmetic operations. An arithmetic formula begins with the equal sign (=) followed by an arithmetic expression. The expression may contain numeric values, cell references, arithmetic operators and parentheses. The arithmetic operators are listed in the table below.

Operation	Symbol	Example
Negation	–	=-A1 (returns the value in A1 with a change of sign)
Percentage	%	Entering 10% is equivalent to entering 0.1
Exponentiation	^	=A1^2 (returns the square of the value in A1) =A1^(1/3) (returns the cube root of A1)
Multiplication Division	* /	=A1 * 2 or =2*A1 =A1/2 (half of A1)
Addition Subtraction	+ –	=A1 + 3 =A1 - A2

Spaces are allowed in a formula to make it more readable. The normal arithmetic rules apply. So =A1 * 2 and =2*A1 are equivalent. Later we shall see that parentheses are needed in some formulas to generate the required result.

We will continue with the price conversion table begun in the previous exercise. A yard is smaller than a metre; the conversion factor to convert to square yards from square metres is 0.836.

(a) On Sheet1 of the CHAP2.XLS workbook, in B3 enter the formula =A3 * 0.836. Do not overlook the equal sign. The spaces around the multiplication operator are optional but they do make the formula more readable. If you type lower case letters for a cell reference, Microsoft Excel automatically converts them to upper case. The cell displays the value 8.36.

(b) We need to copy this formula down to B13. Select B3, capture the fill handle and drag it down to B13. The values in B3:B13 will now be close to those in Figure 2.1 but they will display more decimal places and will be right aligned. We format the values in the next exercise.

Of course, this is not the only way to copy an entry. We could have used any of the Windows copying techniques: (1) the Copy and Paste commands from the Edit menu; (2) the shortcuts Ctrl+C and Ctrl+V; or (3) the Copy and Paste buttons on the standard toolbar. Another, Excel-specific method is shown in Exercise 2 of Chapter 3.

You will notice that the formula is modified as it is copied. The original formula in B3 was =A3 * 0.836. This became = A4 * 0.836 in cell B4 and =A5 * 0.836 in B5, and so on. Microsoft Excel has interpreted =A3 * 0.836 in B3 as meaning 'multiply the value in the cell one column to the left by 0.836' and it 'intelligently' recognized that the formula needed modification as it was copied. We examine this feature in detail in the next chapter.

(c) Save the workbook CHAP2.XLS.

Exercise 3: Formatting the Results

Our project is almost complete. All that remains is to change the way the results are displayed. Anything that alters the appearance of a worksheet without changing the underlying calculations is called *formatting*. For this project it is inappropriate to display so many digits after the decimal. We require only two decimals since we are working with currency.

(a) Select range B3:B13 on the worksheet of the previous exercise. From the Format command, select Cells. In the resulting dialog box select the Number tab — see Figure 2.3.

(b) Click the Number item in the Category box and change the value in the Decimal Places box to 2 either by using the spinner or by typing. Click the OK button to close the dialog box. The cells now displays values to two decimal places.

The Undo tool

(c) There is another way to do this. Click the Undo button on the standard toolbar to display the original values.

Removing formats: Formats are readily removed using the menu command Edit|Clear|Format.

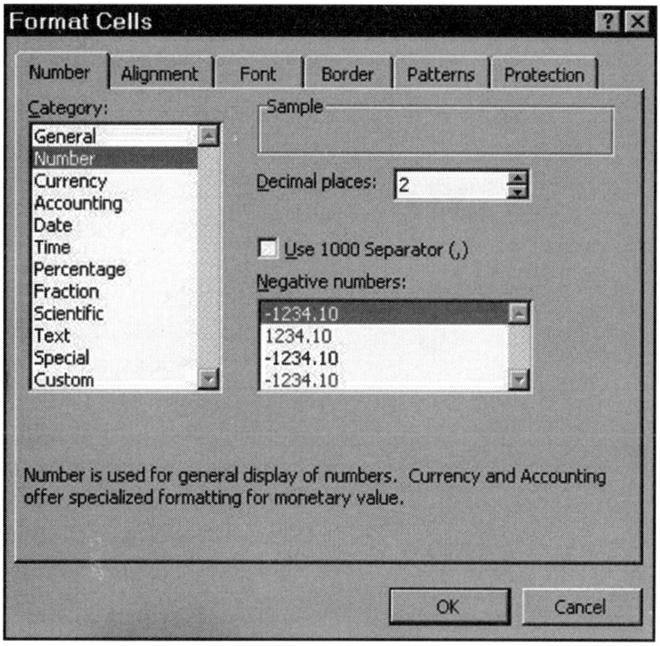

Figure 2.3

(d) Select B3:B13. Click the Decrease Decimals button and note how the number of displayed decimal digits decreases. By experimenting with the Increase and Decrease Decimals tools you will also see that Microsoft Excel automatically rounds numbers when the number of decimals is decreased. *It is important to know that formatting changes the way a value is displayed but does not change the actual value stored in a cell.* Later we will use the ROUND function to change the *stored* value.

(e) With B3:B13 selected, use either the Center Align tool or the menu command Format|Cells|Alignment|Horizontal|Center. Your worksheet should now match that in Figure 2.1. If you wish you may now print the table by clicking on the tool with the printer icon. We explore all the printing options in Chapter 6. Save the workbook CHAP2.XLS.

Exercise 4: Parentheses and Percentages

In this exercise we will see how to handle positive and negative numbers, the use of parentheses in formulas and learn more formatting.

Gourmet Catering is a small catering company. Its income statement is very simple:

Income Statement
Sales
  less expenses
  less depreciation
  less interest
=Profits before taxes
  less taxes
=Profit after taxes
  less dividends (payments to the shareholders)
=Addition to accumulated retained earnings

We will model the income statement for two years and calculate the percentage change in each line item. Our worksheet will resemble Figure 2.4 at the completion of the exercise. We use positive values for inflows of money and negative values for outflows. We have chosen to display the latter as numbers in parentheses.

	A	B	C	D
1	**Gourmet Catering**			
2	**Income Statements for 2000 and 2001**			
3				
4		**2000**	**2001**	**change**
5	Sales	145,000	160,000	10.3%
6	Expenses	(60,456)	(81,234)	34.4%
7	Depreciation	(2,000)	(1,456)	-27.2%
8	Interest	(5,100)	(6,050)	18.6%
9	Profits before taxes	77,444	71,260	-8.0%
10	Taxes	(9,293)	(8,551)	-8.0%
11	Profits after taxes	68,151	62,709	-8.0%
12	Dividends	(45,000)	(50,000)	11.1%
13	To Retained Earnings	23,151	12,709	-45.1%

Figure 2.4

(a) Open the file CHAP2.XLS and click on the Sheet2 tab.

Merge and Center tool

B Bold tool

(b) Enter the heading Gourmet Catering in A1. Select the range A1:D1 and click on the Merge and Center tool. Use the Bold tool to highlight the title. Use the same method to enter the subtitle.

Right Align tool

Column Auto Width shortcut: A very useful shortcut (not applicable here) is to double click on the divider to the right of the column header.

(c) Enter the labels in A5:A13 but do not align them at this time. Column A is not wide enough to hold the text in most of these cells. Select A5:A13 and use the command Format |Column|AutoFit Selection to make the column the right size. Now use the Right Align tool on A6, A7, A8, A10 and A12. We might have opted to click on the A column heading to select all cells in the column before using the Auto Fit command but in our case the wide labels in the headings (cells A1 and A2) would have made the column too wide. It is also possible to set the column width to a specific value with Format|Column|Width. The width of a column on a new worksheet is 8.43 units. Alternatively, one can place the mouse pointer over the line between column headings and, when the pointer changes its shape to show a double headed arrow, click on the divider and drag it to the required position. Similar techniques may be used to alter row heights.

(d) Enter the column headings in row 4 and right align them.

(e) In B5:B8 enter the values 145000, -60456, -2000, and -5100. The last three values will be displayed with negation signs; we will format these values in step (k) to display them in parentheses.

(f) The formula required in B9 for pre-tax profits is =B5 + B6 + B7 + B8. We use addition here because our outflows were entered as negative values. As an alternative to this lengthy formula, we will use =SUM(B5:B8), giving us a preview of a worksheet *function*.

(g) For the purpose of the exercise, let Gourmet's tax rate be 12% of the pre-tax profit. In B10, enter the formula =-B9*12% to compute the taxes payable for 1997. Note that this is equivalent to =-B9*0.12.

(h) The after-tax profit is computed in B11 using =B9 + B10. For a change of pace, we will enter this formula with very little typing. Click on the = symbol on the formula bar, then on cell B9, type the plus sign and click on the cell B10. Complete the formula by clicking the Enter icon (green check mark) on the formula bar.

(i) In B12, enter the value -45000. This is the dividend the board of directors agreed to disburse to the shareholders. Clearly, in B13 we need =B11 + B12.

(j) The data in column C is entered in the same way using the values 160000, -81234, -1456, -6050 and -50000 in cells C5, C6, C7, C8 and C12, respectively. Remember that you need not retype the formulas in C9, C10, C11 and C13; these may be copied from the corresponding cells in column B.

(k) Now we are ready to format the values. While Microsoft Excel offers a wide range of numeric formats, it cannot anticipate everyone's wish. So it provides a way for the user to make his/her own custom formats.

Format Cells shortcut: To quickly open the cell format dialog box, right click on the cell to be formatted and select Format from the popup menu. The selction may be made with the mouse or by using the F key (the letter underlined on the menu).

We require negative values to be displayed in parentheses and zero values to show as a dash. Select the range B5:C13 and use the command Format|Cells. On the Number tab of the resulting dialog box (see Figure 2.5) select the Custom category. We need a format specification #,### ; (#,###) ; "-". If this format is not present, enter it in the Type box. A format specification is composed of three parts separated by semi-colons. The first part sets the format for positive values, the second for negative and the third for zero values. We could use #,##0.00; (#,##0.00) ; "-" should we wish to display two decimal places. The specification [Blue]#,##0.00; [Red](#,##0.00); "-" displays positive numbers in blue and negative values in red; both with two decimal places. Note the use of square brackets around the colour names.

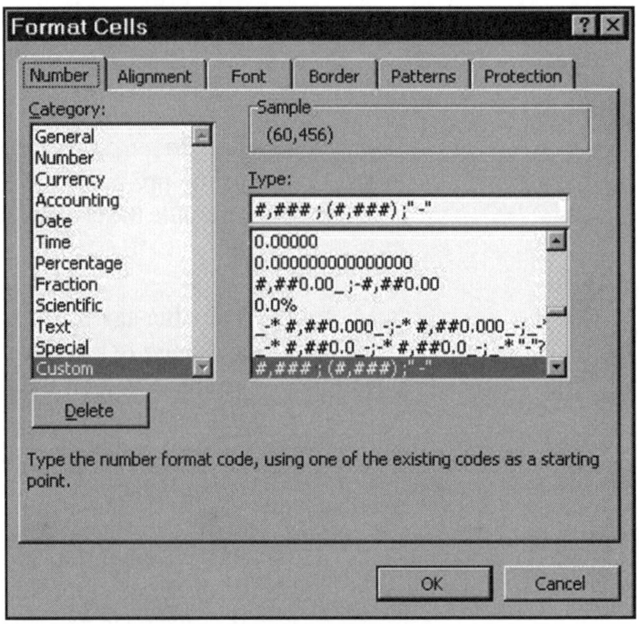

Figure 2.5

 Percentage tool

 Increase Decimals tool

(l) To complete the worksheet, we need to calculate the percentage changes. The fractional change in Sales is calculated with $\frac{\text{2001 Sales - 2000 Sales}}{\text{2000 Sales}}$. We would write the equation on one line as (2001 Sales – 2000 Sales) / 2000 Sales, using parentheses to clearly indicate that the 2000 Sales value is to be divided into the difference of the two values in the numerator. We use a similar approach in Excel when, in cell D5, we use =(C5 – B5)/B5. This gives the value 0.103448. We need the value as a percentage. We may (i) modify the formula to =(C5 – B5)*100/B5, or (ii) format the cell with the percentage tool. We will opt for the latter. This displays the value as 10% in D5. With D5 as the active cell, click on the Increase Decimal tool once to display the value 10.3%. Copy the formula in D5 down to D13. Note how when you copy a cell, the target cells are given the same format as the source cell.

(m) The numbers in columns B and C seem crowded. Select B4:C4 and use the command Format|Column|Width to set the width to 12.

(n) Save the workbook CHAP2.XLS

Exercise 5: More About Formulas

Operators' order of precedence

- – negation
- % percentage
- ^ exponentiation
- * / multiplication and division
- + – addition and subtraction

In cell D5 in the previous exercise we used the formula =(C5 – B5)/B5 where the parentheses ensured that B5 was divided into the quantity C5 less B5. Had we not used the parentheses, Microsoft Excel would evaluate the formula =C5 – B5/B5 by first dividing B5 by B5 and then subtracting the result from C5. To refer to this behaviour we speak about the *order of precedence* of operators. Negation has the highest level (see sidebar) while addition and subtraction rank equally at the lowest level. If a formula contains operators with the same precedence (for example, if a formula contains both a multiplication and division operator) Microsoft Excel evaluates the operators from left to right.

It is sometimes helpful to know this order of precedence but it is more important to know that parentheses can be used to override it. Whenever you are in doubt of how Excel will perform the evaluation, use parentheses to ensure it does it your way. Not only will this produce the required result, it will also make the formula easier to understand by another user — or by yourself at a later date.

New Excel 2002 feature

In this exercise we look at a new Excel 2002 feature: Formula evaluation which can be very helpful in ensuring a formula has been constructed correctly.

(a) Return to Sheet2 of CHAP2.XLS and make D5 the active cell. Using command Tools|Formula Auditing| Evaluate Formula, bring up the Evaluate Formula dialog box shown in Figure 2.6.

(b) Click on the Evaluate button of the dialog box while observing the Evaluation window. This will show a series of formulas and finally a result: first (C5-B5)/B5 then (16000-B5)/B5, later (15000)/B5 and finally 10.3%. This confirms what we have learned about the use of parentheses to overwrite the order of precedence.

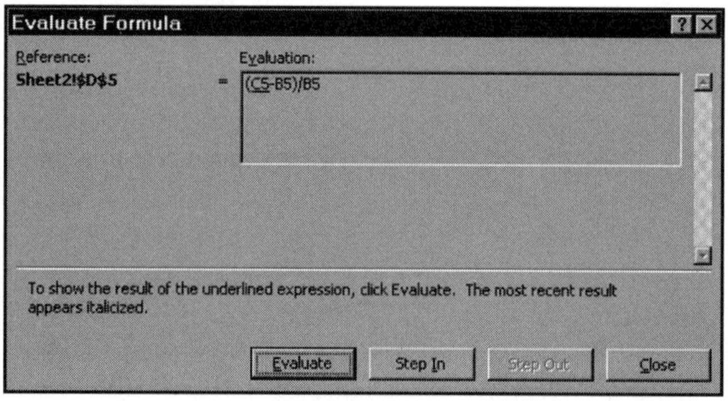

Figure 2.6

You may wish at a later date to experiment with some of the other items on the Format Auditing menu — for example, the Trace Precedence and Show Watch Window.

Exercise 6: Copy and Paste

So far we have use dragged the fill handle when we wished to copy a cell's contents. We have spoken about Copy and Paste but have not experimented with it. In this exercise we find that Excel's Copy and Paste (and Cut and Paste) is not quite like that in other Windows applications. In preparation for Exercise 7, we will make a worksheet that resembles that in Figure 2.7. We shall use both the fill handle drag and the Copy and Paste methods.

(a) On Sheet3 of CHAP2.XLS, enter the text Currency format in B1. Select B1:E1 and use the Merge and Center tool. Enter the text in A2:E2. Select B1:E1 and use the Right Align tool.

(b) Enter the values 123.45 and 12345.67 in A3 and A4, respectively. Select these cells and drag the fill handle to the right as far as column E. The first four rows of your worksheet should resemble those in the figure.

(c) In B6 and B11 enter the text Accounting formats and Custom formats, respectively. Use the Merge and Center tool to centre the text over columns B and E.

(d) Now we shall use Copy and Paste. Select A2:E4 and click on the Copy tool; alternatively, use Edit Copy or the shortcut Ctrl+C. This places the copied material on the Clipboard.

	A	B	C	D	E
1		Currency formats			
2	Currency tool	Dollars	Pounds	Francs	Euros
3	123.45	123.45	123.45	123.45	123.45
4	12345.67	12345.67	12345.67	12345.67	12345.67
5					
6		Accounting formats			
7	Currency tool	Dollars	Pounds	Francs	Euros
8	123.45	123.45	123.45	123.45	123.45
9	12345.67	12345.67	12345.67	12345.67	12345.67
10					
11		Custom formats			
12	Currency tool	Dollars	Pounds	Francs	Euros
13	123.45	123.45	123.45	123.45	123.45
14	12345.67	12345.67	12345.67	12345.67	12345.67

Figure 2.7

(e) We wish to copy the material to A7:E9, so click on A7 to make it the active cell. To paste the material from the Clipboard use the Paste tool; alternatively, use Edit|Copy or the shortcut Ctrl+C.

Note that the copied area (A2:E4) — also called the source — is ringed by an animated dotted border, informally called the 'ant track'. This shows what material is on the Clipboard. If you do some work on the worksheet (enter values in a cell, format a cell, etc.) the ant track disappears and the material is removed from the Clipboard. This generally does not happen in other applications but the Microsoft programmers want to be cautious. Numeric errors are often harder to detect than textual ones. Furthermore, pasting in Excel can cause data loss if the target area already contains data.

New Excel 2002 feature

Paste option smart tag

If you are using Excel 2002 there will be a smart tag next to the target area. Click it to view the paste options — none of which are applicable here — see Figure 2.8. One very useful option permits you to copy material in such a way that the target cells contain new values but keep their original formats. The Excel 2002 Paste tool also has a new feature. When a range has been selected (has an ant track), the Paste tool gains a downward pointing area. Click the tool and a menu appears — Figure 2.9 — with options similar to those in the smart tag.

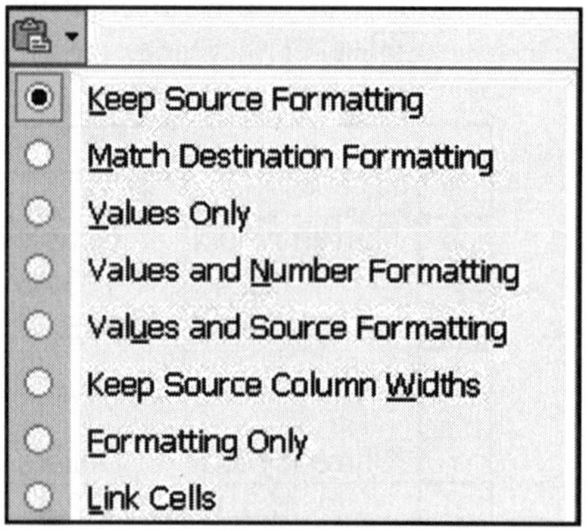

Figure 2.8

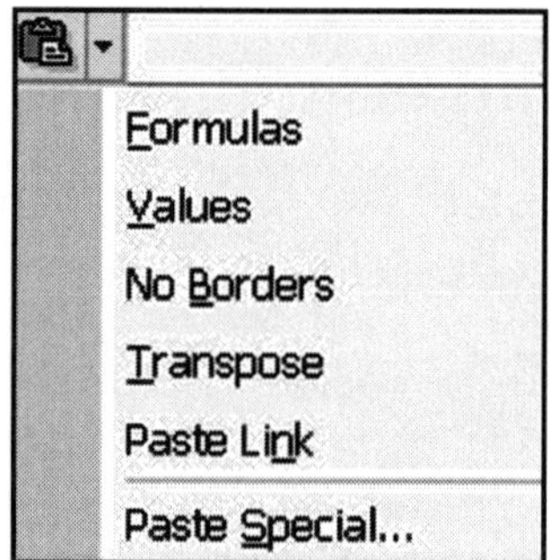

Figure 2.9

You will be familiar with the concept of the Clipboard from other applications. Microsoft Office also has its own Clipboard. Whereas the system Clipboard holds only one copied or cut item, the Office Clipboard can hold up to 24. We do not have space to pursue this topic but private experimentation might be helpful. The reader may also wish to experiment with Paste Special (on the Edit menu) when the basic Excel material has been mastered.

Exercise 7: Formatting Money

Caution: If you wish to experiment with Regional Settings, close all programs before making any changes. Do not open any important documents while conducting the experiment.

In this exercise we will construct a worksheet similar to that in Figure 2.10. This allows us to compare the results of the Currency Style tool, and the Currency and the Accounting formats. We also learn how to make Custom formats. We will find that Excel provides a wide range of currency symbols such as \$, £, € and letter abbreviations such as F, DM, SFr, FB, fl, etc.

Most of the time the Currency Style tool will be used to format monetary values. The symbol for this depends on your Windows Regional Settings and the language options of your version of Excel. For North Americans (and some others) the symbol is a dollar sign. The general symbol is a pile of coins on a bank note.

If you do a lot of work involving the euro currency, you should instal the Euro Currency tools add-in to put this style on your formatting toolbar along with your local currency tool.

	A	B	C	D	E
1		Currency formats			
2	Currency tool	Dollars	Pounds	Francs	Euros
3	$ 123.45	$123.45	£123.45	123.45 F	€ 123.45
4	$ 12,345.67	$12,345.67	£12,345.67	12,345.67 F	€ 12,345.67
5					
6		Accounting formats			
7	Currency tool	Dollars	Pounds	Francs	Euros
8	$ 123.45	$ 123.45	£ 123.45	123.45 F	€ 123.45
9	$ 12,345.67	$ 12,345.67	£ 12,345.67	12,345.67 F	€ 12,345.67
10					
11		Custom formats			
12	Currency tool	Dollars	Pounds	Francs	Euros
13	$ 123.45	123.45 $	£ 123.45	123 Franc	€ 123.45
14	$ 12,345.67	12 345.67 $	£12 345.67	12 346 Franc	€ 12 345.67

Figure 2.10

(a) Open Sheet3 of CHAP2.XLS where you did Exercise 6.

General Currency Style tool

Dollar Style tool

(b) Click on the A column heading and on the Currency Style tool. This is quicker than formatting the three ranges separately and has no detrimental effect on the text vales. The figure shows the $ symbol since the author is in Canada; your worksheet will show your local currency.

Shortcut method: To open the Format Cells dialog, right click on the cell and select the appropriate item from the pop-up menu.

(c) To apply the Currency format to B3:E4, select pairs of cells in turn (B3:B4, C3:C4, etc.) and right click. From the pop-up menu select Format Cells. In the Format Cells dialog box locate the Currency category and in the symbols box select the appropriate currency symbol — see Figure 2.11.

(d) Repeat step (c) with the cells in B8:E9 but this time use the Accounting category.

We will have made a number of observations by now:

1. The Currency Style tool generates the same results as the Accounting format.

2. The $ and £ symbols are placed to the left of the value but most other currency symbols are placed to the right. Excel offers both options with the euro to satisfy local customs.

3. With $ and £ symbols, the Currency format aligns the value to the left of the cell with no space between the currency symbol and the first digit. In contrast, the Accounting format left aligns the currency symbol but right aligns the numeric value with a space after the last digit.

4. With the Currency format, there are options for how a negative number is to be displayed.

If neither the Accounting nor the Currency format satisfies your need, then you must use a Custom format. Before we experiment, let's review how you obtain symbols that are not present on your keyboard. If you are using a US 101 keyboard, the £ and € symbols are generated using Alt+0163 and Alt+0128, respectively. Of course, the numeric keypad must be used for the digits. The euro symbol is produced with AltGr+4 on the UK keyboard and with AltGr+5 on the US International keyboard.

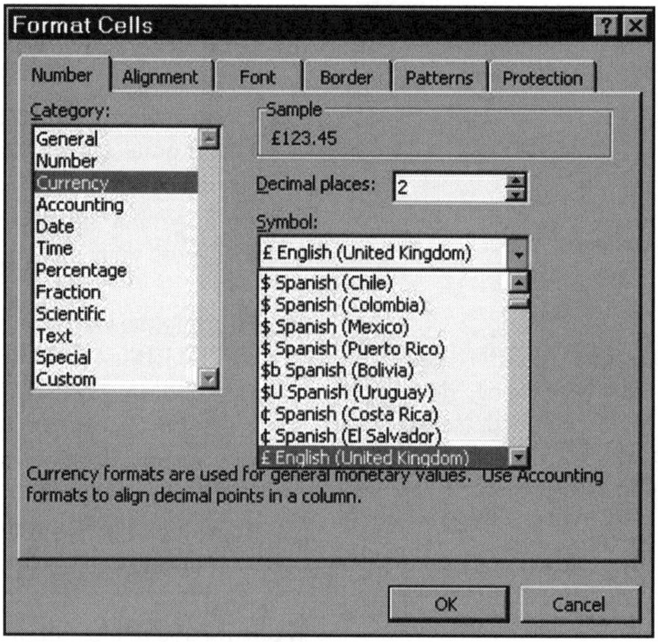

Figure 2.11

(e) Select B3:B14 and open the Format Cells dialog using the shortcut Ctrl+1 or one of the methods we have used before. Locate the Custom category at the bottom of the Category list and in the Type box enter # ##0.00 $ — see Figure 2.12. Note the two spaces in this text. Once you have constructed a custom format it will be available for use at any time by selecting it from the list under the Type box.

(f) Repeat the last step with the other three pairs of values. The Custom formats are £# ##0.00 in C3:C14, ### 000 "Franc" in D13:D14 and €* ### ###.00" " in E13:E14.

(g) Save the workbook.

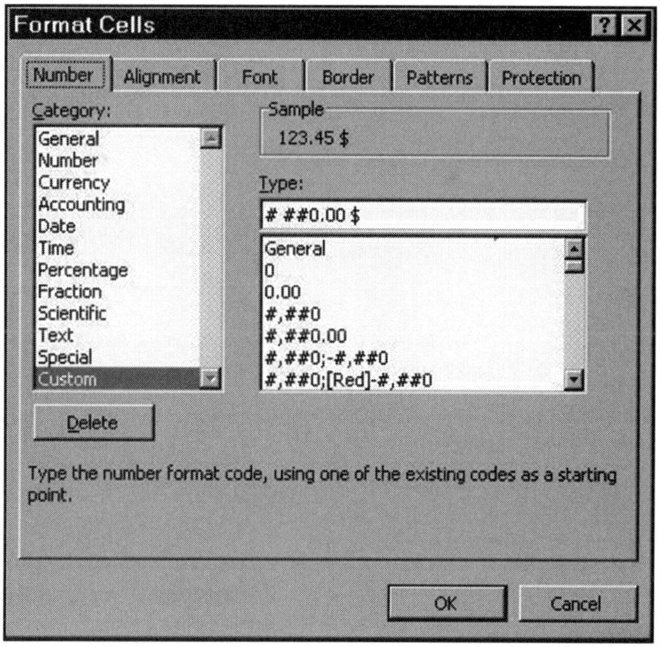

Figure 2.12

The # and 0 symbols in # ##0.00 $ are place holders. The three zero symbols ensure that if the value is zero then it will be displayed as 0.00 $. We needed to place the text Franc in quotations since it is not an Excel currency abbreviation. The asterisk (*) in the last Custom format places the currency symbol to the left of the cell as in the Accounting format. Use Help to learn more about Custom formats (type *Create a custom format* in the Answer Wizard or Question box), and do experiment!

Exercise 8: Displayed and Stored Values

The purpose of this exercise is to demonstrate that while formatting may be used to change how a value is *displayed*, the *stored* value is unaltered. We also note that sometimes a cell with a simple formula inherits another cell's format. When completed the worksheet will resemble that in Figure 2.13.

(a) Open the workbook CHAP2.XLS. We wish to work on Sheet4 so you may need to add another sheet since normally Excel is set to open a workbook with three sheets. Use the command Inset Worksheet. Click on the newly created Sheet4 tab and drag it to the correct place following Sheet3. Click on the Sheet4 tab to open it.

	A	B	C	D
1	Displayed and stored values			
2	a) Enter formulas before formatting A4			
3	Value	=Value	=2+Value	=2*Value
4	1.2	1.234	3.234	2.468
5				
6	b) Enter formulas after formatting A7			
7	Value	=Value	=2+Value	=2*Value
8	1.2	1.2	3.2	2.468

Figure 2.13

(b) Begin by typing the text in A1:D3. Entering the text in B3:D3 presents a small problem. The equal sign alerts Excel to use a formula but this is not what we want. We solve this by typing a single quote (an apostrophe) before the equal sign to indicate that we wish to enter text — the quote symbol will not be displayed. If a cell displays the #NAME? error value, you have forgotten the apostrophe.

Note: In some spreadsheet applications, the format of a cell is revealed in the equivalent of the Name box. It is unfortunate that Microsoft Excel does not have this feature.

(c) In A4 enter the value 1.234. In B4 enter the formula =A4, in C4 enter =2+A4 and in D4 enter =2*A4.

(d) Now format A4 to display one decimal place. This could be done by opening the Format Cells dialog as in the previous exercise. But we will use the Decrease Decimals tool for this simple operation. The cells A4:C4 should now be in agreement with Figure 2.7.

(e) Make A4 the active cell. The value displayed in A4 is 1.2 but from the formula bar we see that the stored value is 1.234. Unfortunately, one cannot see the applied format by looking here. You may check how a cell is formatted by selecting the cell and using the Format|Cells|Number command. Cells B4 and C4 have not been formatted, so they correctly show 1.234 (=A4) and 2.468 (=2*A4), respectively.

If we wish to have a value stored with a set number of decimal digits, we use the ROUND function which is discussed in a later chapter. It is possible to use the Tools|Option command to have Excel use the same precision as the displayed value but this is not recommended for the novice user.

In the next part of the exercise we see an oddity of Microsoft Excel. When a formula is typed into a cell which has not been previously formatted (i.e. it has the General format) and the formula contains (i) only references to one or references to more cells with identical formats and (ii) either no operator, or only the addition or subtraction operator, then the cell with the formula gets the number format of the referenced cells.

(f) Either type the text in A6:D7 or use Copy and Paste and edit A6. Enter the value 1.234 in A7 and format it to one decimal place.

(g) In B7 enter the formula =A7. The value 1.2 is displayed. Cell B7 has taken on the number format of A7 because the formula is a simple reference to a formatted cell. We may format the cell to restore the value of 1.234 if that is required.

(h) In C7 enter =2+A7. Again the value is displayed with one decimal place since both referenced cells have this format. The formula =A7+B7 would display 2.5 since both cells are formatted for one decimal. In D7 enter =2*A7. Now we get 2.468 — three decimal places. Because the formula contains a multiplication operator, the format of A7 is not copied to D7.

(i) If you now reformat A7 to display three decimals, the values in B7 and C7 are unchanged! Something to be wary off. Save the workbook.

Exercise 9: Borders, Fonts and Patterns

In this exercise, we learn to embellish the appearance of a worksheet. We may change the typeface used in a cell, display information in colour, fill the cell with a solid colour or a pattern, add borders around a cell, etc.

For the purpose of this exercise, we will assume that the manager of Gourmet Catering wishes to produce an enhanced worksheet showing the company's revenue sources. Perhaps the worksheet is to be displayed at a staff meeting, or the data is to be imported into a word processing application to generate a printed report, or the data is to be imported into an application that will create a slide show to be used to persuade the bank to lend more money! Importing worksheet data into other applications is discussed in Chapter 12.

Gourmet Catering Revenue Sources for 2000				
Item	Number	% of Total	Revenue	Percentage
Private parties				
Buffets	12	15%	14,000	9%
Dinners	15	19%	25,000	16%
Children's parties	8	10%	2,400	2%
Corporate Events				
Dinners	20	25%	50,000	31%
Receptions	23	29%	54,000	34%
Conferences	2	3%	14,600	9%
Total	80		160,000	

Figure 2.14

(a) Open the workbook CHAP2.XLS. If necessary, create Sheet5.

(b) Since this book does not use colour, the example of the finished worksheet as displayed in Figure 2.14 contains few embellishments, but provides a place from which you can begin to experiment. As before, begin with the headings in A1 and A2 and use the Merge and Center tool on them. Enter the other values shown in the figure except for the cells listed below which contain formulas:
B13: =B6 + B7 + B8 + B10 + B11 + B12;
D13: =D6 + D7 + D8 + D10 + D11 + D12;
C6: =B6 / $B$13
(this is copied down to C12 and then C9 is deleted);
E6: =D6 / $D$13
(this is copied down to E12 and then E9 is deleted).
Format E6:E13 with the Percentage tool. The purpose of the dollar signs in the formulas is explained in the next chapter.

(c) The simplest format to apply is removing the worksheet's gridlines. Start with the command Tools|Options and open the Views tab. Locate the Gridlines box and click in it to remove the check mark. Exit the Option box by clicking OK. This Option applies only to the current worksheet. Be careful when using this dialog box that you do not make changes without full knowledge of the consequences.

(d) The cells in Figure 2.11 have been formatted to be displayed in a font other than Excel's default Arial font. Selected cells may be assigned a typeface, size and colour by using either the Format|Cells command, or the first and second tool on the Formatting toolbar for typeface and size and the penultimate tool for font colour. Similarly, the Format|Cells command may be used to fill a cell with colour and pattern while the last tool on the Formatting toolbar may be used to fill a cell but not to add a pattern. The reader is encouraged to experiment with combinations of these effects.

To select all the cells in a worksheet, click on the box at the intersection of the column and row headers. There is a handy shortcut method to select a range: click on the top left cell (say A1) and hold [⇧ Shift] down, then click on the bottom right cell (say E13).

(e) Let us assume you have made various formatting changes to A1:E13. Now you would like to remove all of the effects but leave the cell contents intact. Select the range to be de-formatted and use the command Edit|Clear|Formats. You may wish to reformat some of the columns of numbers before proceeding.

(f) Microsoft Excel provides a number of built-in formats for tables like the one we are working with. Select A1:E13 and use the command Format|AutoFormat. Select one of the options and observe the effect on your worksheet. You may find one that looks suitable or which can be made suitable with some fine tuning.

(g) Save the workbook CHAP2.XLS.

Exercise 10: When Things Go Wrong

In this exercise we purposely make some mistakes so that we may learn how Microsoft Excel responds. We shall work with the worksheet of the previous exercise but do not save the worksheet because it may have errors in it when you are finished.

(a) Open the file CHAP2.XLS and open Sheet2.

Error value: ####### is Excel's way of saying that the cell's width is too small.

(b) We begin by seeing what happens when a very large number is entered in a cell. In B5 (the Sales figure for 1997) enter the number 123,456,789,999. The cell B5 and other cells on the worksheet will be filled with ########. This is Excel's way of saying the value in this cell is too large to be displayed in the specified format. This happens as a result of two actions we took in the previous exercise: (i) we have specified a format for the cells and (ii) we have set the column width. Click the Undo tool to reset the value.

Scientific notation: 1.23E+08 means 1.23×10^8.

If you move to a cell to the right of the area we have worked (say H1) and enter a very large number, such as 123,456,789, Microsoft Excel will automatically expand the column to accommodate the value. If in another cell (say I1) you enter the same number without the commas and then make the cell narrower, Excel will display the value as 1.23E+08. This should be interpreted as 1.23×10^8.

Error value: When #VALUE! is displayed, the formula contains a reference to a non-numeric value.

(c) Change the formula in D5 to read =(C5 - B5) / A5. Clearly, this is a gross error since A5 contains textual material and not a numeric value. Excel indicates this by displaying #VALUE!. Again, click Undo to reset the formula.

Error value: When the error value #DIV/0! is displayed, the formula is attempting to divide by zero.

(d) Suppose Gourmet Catering had no interest charges in 1997. What happens to the worksheet? Enter 0 in B8. D8 now displays #DIV/0! to warn you that division by zero is mathematically impossible. Click Undo to reset the cell. This may be a real situation we could run into. We will solve it in a later chapter when we explore the IF function.

(e) The formula in D5 that calculates the change in Sales is =(C5-B5)/B5. Edit this to read =(C5−B5)/D5 — again we are making a deliberate error. Microsoft Excel responds with a message box warning of a circular reference. A formula that refers to its own cell (i.e. references its own value) has a circular reference. Exit the message box. Observe the message in the status bar: Circular D5. Click on the Undo tool to reset the cell.

Circular references are generally errors but there are occasions when the user purposely sets up a circular reference to have Excel perform an iterative (repetitious) calculation.

(f) The Range Finder can be helpful in locating the source of errors in a large worksheet. Double click on D5 (or make D5 the active cell and click in the formula bar). Note that (i) the formula is colour coded with each cell reference in a separate colour, for example C5 is blue, and (ii) there is a border around each of the cells referred to and the colour matches that in the formula, so there is a blue border around C5.You can edit a formula by dragging the cell's border to a new position.

Summary

Formulas

A formula consists of an equality symbol (=) followed by an arithmetic expression. A mathematical expression is composed of numeric values, cell references and arithmetic operators. In a later chapter we will look at textual expressions.

Operators

The mathematical operators in order of precedence are: – (negation), % (percentage), ^ (exponentiation), * (multiplication), / (division), + addition and – (subtraction). The operators * and / have the same order of precedence, as do the operators + and –. Excel executes two operators of the same order in the order left to right. Parentheses override the order of precedence and can also be used to clarify a formula.

Error values

When a cell is filled with #### symbols, Microsoft Excel is signalling that the cell's column is not wide enough to display the value. Three other error values are: #VALUE! (there is something that prevents evaluation of the formula — usually a reference to a cell with a non-numeric value); #DIV/0! (the formula cannot be evaluated because it uses division by a zero value); and the Circular Reference error (a formula refers to its own cell).

Formatting

A cell may be formatted to change the way in which its value is displayed. We use numeric formatting to change the way a number is displayed. For example: the number of decimals, with a currency symbol, with thousands separators, etc. Formatting a cell does not alter the value stored in that cell. Other formatting alters the font (typeface) used to display a cell, the alignment within the cell (left, right or centred), the colour of the value or the cell's background. Formatting may also be used to add borders to a range. We also saw how to change a column's width or a row's height. The Merge and Center tool is used to improve the appearance of a worksheet.

AutoFill

This feature is used to generate a series of values such as the days of the week or the months of the year, or a numeric series such as 2, 4, 6, 8.

Problems

1.* Gourmet Catering pays its six employees weekly, our task is to develop a worksheet for the manager to calculate each person's wages. Everyone pays $5 health insurance and is taxed at 10%. As you work on the problem, note how many steps are the same as you would use with a pencil and paper approach. Figure 2.12 shows how it will appear upon completion.

	A	B	C	D	E	F	G	H
1				Gourmet Catering				
2								
3	Employee	Hours	Rate	Pay	Insurance	Tax	Deductions	Net Pay
4	Joe	32	15.50	496.00	5.00	74.40	79.40	$ 416.60
5	Mary	32	15.50	496.00	5.00	74.40	79.40	$ 416.60
6	Fred	32	12.00	384.00	5.00	57.60	62.60	$ 321.40
7	Jane	25	12.00	300.00	5.00	45.00	50.00	$ 250.00
8	George	20	10.00	200.00	5.00	30.00	35.00	$ 165.00
9	Jill	32	8.00	256.00	5.00	38.40	43.40	$ 212.60
10		Totals		$2,132.00	$ 30.00	$319.80	$ 349.80	$1,782.20

Figure 2.15

The cells in columns D, F, G and H of the main part of the worksheet clearly need formulas. What are the formulas in D4, F4, G4, H4 and D10?

Can you see a flaw in our worksheet? If someone has the week off (Hours = 0) then the Net Pay will be a negative value! We learn how to solve this type of problem with the IF worksheet function in Chapter 5.

2.* A book on corporate finance states that the approximate yield of a bond may be found using the following formula:

$$\text{Yield} = \frac{\text{Coupon} - (\text{Face Value} - \text{Price}) \ / \ \text{Maturity}}{(\text{Price} + \text{Face Value}) \ / \ 2}$$

Referring to Figure 2.16, what formula would you use in E4 to compute the yield?

	A	B	C	D	E
1	Yield to Maturity				
2					
3	Coupon	Face value	Price	Maturity	Yield
4	$80	$1,000	$955.14	6	8.95%

Figure 2.16

3
Cell References and Names

Objectives

Upon completion of this chapter you will:

- be familiar with the concept of relative cell references and understand how a formula with a relative address changes when the formula is copied;
- understand how absolute cell references are constructed and when to use them;
- be able to use mixed references in a formula;
- be able to name a cell or a range of cells, and use these names in formulas;
- know what to expect when a formula is copied;
- appreciate what is meant by 'what-if' analysis and be able to save scenarios.

Exercise 1: Relative References

In formulas such as =A1*2 or =(A1+A2)/2, the terms A1 and A2 are called *relative references*. If the formula =C1*2 is located in cell E2, Microsoft Excel treats the reference C1 as being the cell that is one row above and two columns to the left of the cell containing the formula. The cell C1 is a relative location and not an absolute one. The effect of this is apparent only when a formula is copied.

Let us try to think of the formula =C1*2 in E2 as meaning =(cell one row up, two columns to left) * 2. Now let us copy the formula in E2 to G5 where it will still be evaluated as =(cell one row up, two columns to left) * 2. What will we see in G5? We can answer this by locating the cell which, relative to G5, is one row up (i.e. row 4) and two columns to the left (i.e. column E). So we expect, quite correctly, that the new formula will read =E4*2.

(a) Open a new workbook and, referring to Figure 3.1, enter the numbers shown in C4:F7.

(b) In D9, enter the formula =E4*2. This evaluates to 6.

The Copy tool

(c) With D9 as the active cell, click the Copy tool. Note that this causes a flickering dotted box around the cell — the ant track!

	A	B	C	D	E	F
1						
2	#REF!					
3						
4			1	2	3	4
5			5	6	7	8
6			9	10	11	12
7			13	14	15	16
8						
9		0		6		
10						
11		18				
12					32	

Figure 3.1

The Paste tool

(d) Move to B11 and click on the Paste tool. If you are working with Excel 2002, the Print Option smart tag will appear near cell B11 as discussed in Exercise 6 of Chapter 2 — ignore it for now.

The original formula in D9 references the cell E4 which is one column to the right and five rows above the cell containing the formula. So we expect the new formula in B11 to reference a cell one column to the right (column C is one to the right of B11) and five rows above (row 6 is five rows above B11). We therefore expect the reference to E4 to have changed to C6 giving the formula =C6*2. Check in the formula bar to see that this is the case.

(e) We are now going to copy the formula in D9 to E12. Before you perform this operation, write down on a scrap of paper what you predict the formula will be in E12. If D9 is still surrounded by the ant track you may now move to E12 and again use the Paste tool (or the shortcut Ctrl+V) to put the formula into E12. Otherwise, you must return to D9 and use the Copy tool before going to E12 and pasting.

Do you understand why E12 now has the formula =F7*2 which evaluates to 32? If not, please re-read the introduction to this exercise.

(f) Now copy the formula in D9 to A9. This results in =B4*2 but since B4 is empty, the formula evaluates to 0.

(g) Lastly, copy D9 to A2. The cell displays the error value #REF!. The formula bar shows =#REF!*2. Recalling that the formula in D9 references a cell five rows above D9, you can see that trying to copy the formula to A2 cannot yield a valid formula — there is no row five above row 2! The error value #REF! is signalling an invalid cell reference.

Error smart tag

If you are using Excel 2002, the top lefthand corner of A2 will display a green triangle to indicate an error (a strange colour choice for an error?) and, when A2 is the active cell, an Error smart tag (exclamation mark within a yellow diamond) will appear near A2. Click on the Error smart tag and you will open a menu, one item of which is an offer of help with the problem.

(h) You may wish to experiment with copying other cells and checking the results with your predictions. When you are ready, save the workbook as CHAP3.XLS.

Exercise 2: Absolute References

We now know that a formula such as =A1*2 will change when it is copied. But there are occasions when we do not want this to happen. This exercise explains the use of *absolute references* (for example, =$A$1*2) that preserve cell references when a formula is copied.

Keeping floors clean in a catering establishment is essential and the manager of Gourmet Catering is considering contracting out this task. She is looking at two cleaning companies. Floors-R-Us state they will do the job for a flat rate of £10 plus £0.50 a square metre while Acme Cleaners want £0.70 a square metre. Our task is to construct a worksheet to compare the two bids. Figure 3.2 shows our final product.

	A	B	C	D	E	F
1	**Floor cleaning**					
2					Cost / sq. m	
3					Floors-R-Us	Acme
4	room	length	width	area	£0.50	£0.70
5	main kitchen	8	7	56.00	28.00	39.20
6	small kitchen	5.5	5	27.50	13.75	19.25
7	dry stockroom	4	4	16.00	8.00	11.20
8	veg stockroom	4	3	12.00	6.00	8.40
9	hallway	12	1.25	15.00	7.50	10.50
10	office	4	4	16.00	8.00	11.20
11				variable cost	71.25	99.75
12				fixed cost	10.00	0
13				total	£81.25	£99.75

Figure 3.2

(a) On Sheet2 of the workbook CHAP3.XLS, begin the exercise by entering the text and values shown in A1:F4. Use the Merge and Center tool on E2:F2. Do not format E4:F4 to display currency at this time. You may need to adjust the width of column E to hold the text in E3.

(b) Enter the text and values shown in A5:C10. Widen column A and align the text in A5:A10 to the right.

(c) We will enter the required formulas in D5, E5 and F5 and copy them down to row 10. The formula to compute the area in D5 is =B5*C5. Format this to show two decimal places using the Increase or Decrease Decimals tools.

(d) The formula in E5 to compute the cost of having Floors-R-Us clean this floor is =D5*E4. This would give the correct result but think what will happen when we copy it down to the next row. We will get =D6*E5 but we would like the reference to E4 (the unit cost from Floors-R-Us) to remain unchanged when the formula is copied. To achieve this we use =D5*$E$4.

The reference $E$4 is said to be *absolute*. The dollar symbol before the E may be interpreted as an instruction to Microsoft Excel not to change the column label (E) when copying the formula. Likewise the second $ prevents the row number (4) from changing when the formula is copied.

(e) In the same manner as above, the formula needed in F5 is =D5*$F$4. Rather than simply typing this formula we will use the mouse pointing method. With F5 as the active cell, click on the = symbol in the formula box. Next click on D5 giving the incomplete formula =D5. Type the multiply symbol (*) and click on F4 to give the formula =D5*F4. To add the dollar symbols to make the reference to F4 absolute, tap the F4 key once to give the required formula =D5*$F$4.

If you inadvertently tap the F4 key more than once, you may get just one dollar symbol. Tapping the key cycles through the references $F$4, F$4, $F4 and back to $F$4.

(f) Now we are ready to copy D5:F5 down to row 10. We can do this by selecting the range D5:F5 and pulling down the fill handle (the block at the lower right of the box around the selected range). Alternatively, since we are making a vertical table, we can use the shortcut of double clicking on the fill handle after selecting the range D5:F5.

(g) A few steps more and the worksheet is ready. Enter the text variable cost in C11, select C11:D11 and use the Merge and Center tool. Finally click on the Align Right tool. Repeat these steps with the next two pieces of text.

Σ The AutoSum tool

(h) In E11 enter the formula =SUM(E5:E10). If by now you have discovered that the AutoSum tool may be used to enter the SUM formula, please ensure you have not entered =SUM(E4:E10) in error! Enter the fixed cost (10) in E12 and in E13 enter =E11+E12 to compute the total cost. Copy E11:E12 to column F and then adjust the fixed cost in F12 to 0 (Acme Cleaners do not have this charge).

(i) Finally, use Format|Cells|Currency on the ranges E4:F4 and E13:F13. You may prefer to format the cells with your own local currency symbol. Save the workbook as CHAP3.XLS.

If you want the final worksheet to be closer to that in Figure 3.2 you will need to (1) use Tools|Options|View and remove the check mark in the Gridlines box, and (2) use the Border tool to add borders to some of the cells. Remember, you can use Edit|Clear|Format to remove any border added by mistake.

Exercise 3: What-if Analyses

Having developed the worksheet, the manager is now able to do some 'what-if' analyses. For example, she might ask 'What if I could negotiate with Acme to bring their price down to 60 pence/square metre — will that alter my decision on who gets the contract?' Clearly she can answer this question very quickly by entering the value 0.60 in cell F4. Alternatively, her question might be 'What if we use our staff to clean the hallways and office?' Rather than delete the information for these two areas, she can simply enter the value 0 into cells B9 and B10. Experiment with this and other possible 'what-ifs'; for example, 'What if next year the contractor increases the rate per square metre by 10%?'

Exercise 4: Scenarios

We saw in Exercise 3 how to change values in worksheet cells so as to answer 'what-if' questions. One way to share these findings with others would be to print the worksheet with each of the various cell settings. Alternatively, we may display the results on the screen since then we can try other models suggested by co-workers. The manager wishes to share the results of her deliberations with her staff. However, making the changes in various cells as she is talking to her co-workers could be distracting. In this exercise we will show how she can incorporate a number of *scenarios* within one worksheet.

For this exercise we shall make three scenarios: (1) the Basic model as developed in Exercise 2, (2) the Acme Possibility model in which Acme has been persuaded to do the job at a reduced rate (a change in value in F4) and (3) the Minimal model in which local staff wash two areas (a change in value in B9 and B10). We will use A2 to hold the name of the model. So we have A2, B9, B10 and F4 are variable cells. It is imperative to ensure that the Changing Cells box for each scenario references all the cells changed in all scenarios; this will become clear later.

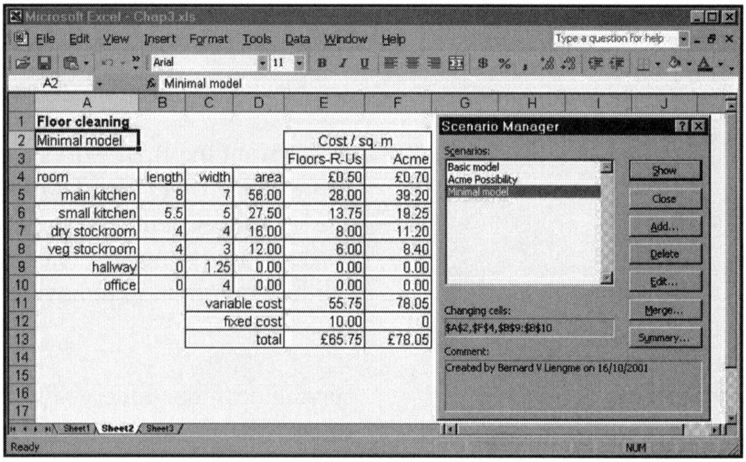

Figure 3.3

(a) Open the workbook CHAP3.XLS and move to Sheet2. In A2 enter the text Basic model.

(b) Use the command Tools|Scenarios to bring up the Scenario Manager — see Figure 3.3. Click on the Add button and in the Add Scenario dialog box (Figure 3.4) name this first scenario Basic model. In the Changing Cells box enter A2, F4, B9: B10, E14. Click on the OK button. In the Scenario Values dialog box enter the values as shown in Figure 3.5 and click on the OK button.

(c) We will now add the second scenario answering the question 'What if Acme can be persuaded to lower its price to 60p/sq.m?' If the Scenario Manager is not visible, open it with Tools|Scenarios. Repeating the steps as in (b) above, add a new scenario named Acme Possibility. In the Scenario Values dialog, you should give A2 the value Acme Possibility and F4 the value 0.6.

(d) Make the last scenario in the same manner using the values: Minimal model in A2, 0.7 in F4 and 0 in both B9 and B10.

(e) Figure 3.3 shows the current state of your worksheet. By selecting one of the models, and clicking the Show button, it is possible to have the worksheet show any one of the three scenarios.

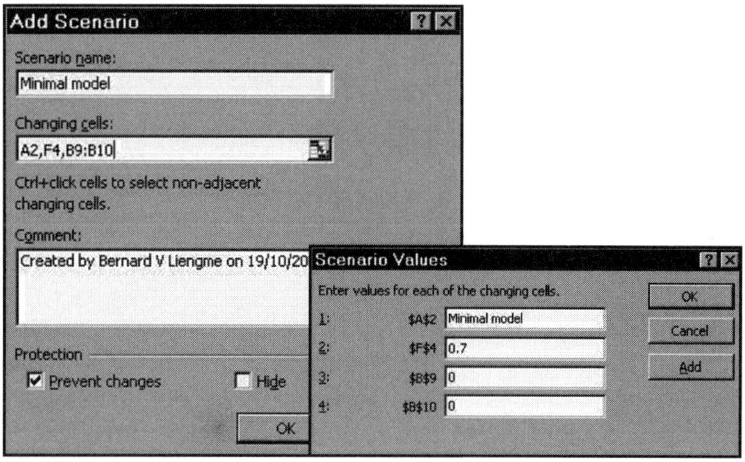

Figure 3.4 **Figure 3.5**

Exercise 5: Mixed Cell References

In Exercise 1 we worked with relative cell references such as =A1*2 which change when the formula is copied. In Exercise 2 we explored absolute cell references such as =$A$2*2 which do not change when the formula is copied. Now we will explore the middle ground using formulas in which either the column or the row designation of a cell reference is allowed to change when the formula is copied. Examples of mixed references are =$A1*2 and =A$2*2.

Frequently the interest rate is given as an annual value but the compounding term is not annual but monthly or quarterly — see Problem 1 at the end of the chapter. However, in this exercise we will use a simple case of an investment which has annual compounding. In Chapter 4 we look at Microsoft Excel worksheet functions which may be used in various problems relating to the value of money.

It is interesting to note that from the Middle Ages until recently, compound interest tables were indispensable tools for the business person. Electronic calculators and computers which facilitate the easy calculation of the required data have made these tables all but obsolete except in the educational milieu. We will generate a table, see Figure 3.6, showing the growth of an investment which accumulates interest annually at various rates of interest.

To remove gridlines: Use Tools|Options|View and uncheck the Gridlines box.

To make borders: Use the Format|Cells|Border command or the Border tool .

	A	B	C	D	E	F	G
1	**Compound Interest (annual compounding)**						
2							
3	Principal	100.00					
4							
5				Interest rates			
6	Year	5%	6%	7%	8%	9%	10%
7	1	105.00	106.00	107.00	108.00	109.00	110.00
8	2	110.25	112.36	114.49	116.64	118.81	121.00
9	3	115.76	119.10	122.50	125.97	129.50	133.10
10	4	121.55	126.25	131.08	136.05	141.16	146.41
11	5	127.63	133.82	140.26	146.93	153.86	161.05

Figure 3.6

Let the initial investment be P and the annual interest rate r. At the end of year one the earned interest will be $P \times r$ and the investment will be worth $P + P \times r$ or $P(1 + r)$. At the end of year two its worth will be the starting value of $P(1 + r)$ plus the earned interest of $P(1 + r) \times r$. This sums to $P(1 + r)(1 + r)$ or $P(1 + r)^2$. At the end of n years the value will be $P(1 + r)^n$.

Before we start constructing the spreadsheet, let us work out what formula is needed in B7 with the design in Figure 3.6. To compute the quantity $P(1 + r)^n$ in B7, we could use the formula =B3*(1 + B6)^A7. This will correctly compute the value needed in B7, but incorrect results will be generated if it is copied to the other cells.

First, the B3 term represents P and we wish this reference to remain unchanged when the formula is copied. We achieve this by using $B$3 rather than the simple B3.

The next term, B6, represents the interest rate, r. As we copy the formula down the column we need the row (6) to stay unchanged but as we copy it across the row we want the column (B) to change. In column C, for example, we want the formula to use the 6% values in C6. So the second term becomes B$6.

In like manner, the term A7, which represents the number of years, n, should reference A7, A8, etc. as the formula is copied down the column but should reference A7 as we copy it across the first row. We can ensure this behaviour by using $A7, where the dollar symbol prevents the A part of the reference from changing. Putting everything together, we see that the formula required in B7 is =$B$3*(1 + B$6)^$A7.

(a) Begin your work on Sheet3 of the workbook CHAP3.XLS. Enter the text and values in rows 1 to 6, and in A7:A11. The text Interest Rate is entered in B5 and then, with B5:G5 selected, it is centred with the Merge and Center tool. Similarly, the text Year is entered in A5 and Merge and Center is used with A5:A6 selected. Remember that the AutoFill feature can be used to enter the series 5%, 6%, ... and 1, 2, ... Type in the first two values, select the cells and drag the fill handle. Complete this stage by selecting A5:G11 and adding borders.

Tip: The pointing method helps avoid typos with long formulas.

(b) Next we will enter the formula =$B$3*(1 + B$6)^$A7 in B7. With long formulas there is always the possibility of typo errors so we will use the pointing method to make the cell references. Begin by typing the = symbol then use the mouse to click on cell B3. This gives =B3. Press F4 to change this to =$B$3. Use the keyboard to expand this to =$B$3*(1+ and then point to B6 to get =$B$3*(1 + B6. Tap F4 to change this to read =$B$3*(1 + B$6. Continue in like manner until you have the complete formula =$B$3*(1 + B$6)^$A7.

(c) Format cell B7 to display two decimal places.

(d) Copy this cell down to row 11 by double clicking on its fill handle. With B7:B11 selected, drag the fill handle to the right to copy the formulas to column G. The values in B7:G11 of your worksheet should agree with those in Figure 3.6.

(e) Save the workbook CHAP3.XLS.

Exercise 6: Using Names

We shall see shortly how to give a name to a cell or to a range of cells. We shall begin by naming B3 as *Principal*. There are a number of advantages to working with named cells: formulas are more readily understood; the likelihood of typo errors is decreased; it is easier to remember the name of a cell especially when the cell is not visible in a large worksheet, etc.

Names are always treated as absolute references. After we name B3 as *Principal*, the formula =$B$3*(1 + B$6)^$A7 in B7 may be entered as =Principal*(1 + B$6)^$A7. Note that no dollar symbols are need with the name.

The two objectives of this exercise are learning how to give a name to a cell or a range and how to incorporate these names into formulas.

In Problem 1 of Chapter 2 you were asked to set up a worksheet to calculate the pay of Gourmet Catering employees. We will modify that worksheet to use named cells and ranges. When completed the new worksheet will resemble that in Figure 3.7.

	A	B	C	D	E	F	G	H
1				Gourmet Catering				
2								
3	Tax rate	15%						
4	HealthIns	5.00						
5								
6								
7	Employee	Hours	Rate	Pay	Insurance	Tax	Deductions	Net Pay
8	Joe	32	15.50	496.00	5.00	74.40	79.40	$ 416.60
9	Mary	32	15.50	496.00	5.00	74.40	79.40	$ 416.60
10	Fred	32	12.00	384.00	5.00	57.60	62.60	$ 321.40
11	Jane	25	12.00	300.00	5.00	45.00	50.00	$ 250.00
12	George	20	10.00	200.00	5.00	30.00	35.00	$ 165.00
13	Jill	32	8.00	256.00	5.00	38.40	43.40	$ 212.60
14			Totals	$ 2,132.00	$ 30.00	$ 319.80	$ 349.80	$ 1,782.20

Figure 3.7

(a) Open CHAP3.XLS and move to Sheet4. If you need to insert a sheet, see Exercise 7 of Chapter 2.

Reminder: If you mistakenly widen a row when attempting to select the row headers, remember the Undo tool will redress the problem.

(b) If you completed Problem 1 of Chapter 2 you can open the workbook and copy the range A1:H14 to the new worksheet in CHAP3.XLS. Remember you can use the Window menu item to move from one workbook to another when more than one is open. Next you need to insert four rows in the new worksheet. Left click on row heading 2, drag the mouse down to highlight four rows, right click and select the Insert menu item.

(c) Enter the text and values shown in A3:B4. Select the range A3:B4 and use the menu command Insert|Names|Create. The Name dialog box appears — see Figure 3.8. Microsoft Excel has correctly assumed that you wish to apply the names in the left column to the cells in the right column, so click on the OK button. You may find the wording 'Create names in' confusing when we are creating names *from* the cells in the left column.

(d) Select B7:H13. Here is a quick way to do that: click on B7, hold down ⇧Shift and click on H13. Use the menu command Insert|Names|Create to open the Name dialog box again. This time Excel has seen that you want the names from the top row.

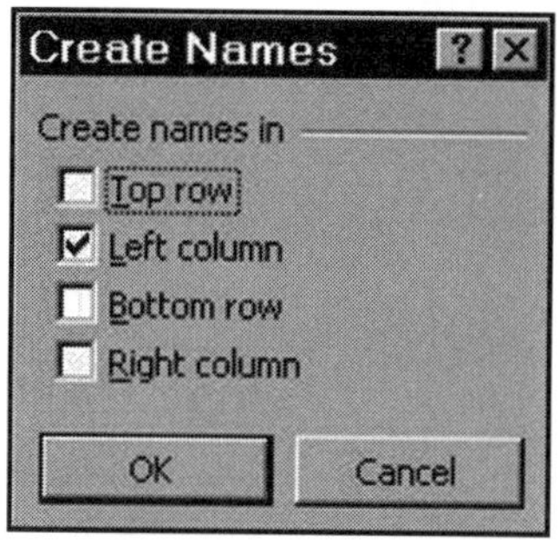

Figure 3.8

(e) Perhaps you would like to see a list of the names you have created. Move to a blank area of the worksheet, say A18. Use the command Insert|Name|Paste and click on Paste List in the resulting dialog box. Figure 3.9 shows the result. Excel is not keen on having blank spaces in names and has named B3 as Tax_rate and the range H8:H13 as Net_Pay, with an underscore character in place of the space.

Deductions	=Sheet4!$G$8:$G$13
HealthIns	=Sheet4!$B$4
Hours	=Sheet4!$B$8:$B$13
Insurance	=Sheet4!$E$8:$E$13
Net_Pay	=Sheet4!$H$8:$H$13
Pay	=Sheet4!$D$8:$D$13
Rate	=Sheet4!$C$8:$C$13
Tax	=Sheet4!$F$8:$F$13
Tax_rate	=Sheet4!$B$3

Figure 3.9

In the next two steps we see how to use the names just created. First, we will start with a black cell and see how we would construct a formula from scratch. This can be done in a variety of ways: (i) simply type the entry including the name, (ii) use the pointing method seen in Exercise 5, when you point to a names cell Excel inserts the name rather than the cell reference into the formula, (iii) use the Insert|Name|Paste command (the = symbol is automatically inserted if you are starting a formula).

> **Excel 2002:** To the left of the text box in the formula bar in Excel 2002 you will see the Insert Function tool. In previous versions this spot was occupied by the Edit Function tool which could be clicked to start a formula. The author misses the convenience of this.

(f) Select E8:E13 and use Delete to clear the cells. In these cells we need the formula =HealthIns. Use the three methods outlined above to enter the formula in E8:E10. Complete the column by dragging E10's fill handle down to E13. If you mistype the name using method (i), the cell will display a #NAME? error.

We have named the cells after completing the worksheet and we need a more efficient way of changing absolute references to names. We could do this in one step but it is more instructive to break the problem down into stages.

(g) In F8:F13 we wish to change references to $B$3 to Tax_rate. Thus the formula in F8 needs to change from =D8*$B$3 to =D8*Tax_rate. Select F8:F13 and use Insert|Name|Apply. In the Apply Names dialog (Figure 3.10) click on the names so that Tax_rate is selected (it does not matter if others are also selected) and uncheck the two option boxes. Click the OK button. The formulas now use the Tax_rate name.

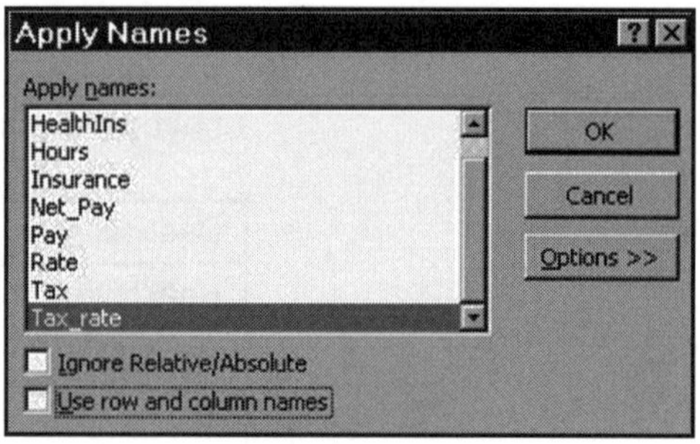

Figure 3.10

(h) You may wish to experiment on your own to have the cells in row 14 use names in place of ranges. For example, change D14 to =SUM(Pay) using any of the methods we have explored.

> **Excel 2002:** When step (i) is completed double click on any cell in D8:D13 as if you wished to edit the formula. This action will display the coloured range finders. In Excel 2002 they will correctly encompass each of the named ranges Hours and Rate. In earlier versions only the two cells to the left of the active cell will be encompassed.

(i) The following advanced step may be skipped. Select D8:D13, use Insert|Name|Apply and in the Apply Names dialog ensure that the names Hours and Rate are selected and that there are check marks in the two option boxes. Click the OK button. The formulas in each cell of the range now read =Hours*Rate. Both these names refer to a range. Normally, they would be used in formulas which take ranges as in =SUM(Hours). But in D8:D13 the two names are being used to refer to single cells. This use is restricted to rows 8 to 13 for the two names since that is the range that was used to define them. DO NOT confuse this with using labels in formulas (see Exercise 7).

(j) Save the workbook CHAP3.XLS.

Formulas Using Labels

Microsoft Excel 97 introduced a feature called *natural language formulas*. This allowed, without explicitly naming ranges, the use of row and column labels in formulas in a manner similar to, but actually subtly different from, range names. When, for example, this feature is active in a worksheet such as that in Figure 3.7, we could use the formulas =hours*rate and =SUM(pay) even if we had not named the ranges.

When it was first introduced it was hailed as a great convenience but it subsequently proved to be a mixed blessing because it led to great confusion and hence erroneous calculations. Microsoft contemplated removing the feature but some users wanted to keep it. The compromise is that when you instal Excel the use of row and column labels in formulas is not permitted. Those who wish to use it must reconfigure Excel.

Some textbooks still promote this feature, but you are strongly advised to stay clear of such muddy waters.

Summary

Relative, absolute and mixed references

1. When a cell with a formula using a relative reference (example =2*A1) is copied to another cell then the reference is changed. No change occurs when the formula is moved to another cell. When the reference is absolute (example =2*$A$1) the reference is unaltered when the cell is copied. Mixed references (example =2*$A2) allow us to specify that only the column or the row is to change.

2. The [F4] key may be used to place $ symbols in a cell reference.

3. When we need the same formula in a range, we can enter the formula in the first cell and pull the fill handle to copy it to the other cells. Excel adjusts the relative cell references. An alternative method is the select the range first, type the formula for the first cell and complete the entry with [Ctrl] +[Enter↵] rather than the simple [Enter↵].

4. Cell references are not altered when a formula is moved with Cut and Paste.

Named cells and ranges

1. We have seen the Insert|Name|Create method to name a cell or a range. One can also use Insert|Name|Define to name ranges and also constants and formulas. See Chapter 8, Exercise 3.

2. A name may have up to 255 characters but short names are more useful. The characters may be letters, digits, periods or underscores. The first character must be a letter or an underscore. Names are not case sensitive; thus SALES and Sales refer to the same named range.

3. If the Insert|Name|Create method is employed and a label to be used as a name contains a space (e.g. Tax rate), the actual name created has the space replaced by an underline symbol (e.g. Tax_rate).

4. If the Insert|Name|Create method is employed and the name to be used could be taken for a cell reference (e.g. X1) then the actual name replaces the space with an underline (e.g. X1_). The letters R and C have meaning for Microsoft Excel (row and column, respectively), so if labels with these single letters are used then the names created will be R_ and C_.

5. When a named cell is the active cell, the name box of the formula bar displays the name rather than the cell reference. When a named range is selected, its name is displayed.

6. Named cells and ranges are automatically adjusted when rows or columns are inserted or deleted.

7. If a range is named on one sheet of a workbook it may be referenced on another. Thus moving to Sheet2 of CHAP3.XLS and entering =Tax_Rate in an unused cell will return the value 15%. Had we used the same name for a cell on Sheet2, its value would be returned. If there is any ambiguity one can use a reference such as =Sheet4!Tax_Rate.

8. If, in Exercise 6, we had selected A8:H13 and used the Insert|Name|Create command, then the horizontal range B10:H10 would be called *Fred* while vertical range F8:F13 would be called *Tax*. A reference to *Fred Tax* (or *Tax Fred*) would return the value 57.60 since this is the value in the cell at the intersection of the two named ranges. The space in *Fred Tax* is called the intersection operator.

9. A reference to a non-existent (or misspelt) name results in a #NAME? error.

10. Use Insert|Names|Paste|Paste List to generate a list of names after ensuring the list will not overwrite existing entries.

11. If a label is changed after naming a cell or range, the name of the cell or range is unchanged. So if the text is changed in A3, the cell B3 retains the name Tax_rate.

Problems

1. In this problem we develop a worksheet to investigate the relationship between nominal and effective rates of interest. A bank, for example, may offer a savings account with 5% interest compounded monthly. We speak of the 5% as the nominal rate or the annual percentage rate (APR) but when the interest is compounded monthly a deposit of £100 earns £5.12 in interest, so the effective annual rate (EAR) is 5.12%.

   If we deposit an amount P, when the nominal rate is r, then with monthly compounding, the interest earned in the first month is $P \times r/12$. The nominal rate has been divided by 12 since the period is one-twelfth of a year. At the end of one month the deposit has grown to $P + P \times r/12$ or $P(1 + r/12)$. This is the starting amount for the second month. When completed the worksheet will resemble Figure 3.11.

	A	B	C	D	E	F	G
1	Principal	100					
2							
3							
4	month	5%	6%	7%	8%	9%	10%
5	0	100.00	100.00	100.00	100.00	100.00	100.00
6	1	100.42	100.50	100.58	100.67	100.75	100.83
7	2	100.84	101.00	101.17	101.34	101.51	101.67
8	3	101.26	101.51	101.76	102.01	102.27	102.52
9	4	101.68	102.02	102.35	102.69	103.03	103.38
10	5	102.10	102.53	102.95	103.38	103.81	104.24
11	6	102.53	103.04	103.55	104.07	104.59	105.11
12	7	102.95	103.55	104.16	104.76	105.37	105.98
13	8	103.38	104.07	104.76	105.46	106.16	106.86
14	9	103.81	104.59	105.37	106.16	106.96	107.75
15	10	104.25	105.11	105.99	106.87	107.76	108.65
16	11	104.68	105.64	106.61	107.58	108.57	109.56
17	12	105.12	106.17	107.23	108.30	109.38	110.47
18							
19	EAR						
20	(A)	5.12%	6.17%	7.23%	8.30%	9.38%	10.47%
21	(B)	5.12%	6.17%	7.23%	8.30%	9.38%	10.47%

Figure 3.11

(i) Row 5 shows the value of the initial deposit. What formula will be entered in B5 so that it may be copied across to G5?

(ii) Row 6 shows the value of the investment after the first month. What formula can we use in B6 such that it may be copied to B6:G17?

(iii)The effective rate of interest can be computed from $\frac{\text{Final Value - Initial Value}}{\text{Initial Value}} \times 100$. If we format B20 as a percentage, what formula may be used here and copied across to G20?

(iv)The EAR may also be computed using the formula EAR =(1 + $r/m)^m$ - 1,where r is the nominal rate and m is the number of compounding periods. What formula may be used in B21 such that it can be copied across to G21.

2.* Acme Manufacturing is considering three sites (A, B and C) for a new factory. The fixed costs of the three sites are shown in B5:D5 of Figure 3.12 and the variable cost for a thousand units are in B6:D6.

	A	B	C	D
1	Factory location problem			
2				
3			Locations	
4	Costs	A	B	C
5	Fixed	140,000	100,000	220,000
6	Variable/thou	8	14	4
7				
8		Total annual costs ($000)		
9	Production (thousands)	A	B	C
10	0	140	100	220
11	2	156	128	228
12	4	172	156	236
13	6	188	184	244
14	8	204	212	252
15	10	220	240	260
16	12	236	268	268
17	14	252	296	276
18	16	268	324	284
19	18	284	352	292
20	20	300	380	300
21	22	316	408	308
22	24	332	436	316

Figure 3.12

(i) What formula will you type in B10 so that it may be copied across to column D10 and down to row 22?

(ii) What conclusions do you reach as to the best site?

To enter the text in A9, type Production, press Alt+Enter and complete the entry by typing (thousands). This is called text wrapping. This problem is examined again in Chapter 7.

4
Using Functions

Objectives

Upon completion of this chapter, you will know:

- what is meant by a worksheet function, an argument and an error value;
- the syntax and behaviour of the common arithmetic functions: SUM, AVERAGE, COUNT, etc.;
- how to use the AutoSum tool to perform a SUM function, and if you are using Excel 2002, some other common functions;
- how to use the common financial functions: PV, FV, PMT, etc.

Introduction to Functions

An Excel worksheet function is often a predefined expression. Thus, for example, the formula =SUM(A1:A5) is equivalent to =A1+A2+A3+A4+A5. Think how useful the SUM function would be if we needed to total 100 cells. Here the worksheet function would save a great deal of typing. In other cases, worksheet functions perform more complex mathematical operations such as computing the payments due on a loan. This saves us delving too deeply into higher mathematics.

Microsoft Excel provides over 300 worksheet functions which are conveniently divided into 10 groups: math and trig, engineering, logical, statistical, date and time, database, financial, informational, lookup and reference, and text. In addition, the user may construct custom functions using the built-in Visual Basic Editor but we shall not explore this topic.

Arguments and syntax

In a formula such as =SUM(A1:A5) the range A1:A5 is called the *argument*. Some functions have a fixed number of arguments while others can have a variable number. If you check with Help, you will find the syntax (the rules) for the SUM functions is written as **SUM(number1**, number2, …) in which number1, number2, etc. are 1 to 30 arguments for which you want the total value or sum. The items in bold (SUM and number1) are required while the other arguments are optional. The ellipse (…) is used to indicate that more arguments may follow the first two. So this function may take one or more arguments. The formula =SUM(A1:A5, B1:B5) sums the values in the two ranges A1:A5 and B1:B5 while =SUM(A1:A5,

B2, 10) sums the range A1:A5, and adds to it the value in B2 and the value 10. Do not overwork this function; =A1+B1 is generally preferable to =SUM(A1:B1).

Figure 4.1 will help you learn the terminology and rules associated with making formulas that use worksheet functions.

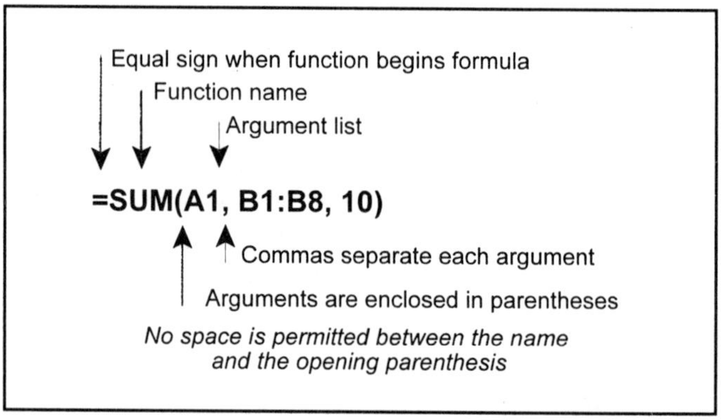

Figure 4.1

When you use Help for information on a function with a variable number of arguments, the required arguments are displayed in bold and the optional ones are in normal weight. The maximum number of arguments is 30 and the number of characters used in the arguments list may not exceed 1,024.

While some functions require specific types of arguments, most functions permit an argument to be a cell reference, a range reference, a constant, an expression or another function. Certain functions require text-type arguments and others require logical arguments. Here are some examples of arguments:

Cell and range
    =SUM(A1, B1:B10) Sum A1 and the range B1:B10
Named range
    =SUM(Xvalues) Sum the named range Xvalues
Cell and constant
    =MAX(A1, 20) The maximum of A1 and 20
Constant
    =LOG10(9.81) Logarithm of 9.81
Expression
    =INT(A1/2) Integer of half the value in A1
Function
    =INT(SUM(A1:A10)) Integer of the sum of the range

Nesting

When a function is used as an argument for another function, we use the term *nesting*. Functions may be nested up to seven levels. An example of two-level nesting is =MAX(SUM(A1:A20), SUM(B1:B20)). To understand this we work from the inside: (1) the function sums two columns of numbers, and (2) it selects the sum with the maximum value. We speak of a function *returning* a value. The function in this example *returns* the larger of the sums of two ranges. A three-level nesting is =INT(MAX(SUM(avalues), SUM(bvalues))). The first two steps for this are the same as before: (1) sum two named ranges and (2) find the sum with the maximum value. Finally, (3) the function returns the integer value of this maximum sum.

Combining functions

Formulas may be constructed from cell references, constants and functions. For example, =2.5 * SUM(A1:A20) / SQRT(B1) is a formula with two functions and a constant. Recall that the spaces around the arithmetic operators are optional.

Using Help

There is not room in this book to discuss all the worksheet functions. The reader is encouraged to use Help and type 'worksheet functions' in the Answer Wizard box and then select 'worksheet functions listed by category' from the topics. You should review the list before constructing a complex formula or worksheet. You do not want to reinvent the wheel!

Some functions are described as *array functions* and need to be entered in a special manner. We examine some of these later.

Error value

Excel displays one of the following error values if a mistake is made when entering a formula.

#DIV/0!	The formula is attempting division by zero — a mathematical impossibility.
#NAME?	A formula contains an undefined variable or function name.
#N/A	No value is available. In addition to being a error value, it can also be returned deliberately by the function NA().
#NULL!	No value to return. Maybe you specify an intersection of two areas that do not intersect.
#NUM!	Numeric overflow; e.g. a cell with =SQRT(Z1) when

	Z1 has a negative value.
#REF!	Invalid cell reference; often this results when a cell (not its contents) has been deleted.
#VALUE!	Invalid argument type; e.g. a cell with =PV(A1, A2, A3) when one of the cells A1, A2, or A3 contains text but the Present Value function expects numeric data.

When a cell having an error value is referenced in the formula of a second cell, that cell will also have an error value.

Constructing formulas

An error you are sure to meet once or twice is the *circular reference* error. Normally, a formula should not contain a reference to the cell address of its own location. For example, it would be meaningless to place in A10 the formula =SUM(A1:A10). If you try this Microsoft Excel displays an error dialog box 'Cannot resolve circular reference' with an OK and a Help button. If you click OK, the value 0 will display in A10 and the status bar will display 'Circular: A10' to warn you of the problem. You will need to edit the formula. There are some specialized uses for circular references.

To make a formula which uses a function you may: (1) type the function, (2) access the function using the Insert Function tool, (3) enter the SUM function, or with Excel 2002 the SUM, AVERAGE, COUNT, MAX and MIN functions, with the AutoSum tool. The first three exercises of this chapter explore the three methods.

Exercise 1: Using the AutoSum tool

We begin by using the AutoSum tool which is found on the standard toolbar. The icon depicts the Greek character sigma (Σ) which is used by mathematicians as the summation symbol.

At the completion of the next three exercises, your worksheet should resemble that in Figure 4.2.

(a) Open a new workbook. Enter the values shown in the first three rows. The word wrap in F3 is achieved with Alt+Enter between the words.

(b) Enter the numeric values in A4:A8 and the text values in C4:C8. Add formatting as required.

(c) Make A9 the active cell A4 and click the AutoSum button on the standard toolbar. If you are using Excel 2002 make sure

Σ Earlier Excel AutoSum tool

Σ▾ Excel 2002 AutoSum tool

New Excel 2002 features

you click the lefthand side of the icon not the downward pointing arrow. AutoSum will select the range A4:A8 for its argument. Click the formula bar's Enter icon (✓) to complete the formula. Cell A4 contains =SUM(A4:A8).

Excel 2002 users will have noticed a blue formula tip appear when the AutoSum tool was clicked. You will see these tips throughout the exercises in this chapter; their purpose is to remind you of the syntax of the functions.

(d) Move the contents of A9 to D4 using the Cut and Paste tools or the shortcuts learned in Exercise 4 of Chapter 1.

	A	B	C	D	E	F
1	**Simple functions**					
2					Results	
3	Data			AutoSum	Manual	Insert Function
4	3		Sum	58	58	58
5	10		Average	11.6	11.6	11.6
6	15		Count	5	5	5
7	26		Max	26	26	26
8	4		Min	3	3	3
9						

Figure 4.2

The AutoSum tool generally locates the range to be added correctly. If it fails to do so you may use the pointing method to correct the formula. If you are not using Excel 2002 move to step (h) of this exercise.

(e) Repeat step (c) but this time click on the down arrow to open the menu attached to the AutoSum tool. Select the AVERAGE function. Complete the formula as before and move it to D5.

(f) Repeat step (e) for the COUNT and MAX functions — rather repetitive but it will help you remember them!

(g) We will place the formula in D3 in a slightly different way. With D3 as the active cell click to open the AutoSum menu and select MIN. AutoSum thinks you want to find the minimum of the three cells above D3. Use the mouse to drag over A4:A8 and so correct the formula. Complete it with the [Enter ↵].

(h) Save the workbook as CHAP4.XLS.

Exercise 2: Entering Functions Manually

The functions we are using in this exercise are rather simple and are most readily entered either with the AutoSum tool or by manually typing them.

(a) In E1 of Sheet1 of CHAP4.XLS type the formula =SUM(A4:D8) and press [Enter↵]. Naturally you get the same answer as before.

Excel 2002 users will again see the formula tip as soon as they have typed =SUM(. Other users may try this: after typing =SUM(, use the key combination [⇧Shift]+[Ctrl]+A. This places the syntax of the function in the cell. However, since this function has optional arguments, this technique makes it more cumbersome to build the formula. With more complex functions it can be very helpful.

Formula tips: If you mistype the word AVERAGE when constructing a formula, no formula tip appears. This is a helpful way of avoiding typo errors with function names.

(b) For the next formula we will use the pointing method that we explored in Exercise 2 of Chapter 3. Begin by typing =AVERAGE(. Now use the mouse to select the range A4:A8 and complete the formula by typing the closing parenthesis and clicking the enter tool on the formula bar.

(c) Repeat step (b) to enter the COUNT formula in E6 but omit the final parenthesis before click the enter tool. Excel automatically adds the missing parenthesis to the formula. In other cases the correction will not be automatic but a dialog box will inform you of an error and suggest a correction that you can accept or decline.

(d) Complete the exercise by adding formulas to E7:E8 and save the workbook.

Exercise 3: Insert Function Dialog

New Excel 2002 feature

The Insert Function or Paste Function tool

Next we will learn how to use less familiar functions. Perhaps we do not know the exact name or are unsure of the syntax.

Excel 2002 introduced some changes in nomenclature. Whereas Excel 97 and Excel 2000 users speak about the Paste Function tool and the Formula Palette, Excel 2002 users talk of the Insert Function tool and dialog box. Also, the location of the tool has been changed. The Paste Function tool is on the standard toolbar while the Insert Function tool is on the formula bar. Functionally, everything works more or less the same in all Excel versions! This exercise uses the terminology of Excel 2002; other users should readily be able to follow the instructions.

Again we are going to construct formulas using the functions SUM, AVERAGE, etc. Since these are very simple functions we shall not need much help from Excel.

(a) Select cell F4 on Sheet1 of CHAP4.XLS. Click the Insert Function tool to open the Insert Function dialog box — Figure 4.3. The Search box, new in Excel 2002, is for use when the user does not know the name of the function. We are not in that position.

Shortcut: To open the Insert Function dialog use ⇧Shift+F3.
Alternative: Use Insert Function.

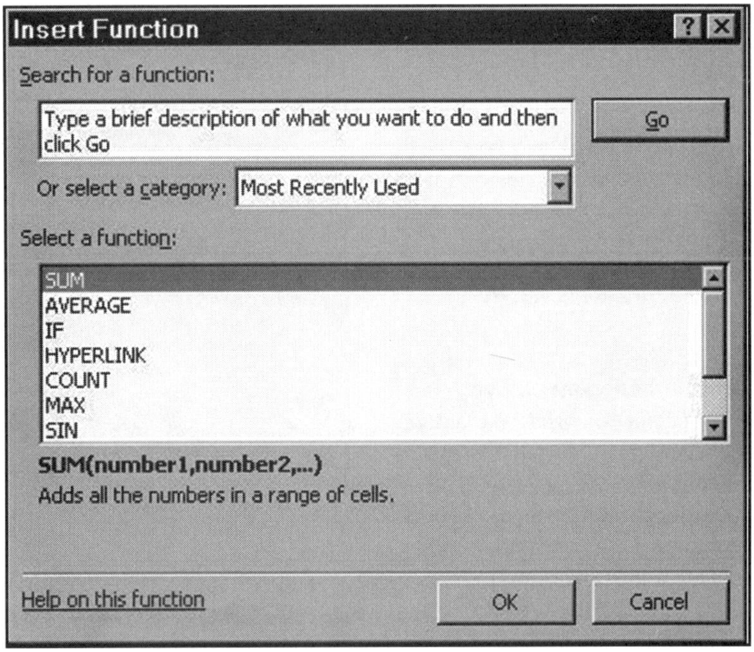

Figure 4.3

(b) Under Function Category you will find a list of the various categories. The dialog starts with *Most recently used* displayed and most likely SUM is in this group. If not, open the *Math & Trig* category and locate SUM. Select SUM with the mouse when you have located it. Note how Excel displays the syntax and a brief description of the function. Click the OK button.

Time saver tip: When searching a category, typing the first letter of the function (here S) will speed up the search.

(c) The Function Argument dialog box (aka Function Palette) shown in Figure 4.4 is displayed. Excel has tried to be helpful and has guessed at the range we wish to use, so the text box initially says A4:E4. Observe the array of values to the right of the text box. We wish to enter A1:A3. We may do this by either typing or by using the pointing method.

The dialog box may be dragged out of the way if needed. However, there is a better way. Click on the icon with a red upwards pointing arrow in the Number1 box to collapse the dialog box. Complete your entry in the box by pointing and resize the dialog box by clicking the red downwards pointing arrow to reopen the dialog.

If you do not collapse the dialog box, Excel automatically collapses and reopens it when you drag over a range to complete an argument box.

Time saver tip: There is no need to delete the current entry — it is in reverse type so it will disappear as soon as new data is entered.

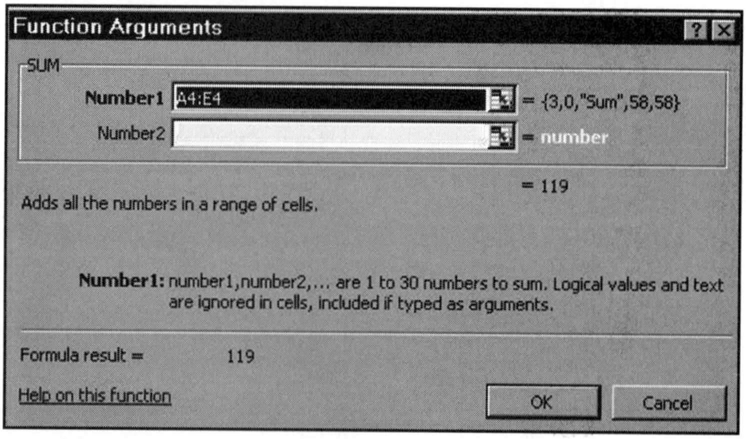

Figure 4.4

Insert Function: If you use Insert Function when the active cell contains a formula using a function, the dialog box will have the argument text boxes completed. This offers a simple way to adjust a formula.

(d) Repeat these steps to add the other formulas. The functions AVERAGE, COUNT, MAX and MIN can be found in the *Statistical* category. For practice, pretend you do not know the function is called AVERAGE. Type a suitable question (e.g. 'How do I find the average') in the Search box, click the Go button and observe the result.

Exercise 4: Mixed Text and Numeric Values

Some functions can tolerate arguments that point to a mixture of numeric and textual values even when numeric values are expected. The functions SUM, AVERAGE and COUNT are amongst these.

(a) On Sheet1 of CHAP2.XLS type some text such as ABC in A2. Observe how the results of the formulas are altered. Change the numeric values to 2 leaving text in one cell. How does the AVERAGE function handle the textual value? Does it ignore it or count it as zero? Use Help to see if your answer was correct.

(b) Experiment in column G with formulas such as =AVERAGEA(A4:A8) and COUNTA(A4:A8). How do these functions differ from their 'cousins'?

(c) How does the formula =A4+A5+A6+A7+A8 behave when one of the values is text?

Exercise 5: Rounding and Truncating Functions

In Exercise 7 of Chapter 2 we saw that formatting a cell changes the way a value is displayed but does not change the stored values. Excel provides a number of functions which either truncate or round a value to a required number of digits or to a multiple of some number. A list of these is given in Figure 4.5.

ABS	Returns the absolute value. =ABS(−12.55) returns 12.55.
CEILING	Rounds a number up (away from zero) to the nearest multiple of significance. =CEILING(1.255, 0.5) returns 1.5.
EVEN	Rounds a number to the nearest even integer. =EVEN(3.25) returns 4.
FLOOR	Rounds a number down (towards zero) to the nearest multiple of significance. =FLOOR(1.255,0.5) returns 1.0.
INT	Truncates a number to the nearest integer. =INT(2.4) returns 2 and INT(−2.4) returns −3. Compare with TRUNC.
MROUND	Returns a number rounded to the required multiple. =MROUND(6.89,4) returns 8 since the multiple of 4 closest to 6.89 is 8. This function is only available when the Analysis Pack is installed.
ODD	Rounds a number to the nearest odd integer. =ODD(4.25) returns 5.
ROUND	Rounds a number to the required number of digits. =ROUND(1.378,2) returns 1.38 (two decimal). =ROUND(123.56,−1) returns 120 (nearest 10). =ROUND(123.56,0) returns 124 (nearest integer).
ROUNDDOWN	Similar to ROUND but always rounds down.
ROUNDUP	Similar to ROUND but always rounds up.
TRUNC	Truncates a number to the nearest integer. =TRUNC(2.4) returns 2 and TRUNC(−2.4) returns −2. Compare with INT.

Figure 4.5

Constant values are used in the examples in this figure to facilitate the discussion. Clearly, the functions would normally be used with cell references or an expression as the first argument. The ROUND function is especially useful when dealing with currency.

	A	B
1	Value of x	1.255
2	ROUND(x, 2)	1.26
3	CEILING(x, 0.5)	1.5
4	EVEN(x)	2
5	FLOOR(x, 0.5)	1

Figure 4.6

(a) On Sheet2 of CHAP4.XLS, construct a worksheet to verify the statements made above. Figure 4.6 shows how to start it.

(b) Enter the text in column A and the value 1.255 in B1.

(c) In the remaining cells of column B, enter the appropriate functions. For example, in B2 enter =ROUND(B1, 2).

(d) Add more examples from the table in Figure 4.5.

(e) Change the value in B1 and ensure you understand the results returned by the functions.

(f) Save the workbook CHAP4.XLS.

Most of us use a simple algorithm for rounding. We examine the first digit to be dropped: (i) if it is less than 5, we drop it and all digits to the right, and (ii) if it is 5 or more, we increase the digit to the left by one. There is a body of thought that believes the rules should be: examine the first digit to be dropped: (i) if it is less than 5, drop it and all digits to the left, (ii) if it is greater than 5, increase the digit to the left by one, and (iii) if it is 5, round the number so that the result will be even. There is currently no simple function in Microsoft Excel for rounding using the 'new mathematics'.

Exercise 6: Rounding the Interest

In Problem 1 of Chapter 3, you computed the value of a savings account accumulating interest monthly and formatted the numbers to display two decimal places to make the worksheet look better. Remember that formatting changes what is displayed, not the stored value. In this exercise we compare three methods of calculating the values: (i) with no rounding, (ii) with rounding to the nearest penny, and (iii) with truncation to the nearest penny. The completed worksheet will resemble that in Figure 4.7.

(a) Begin this exercise on Sheet3 of CHAP4.XLS by entering the text and values in A1:B2. Select A1:B2 and name B1 and B2 as *Principal* and *Rate*, respectively, using Insert|Name|Create.

(b) Enter the text in row 4 and, using the Auto Fill feature, the series in A5:A17.

Time saver tip: The series in A5:A17 has an increment of 1. The quickest way to enter it is (1) enter the 0 in A5, (2) hold Ctrl, and (3) drag the fill handle down to A17.

	A	B	C	D
1	Principal	100.00		
2	Rate	10%		
3				
4	month	no rounding	round	rounddown
5	0	100.0000	100.0000	100.0000
6	1	100.8333	100.8300	100.8300
7	2	101.6736	101.6700	101.6700
8	3	102.5209	102.5200	102.5100
9	4	103.3752	103.3700	103.3600
10	5	104.2367	104.2300	104.2200
11	6	105.1053	105.1000	105.0800
12	7	105.9812	105.9800	105.9500
13	8	106.8644	106.8600	106.8300
14	9	107.7549	107.7500	107.7200
15	10	108.6529	108.6500	108.6100
16	11	109.5583	109.5600	109.5100
17	12	110.4713	110.4700	110.4200

Figure 4.7

(c) In B5 enter =Principal. Remember that the quickest and surest way is to type the = symbol and then to point at the cell B1 — in this context, *point* means to click on the cell. Format the cell to display 4 decimals and copy it to C5 and D5.

(d) The formulas required in row 6 are:

B6: =B5*(1 + Rate/12)

C6: =ROUND(C5*(1 + Rate/12), 2).

D6: =ROUNDDOWN(D5*(1 + Rate/12), 2)

The calculations in B6:D6 are the same but the ROUND function rounds the value to two decimal places (to the nearest penny) and the ROUNDDOWN function truncates or rounds down the value to the nearest penny.

(e) Select B6:D6, format the range to display four decimal places, and copy it down to row 17. The worksheet should now look like Figure 4.7. Save the workbook.

Compare the final values in row 17. When the principal is 100 and the annual rate is 10%, there is a 0.05 difference in the normal rounding and the rounddown methods. The method with no rounding agrees best with the normal rounding method. This is not surprising since the rounding method, on average, rounds up half the time and down half the time. We return to this topic briefly in Exercise 8.

You may be thinking 'There may be a small difference when the principal is only 100 but what about a large value?' Try the what-if analysis for yourself by entering a large value in B1. Even with a principal of one billion (the quickest way is to type 1e9 in B1 and then format the cell with the currency tool), the rounding and the rounddown results differ only by a few pennies.

There is an urban myth that the first computer crime had to do with someone transferring all the fractions of cents resulting from truncation to his own bank account. Now you can see how little he would have made! In E5 enter the formula =C5-D5, copy it down to E17 and use =SUM(E5:D17) in C18 to find the felon's profit on a $1,000,000,000 savings account.

This fairly simple worksheet has enabled us to perform some experiments and draw some interesting conclusions (the major one being that regular rounding versus rounddown has little effect) without doing any sophisticated mathematics.

Exercise 7: Weighed Average Problem

A manager wishes to compute the average salary for his staff. The company pay scheme has 10 steps and each of the 80 employees in the department belongs to a salary group — see Figure 4.8.

(a) Open CHAP4.XLS and move to Sheet4 or insert a new sheet if required. Enter the data shown in A1:C16 of Figure 4.8.

(b) The formula in D4 is =B4*C4. Copy this down to D13.

(c) The formula in C14 is =SUM(C4:C13) and D14 has a similar summation.

	A	B	C	D
1	Average salary			
2				
3	Group	Salary	Employees	Product
4	A	70,000	1	70,000
5	B	65,000	3	195,000
6	C	60,000	4	240,000
7	D	55,000	8	440,000
8	E	50,000	10	500,000
9	F	45,000	15	675,000
10	G	40,000	12	480,000
11	H	35,000	15	525,000
12	I	30,000	8	240,000
13	J	25,000	4	100,000
14			80	3,465,000
15			average 1	43,313
16			average 2	43,313

Figure 4.8

(d) The average in D15 is computed using =D14/C14 and the cell is formatted to show no decimals. Alternatively, one could use =ROUND(D14/C14, 0) to compute the value to the nearest integer.

This is fairly straightforward but there is a quicker way. Use Help to learn about the SUMPRODUCT function. The syntax is SUMPRODUCT(array1,array2,array3, ...), where *array1*, *array2*, etc. are ranges having the same dimensionality (the same number of rows and same number of columns as each other).

To edit a formula: Double click the cell or press [F2]. Note the colour coded range finders and the word *edit* in the Excel status bar.

Use the keyboard and/or mouse to edit the formula. You can work with the formula in the cell or in the formula bar.

To extend the range referenced in a formula, pull down the range finder.

(e) In D16 enter
=SUMPRODUCT(B4:B13, C4:C13) / SUM(C4:C13).
Other than having more decimal places, the result should be the same as in D15. To compute the average to the nearest integer edit the formula to read:
=ROUND(SUMPRODUCT(B4:B13, C4:C113) / SUM(C4:C13), 0)

(f) Save the workbook.

The moral of this exercise is: you cannot be expected to know all the worksheet functions but before developing a worksheet it pays to use Help. The Insert Function dialog also provides information on each function that you highlight.

The Basic Financial Functions

Many financial calculations require the answer to questions like these:

1. If I invest $2,000 at 7.5%, what will it be worth in 5 years?

2. What are the monthly payments needed to retire a $145,000 mortgage in 20 years when the borrowing rate is 8.3%?

3. How much do I need to purchase an annuity that pays $1,000 each month for 18 years, assuming an interest rate of 6.5%?

4. If I make quarterly payments of $100 for five years, I can cash in an investment and receive $2,500; what is the effective annual rate of return?

The 50 or so financial functions of Microsoft Excel provide a very convenient way to solve problems of this type. The basic functions include PV (present value), FV (future value), PMT (payment), RATE (interest rate, rate of return) and NPER (number of payments).

To use these functions we must recognize that the terms present value, future value, rate, etc. are interrelated. For example, in Excel we have a function called PV which is used when we want to compute the present value and an argument called *pv* which is used when we compute another quantity (future value, for example) knowing the present value. It will be helpful if we begin by defining the arguments, which is done in Figure 4.9.

Abbreviation and name	**Description**
fv future value	The value in the future when all payments have been made. For example, the value of a saving bond on maturity.
nper number of payments	The number of payments on a loan (or by an annuity) during the time period of interest.
pv present value	The value at the start of an investment period. For example, the principal amount of a loan.
pmt payment	The amount paid periodically on a loan or by an investment.
rate rate	The interest rate or discount rate for a loan or investment.
type type	Specifies whether payments are made at the beginning or end of the payment period. If *type* is set to 0 (or omitted) the calculation assumes payments are made at the end of the period, If *type* is set to 1, payments are due at the start of the period.

Figure 4.9

The syntax for each of the basic financial functions is shown below. Arguments shown in bold are required; the others are optional. The value of an omitted optional argument is taken to be zero.

Future value	=**FV(rate, nper,** pmt, pv, type)
Number of payments	=**NPER(rate, pmt, pv**, fv, type)
Payment	=**PMT(rate, nper, pv,** type)
Present value	=**PV(rate, nper,** pmt, fv, type)
Rate	=**RATE(nper, pmt, pv**, fv, type, guess)

Note how each function uses as its arguments the other four quantities plus the type argument. Clearly all five quantities (fv, pv, rate, nper and pmt) are interrelated and one must know four of them (even if some are zero) to compute the fifth. The Microsoft Web site may be consulted to see the mathematical functions used by each worksheet function.

There are two important points to remember about arguments.

(i) It is essential that you are consistent with the units used in the arguments. For example, suppose we wish to calculate the future value of $100 deposited in a savings account for 5 years at an annual rate of 8%. If the interest is compounded monthly then the *rate* argument for this problem should be entered as 8%/12 while *nper* should be 5*12.

(ii) Use positive values for cash received (inflows) and negative values for cash paid out (outflows). The financial functions will automatically format their cells such that negative results are displayed in red.

Here are some examples of the use of the functions.

Future value

At the end of each month, $100 is deposited in a savings account that pays an annual interest rate of 8%. What will be the value of the investment after 5 years if interest is accrued monthly? Clearly this is a future value question.

rate	8%/12	the monthly interest rate
nper	5*12	the number of monthly payments
pmt	-100	the monthly payments; negative since it is cash paid
pv	0	there was no money in the account beforehand
type	0	payments are due at the end of the month

The syntax is =**FV(rate, nper, pmt**, pv, type). So we may use =FV(8%/12, 5*12, -100, 0, 0) or, since both *pv* and *type* are optional and have zero values, =FV(8%/12, 5*12, -100). The result is $7,347.69 in either case.

Another example of future value: what will be the value of £1,000 invested at 6% per annum for 5 years if interested is paid monthly? In this case the £1,000 (or strictly -1,000 since is was paid into the account) is the present value and the payments will be zero. Hence the formula needed is =FV(6%/12, 5*12, 0, -1000) which returns the value £1,348.85.

An aside: the Help feature in Excel 97 shows the *pmt* argument as optional but other versions do not. It may be omitted only when a *pv* value is entered in the formula. So =FV(6%/12, 5*12,-1000) is acceptable.

Number of payments

I need to borrow $4,000. The annual rate on the loan is 9% compounded monthly and I can afford payments of $300 a month. How long will it take to repay the loan? The formula to solve this problem is =**NPER(rate, pmt, pv**, fv, type) or =NPER(9%/12, -300, 4000). The optional *fv* and *type* arguments have been omitted. The *future value* is 0 since I plan to pay off all the loan and *type* is 0 since payments will be made at the end of the month. This returns a value of 14.1 so I could pay off the loan in just over 14 months. Use PMT to compute the actual monthly payment on the 14-month loan.

Be forewarned: NPER has a nasty habit of surprising people. You might, for example, try to find how many monthly £100 payments are needed to replay a £10,000 loan when the rate is 10% pa. The formula =NPER(10%/12, -100, 10000) returns the error value #NUM!. The monthly payment is not enough to cover the monthly interest charges so the loan keeps growing and can never be repaid.

Payment

Can I get a more realistic answer to the above problem? What will be the monthly payment on a $4,000 loan at an annual rate of 9% compounded monthly if it is to be paid off in 14 months? The *rate*, *nper* and *pv* are clearly 9%/12, 14 and 4000, respectively. Since the loan is to be totally paid off, the future value will be 0. We assume that payments are due at the end of the month so *type* = 0 and may therefore be omitted. The required formula is =**PMT(rate, nper, pv,** type) or =PMT(9%/12, 14, 4000) which returns the value

-$302.05. In the problem, we stipulated that we could afford $300 a month; if we can find an extra $2.05 we can pay the loan off in 14 months.

Note that if you use PMT to compute mortgage payments, the resulting value may not totally agree with what the bank requires because the PMT does not include taxes and insurance.

Present value

You have some property to sell. Buyer A offers to pay £100,000 while buyer B offers five yearly payments of £30,000. Which is the better offer if you assume an annual discount rate of 8%? The present value of A's offer is exactly £100,000. The present value of B's offer can be found using =**PV(rate, nper,** pmt, fv, type) or =PV(8%, 5, -30000, 0, 1). The last argument sets *type* to 1 since the payments will begin immediately. The formula returns a value of £129,364. So B's offer is worth more than A's. The amount £129,364 is sometimes called the discounted value of the three future payments of £30,000.

Rate

Your are planning your retirement investment. You currently have $25,000 and can afford to invest $5,000 every year. You would like to retire a millionaire in 25 years' time. What interest rate would be needed? The syntax for Rate is =**RATE(nper, pmt, pv,** fv, type, guess). Using =RATE(25, -5000, -5000, 1000000, 1) you find that the annual rate must be 11.1%. The final argument of 1 in the formula is the type and indicates you will make the $5,000 investment at the start of each year. An alternative formula =RATE(25*12, -5000/12, -25000, 1000000)*12 could be used if the $5,000 was paid in 12 instalments at the end of each month. Note that the value returned by the function is multiplied by 12 to give an annual rate. This produces a value of 10.8%.

The *guess* argument needs a word of explanation. Whereas the other functions use a simple substitution method to compute their values, the RATE function uses an iterative method. If a value for *guess* is omitted, a value of 10% is used as the starting value. If the successive results of RATE do not converge to within 0.0000001 after 20 iterations, RATE returns the #NUM! error value. Providing it with a starting value (the *guess* argument) can help the solution process but, in this example, it was not necessary.

Exercise 8: Another Savings Plan

In this exercise we show how the result of Exercise 6 may be obtained by using the future value function. We also compute the final value of a regular deposit savings plan. Our worksheet will resemble that in Figure 4.10 upon completion.

	A	B	C	D	E
1	Future value calculations				
2	=fv(rate,nper,pmt,pv,type)				
3					
4	A one-time deposit				
5	deposit	100	one time		
6	rate	5%	annual	FV	$105.12
7	payment	0	monthy		
8	Periods	1	years		
9					
10	Monthly deposits				
11	deposit	0	one time		
12	rate	5%	annual	FV	$1,227.89
13	payment	100	monthy		
14	Periods	1	years		

Figure 4.10

(a) On Sheet5 of CHAP4.XLS begin by entering the text and values in A1:D14. A single quote must be typed before the equals sign to display the text in A2. Note that A11:D14 can be quickly entered by copying A5:D8 and then editing a few cells.

(b) To compute the first FV we will use the formula =FV(B6/12, B8*12, -B7, -B5) in E6. The term -B7 may seem redundant when B7 has a zero value but we are going to copy this formula later. We will use the Insert Function tool to enter this formula but since we know the name of the function we will use a shortcut. In E6 type =FV. Press the keys Ctrl +A to bring up the dialog box similar to Figure 4.11.

Enter the values shown. Remember that simple cell references can be entered by pointing with the mouse. Note how the dialog box reports the computed value of 105.1161898 just below the FV box, and the formatted returned result of $105.12 at the bottom of the dialog box. The value 105.116... agrees with our value in column B of Exercise 6. Clearly, Microsoft Excel performed the calculation using a simple mathematical formula with no intermediate rounding.

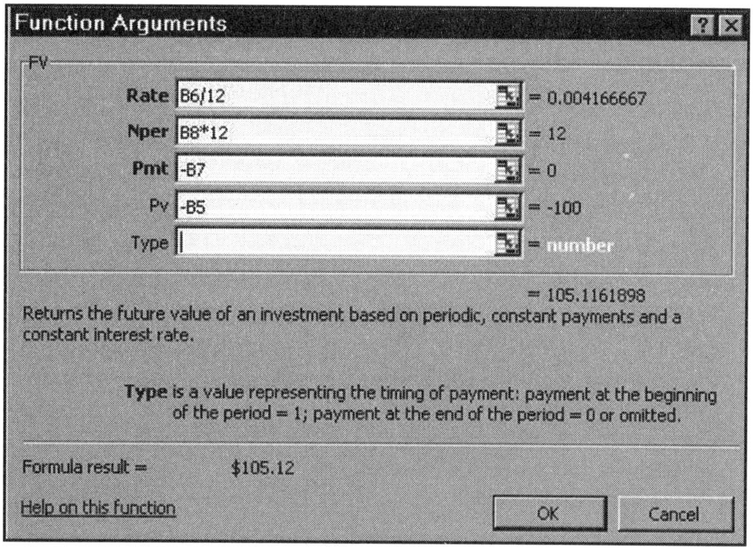

Figure 4.11

(c) Copy the formula from E6 to E12 to compute the future value of a monthly series of deposits to a savings account.

(d) Save the workbook CHAP4.XLS.

Exercise 9: A Decision Model

Engineers often make physical models to test a design. A model aircraft in a wind tunnel is an example. Computers allow us to build mathematical models and to conduct 'experiments'. We often call these 'what-if' scenarios. In this exercise we develop a simple model to help an entrepreneur make an investment decision.

Ms Jones has the opportunity of acquiring some rental property. The figures are not finalized but she makes a note of the factors to be considered — see Figure 4.12. Even without exact figures, Ms Jones can make some educated guesses. Only if it looks like a good investment, will she go to the trouble of getting exact data.

Mortgage:	$350,000 at 9% (hopefully) annual over 15 years	
Property taxes:	Check with Town Hall for assessment value	
Expenditure:	mortgage payment	(to be computed)
	property taxes	(about $1.75 /$100 assessment)
	insurance	(about $2.00/$1,000 value of property)
	maintenance	(about 0.05% of value of property)
Income:	rental on 6 units	($650 a month each)

Figure 4.12

(a) Open CHAP4.XLS and move to Sheet6. Our final worksheet will be similar to that in Figure 4.13. Enter the text in the first three rows. Use the Merge and Center tool as needed. If you make a mistake using this tool, select the cells and use the command Edit|Clear|Format. Excel 2002 users have the advantage that the Merge and Center tool works both ways.

Percentage: Excel is sometimes too helpful! After you have typed three values ending with a percent sign, it gratuitously add the % when you enter the 650. Use Format|Cells to format this as General.

To turn off this feature: use Tools|Options, open the Edit tab and uncheck *Enable automatic percentage entry*.

	A	B	C	D	E
1	Rental property 121 Main Street, Anytown				
2					
3	VARIABLES			EXPENDITURE	
4	Mortgage			Mortgage	3,549.93
5	principal	350,000		Taxes	500.00
6	rate	9.00%		Insurance	145.83
7	term	15		Maintenance	291.67
8	Assessment	300,000		TOTAL	4,487.43
9	Tax rate	2.00%			
10	Insurance rate	0.50%		INCOME	3,900.00
11	Maintenance %	1.00%			
12	Rent per unit	650		NET	-587.43

Figure 4.13

(b) Enter the text and values in columns A, B and D of rows 3 to 12. The values in B5:B12 are Ms Jones's estimates. You may need to format the cells to show the values as in the figure.

(c) Enter the formulas shown below in column E.

E4:	=-PMT(B6/12, B7*12, B5)	the minus sign gives a positive value in the cell
E5:	=B8*B9/12	division by 12 to give monthly amount
E6:	=B5*B10/12	
E7:	=B5*B11/12	
E8:	=SUM(E4:E7)	use the AutoSum tool
E10:	=B12*6	there are 6 units
E12:	=E10-E8	income less expenditure

Format these as Currency with no symbol to get the thousands comma separator, two decimal places and the negative sign. You may wish to choose the option to show negative values in red.

At this stage Ms Jones knows that this is not a good investment. The monthly return is negative. But the worksheet permits 'what-if' scenarios. The rent could be raised, perhaps she can negotiate a better mortgage rate or a lower purchase price. Are there any *reasonable* changes that would make this a good investment?

(d) Change some of the variables to see what happens to the bottom line figure. What if the purchase price was $300,000, or the rent was raised to $800? Notice how we do not change any formulas, only the simple values like the term of the mortgage, the rent, etc. Save the workbook.

Exercise 10: A Loan Amortization

The PMT function may be used to compute the payment on a loan but it is sometimes useful to know how much of the payment goes towards the interest and how much pays off the principal. In this exercise we introduce two functions that compute these quantities.

Whereas the function PMT returns the periodic payments, PPMT returns the amount of each payment that is applied to the principal and IPMT returns the amount that is applied to interest. Clearly for any period PPMT + IPMT = PMT but the actual values of PPMT and IPMT vary with the period in question.

The syntax for the PPMT function is **=PPMT(rate, per, nper, pv,** fv, type), where *per* is the period. Thus if the payments are made monthly we would use a *per* value of 1 for the first month, 2 for the second, etc. With loan or mortgages of long length a large worksheet is needed if we are to see the complete amortization data. We return to this topic again in Chapter 8.

Word Wrap: Select empty cells G1:G2. Use Format|Cell, open the Alignment tab and check the Wrap Text and Merge Cells boxes. Close dialog and type text.

	A	B	C	D	E	F	G
1	**Loan Amortization**				Payment on		Total
2				Month	Interest	Principal	Payment
3	principal	200,000		1	$1,500.00	$1,033.52	$2,533.52
4	APR	9%		2	$1,492.25	$1,041.27	$2,533.52
5	years	10		3	$1,484.44	$1,049.08	$2,533.52
6	payment	-$2,533.52		4	$1,476.57	$1,056.94	$2,533.52
7				5	$1,468.64	$1,064.87	$2,533.52
8	=pmt(rate, nper, pv, fv, type)			6	$1,460.66	$1,072.86	$2,533.52
9	=ipmt(rate, per, nper, pv, fv, type)			7	$1,452.61	$1,080.90	$2,533.52
10	=ppmt(rate, per, nper, pv, fv, type)			8	$1,444.50	$1,089.01	$2,533.52
11				9	$1,436.34	$1,097.18	$2,533.52
12				10	$1,428.11	$1,105.41	$2,533.52
13				11	$1,419.82	$1,113.70	$2,533.52
14				12	$1,411.46	$1,122.05	$2,533.52
121				119	$37.58	$2,495.94	$2,533.52
122				120	$18.86	$2,514.66	$2,533.52
123				Totals	$104,022	$200,000	$304,022

Figure 4.14

(a) Open CHAP4.XLS and on Sheet7 begin the worksheet by entering the data shown in A1:A6 and D2:G2 of Figure 4.14. The optional text in A8:A10 is for documentation; remember to start the formulas with a single quote.

Missing rows: To save space, some rows are not shown in the figure. Select the row header (15:121) of rows to be hidden, right click and use the Hide item on pop-up menu. Drag line between row headers 121 and 122 to widen row, so readers will note missing rows.

(b) Select A3:B6 and use Insert|Name|Create to name B3:B6.

(c) Enter the values in B3:B5.

(d) In B6 enter =PMT(ARP/12, years*12, principal). You should use Insert Function to do this. The result will be returned in red as a negative number to indicate an outflow of cash.

(e) In D3:D122 enter the series 1, 2, 3 … 120 using the AutoFill feature. Alternatively, since this is a long series, you may wish to experiment with Edit|Fill|Series to enter these values.

(f) In E3 use the formula =-IPMT(ARP/12,D3,years*12,principal). The negative sign is used to get a positive value — we know this is an outflow of cash!

(g) Similarly, in F3 enter =-PPMT(ARP/12,D3,years*12,principal).

(h) In G3, enter =E3 + F3. As expected, the sum of the interest payment and principal payment equals the monthly payment on the loan.

(i) Copy E3:G3 down to row 122. Add text and formulas in row 123. Save the workbook.

As expected, the loan is paid off in 120 months. The total interest payments are about 50% of the initial amount borrowed when the APR is 9% and the total period of repayment is 10 years. You may wish to play some what-if 'games' with the worksheet. For example, if the loan was for 30 years, how much is paid off after 10 years?

Summary

Functions are predefined formulas ranging from the very simple such as SUM to the more complex business functions. A function is included in a formula either on its own or in an expression. For example, we may use =SUM(A1:A10) and =2*SUM(A1:A10).

The syntax of a function is FunctionName(argument1, argument2, …). Some functions have a fixed number of arguments. In the syntax information is displayed by Help, the required arguments are shown in bold.

A function may serve as an argument of another function. This is called *nesting*. For example, =INT(SUM(A1:A10)). To unravel a nested formula, work from the inside. In the example, the first quantity to be calculated is the sum of a range. Then the integer value of the sum is calculated.

Insert Function provides an easy way to enter functions. We can call this up using the command Insert|Function or with the appropriate tool. The shortcut is Ctrl+F3. The shortcut Ctrl+A is very useful when you know the name of the function to be used but wish to use the dialog box to complete the argument list.

The AutoSum tool is a quick way of entering a SUM formula. In Excel 2002 it can also be used for AVERAGE, COUNT, MAX and MIN.

It is a good idea to become familiar with the various error values that can result when a mistake is made in a formula using a function. These are listed in the introduction to this chapter. In Excel 2002, an error also results in an Error tag being displayed. This can help locate the error.

The functions we have met so far return a single value. Other functions return results in a range of cells. These are called *array functions* and must be completed using ⇧Shift+Ctrl+Enter↵. Using a simple Enter↵ or clicking the green check mark in the formula bar is not enough.

Problems

1. What is meant by the *arguments* of a function?

2. You have entered =AVG(A1:A0) in cell A11 and the error value #NAME? was displayed. Why?

3. When you know the name of the function you wish to use, what is the shortcut to bring up the Insert Function dialog box?

4. When you know the name of the function you wish to use, what is the shortcut that will display the function's syntax?

5.* What error value will display in A10 if it contains the formula =SUM(A1:A10)?

6.* You have just won the *Book Lovers* magazine annual competition and have been offered a choice of prizes. The first is a cheque for £100,000 while the second will give you an income of £1,000 for the next 20 years. What formula will you type into A1 of a worksheet to find which prize is worth more? Assume the annual interest rate is 8% and that neither prize is subject to taxation.

7.* The range A1:A100 holds an unordered series of numeric values. You wish to know the sum of the numbers with the top three and bottom three left out. What formula will you use?

8.* George had two jobs last year. The first earned him $12,000, the second $15,000. He paid $9,000 in taxes. To compute the percent he lost in taxes he enters the formula =9000/12000+15000 in A1 and formats it as a percentage. What has he done wrong?

9.* Alice has the formula =SUM(A1:A10) in B1 and it displays 12.44. It represents the number of people needed to perform a series of tasks. To use in other calculations, it *must be a whole number*. How should you modify the formula?

5
The Decision Functions

Objectives

Upon completion of this chapter you will be able to:

- construct a condition using the comparison operators =, >=, >, <= , < and <>;
- construct a formula using the IF function;
- use the logical functions AND, OR and NOT;
- use the table look up functions VLOOKUP, HLOOKUP, INDEX and MATCH;
- use the conditional functions COUNTIF and SUMIF;
- name a table and a column using Insert|Name|Define;
- copy and protect a worksheet.

Decision Functions

The functions introduced in this chapter are useful when making decisions. They include the IF function, the logical functions AND, OR and NOT which enable one to make compound tests, and functions such as VLOOKUP, INDEX and MATCH that look up values from tables in the worksheet.

The IF function is used when you want a formula to return different values depending on the value of a *condition.* As a simple example, suppose A2 contains the percentage increase in sales and you wish to have the word ‘Good’ or ‘Poor’ in B2 depending on whether the increase is greater than or equal to 20%. The formula =IF(A2>=20%, "Good", "Poor") will achieve this. The figure below shows the syntax for a formula using the IF function.

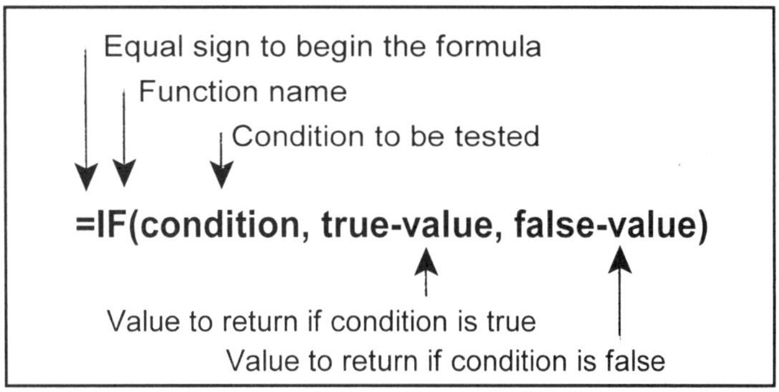

Figure 5.1

A *condition* has the form:

Expression-1 Comparison Operator Expression-2

Expression-1 and Expression-2 are any valid Excel expressions composed of cell references, constants and functions. Examples of conditions are: A1>10, A1*2>=50, and A1–B1<>2*C1. Essentially, an expression is a formula without the equal sign. Thus to test if cell A3 has a value of 5 the condition is A3=5. A condition is said to be either *true* or *false*.

The objects that Microsoft Excel calls *comparison operators* are generally called *relational operators* in computer languages. Excel recognizes this fact; a search in Help for *relational operators* brings up the *comparison operators* information.

The comparison operators are:

=	equal to
>	greater than
>=	greater than or equal to
<	less than
<=	less than or equal to
<>	not equal to.

Examples of IF formulas:

(a) =IF(A2<0, "Negative", "Positive")
Returns the text *Negative* if A2 has a value less than 0, otherwise returns *Positive*.

(b) =IF(A10–B10<=0.001, 0, 1)
Returns 0 if the quantity (A10–B10) is less than or equal to 0.001, otherwise returns 1.

(c) =IF(A2>0, (B2–A2)/A2, " ")
This returns the ratio (B2–A2)/A2 when A2 is greater than zero but it returns nothing otherwise. This avoids the #DIV0! error. See Exercise 4 of Chapter 2 for an example of where it could be used.

(d) =IF(SUM(A12:A20)>0, SUM(A12:A20), "Error")
If the sum of the range is greater than 0, that value is returned, otherwise the text *Error* is displayed.

(e) =IF(D2<0, NA(), D2)
When D2 is negative, the function NA() causes the Excel value #N/A (meaning 'not available' or 'not applicable') to be displayed. Sometimes we use this to mean 'Display something is wrong.'

The *logical functions* AND(), OR() and NOT() may be used alone or to construct compound conditions. Some examples follow. In Exercise 5 we look at these functions in more detail.

(a) =AND(A2>=1, A2<=10)
Returns the value TRUE when A2s value lies between 1 and 10, inclusive. Otherwise, it returns the value FALSE.

(b) =OR(A2<1, A2>10)
Returns the value TRUE when A2s value is less than 1 or greater than 10. Otherwise, it returns FALSE.

(c) =A1=A2
This example may look like a typo, indeed it is something we might mistakenly enter for =A1+A2. However, in this context the formula is correct. It compares the values in two cells and returns TRUE or FALSE.

(d) =NOT(A1=A2)
This formula also compares the values in two cells but it returns TRUE when the values are not the same and FALSE when they are equal.

(e) =IF(AND(A2>0, A2<11), A2, NA())
The value of A2 is returned if A2 is greater than 0 and less than 11. Otherwise, the function NA() returns the error value #N/A.

(f) =IF(OR(A2>0, B2>A2/2), 3 , 6)
Returns the value 3 if either A2>0 or B2>A2/2. If neither condition is true, the value 6 is returned.

(g) =IF(NOT(A2=0), TRUE, FALSE)
This is the same as IF(A2=0, FALSE, TRUE) or, simply =NOT(A2=0).

(h) =IF(NOT(OR(A1=1, A2=1)), 1, 0)
This is a somewhat contrived example. It returns 1 if both A1 and A2 have a value that is not 1.

IF functions may be *nested*. This means that within one IF function, we may use another IF function for either or both returned values. Nesting up to seven levels is permitted provided the total number of characters in the cell does not exceed 256. Remember that spaces in a formula helps make it more readable.

(a) =IF(A1>10, IF(A1>100, "Big", "Medium"), "Small")
For the moment, ignore the second (the inner) IF. It is clear that when the condition A1 >10 is false then the first IF returns *Small*. What happens if the condition is true? The second IF comes into play. When A1 >100, the inner IF returns *Big*, otherwise it returns *Medium*.

(b) =IF(A1>10, IF(A1>50, "Big", "Medium") IF(A1<0, "Negative", "Small"))
Here both the true-value and the false-value of the outer IF are themselves IF functions.

Compound conditions may also be constructed using the * and + operators. This is better understood if we treat a TRUE result as having the value 1 and FALSE having a value 0.

(a) =IF((A1>=0)*(A1<=10), "ok", "ERROR")
This returns *ok* when both conditions are true. Suppose A1 has a value of 5, then both conditions are true. Since 1*1=1, the compound condition is true and the function returns *ok*. If either condition is false, the compound condition becomes 0 or false because 0*1=0, 1*0=0 and 0*0=0. From this we see that the * operator in a condition is similar to the AND function.

(b) =IF((A1=D1)+(A1=E1), "ok", "ERROR")
This formula returns *ok* when at least one condition is true. Suppose the first condition is true and the second is false, we evaluate the compound condition as 1+0 which gives 1 or true. From this we see that the + operator in a condition is similar to the OR function.

Exercise 1: A What-if Analysis

Acme Manufacturing makes corkscrews which are tested before being sold. The testing gives two values, *P* and *Q*. The requirements are that *P* be at least 1.25 and *Q* be no more than 0.5. Using some sample data, Acme wishes to know how many corkscrews pass the tests and how the results would change if the specifications were to be altered slightly. For this exercise, we will use only 10 data sets but in a real case there might be hundreds. The results of this small sample of corkscrews are shown in Figure 5.2.

(a) Start a new workbook. On Sheet1 enter the text and values in A1:E5. Name the cells C2 and C3 as *pmin* and *qmax*, respectively.

(b) Enter the values in A6:B15.

(c) Enter these formulas:

C6: =IF(A6>=pmin, 1 ,0)
D6: =IF(B6<=qmax, 1 ,0)
E6: =IF(AND(A6>=pmin,B6<=qmax), 1 ,0)

Each of these formulas returns a value of 1 if a condition is met, otherwise they return 0. The first tests the *P* value, the second tests the *Q* value, and the third tests both values.

(d) Copy the three formulas down to row 15.

(e) Enter the text in B16 and right align it.

	A	B	C	D	E
1	Quality control				
2		pmin	1.25		
3		qmax	0.5		
4					
5	P	Q	P result	Q test	Two test
6	1.24	1.08	0	0	0
7	1.36	0.50	1	1	1
8	1.44	0.40	1	1	1
9	1.57	0.54	1	0	0
10	1.09	0.82	0	0	0
11	1.52	0.65	1	0	0
12	1.23	0.75	0	0	0
13	1.65	0.62	1	0	0
14	1.24	0.36	0	1	0
15	1.05	0.55	0	0	0
16		Pass	50.0%	30.0%	20.0%

Figure 5.2

(f) In C16, we wish to know the percentage that passed the first test. The number that passed could be found with =SUM(C6:C15) while the total number could be found with =COUNT(C6:C15). Clearly then, the fraction that passed would be given by =SUM(D6:C15)/COUNT(C6:C15) but this is the same as the average value of the range. In C16 enter the formula =AVERAGE(C6:C15) and format the cell with the percentage tool. Copy C16 to the two cells to the right.

(g) We are now ready to play the what-if game. By changing the value in C2, we can get answers to questions such as 'What percentage of corkscrews would pass if the acceptable value of

P was (i) raised to 1.6 or (ii) lowered to 0.22?' We can also change the acceptable value for *Q*.

(h) Save the workbook as CHAP5.XLS.

Exercise 2: Nested Ifs

The salary budget of the Sales Department has been increased by $12,000. The manager is trying to devise a way of apportioning these funds to the sales team. She thinks of two plans:

I: everyone who sold more than $250,000 gets a 5% increase; or

II: those who sold more than $200,000 get a 4% raise and those who sold more than $500,000 get 6%.

Our task is to develop a spreadsheet for her to try various values for X, Y and Z. When completed, your worksheet should resemble that in Figure 5.3.

	A	B	C	D	E
1	**Salary increases**				
2				amount	raise
3			X	250,000	5%
4			Y	200,000	4%
5			Z	500,000	6%
6			Budget	12,000	
7					
8				Plan I	Plan II
9	Salesperson	salary	sales	increase	increase
10	Anne	35,000	250,350	1,750	1,400
11	George	40,400	450,670	2,020	1,616
12	Mary	45,000	560,300	2,250	2,700
13	William	45,350	450,000	2,268	1,814
14	James	37,750	350,400	1,888	1,510
15	Helen	52,000	499,000	2,600	2,080
16				12,775	11,120
17				High	OK

Figure 5.3

(a) Begin your work on Sheet2 of CHAP5.XLS. Enter the information in A1:E6.

(b) Enter the text and values in A9:C15, and the text in D8:E9.

(c) The formula in D10 is =IF(C10>=$D$3,B10*$E$3,0). Making the references to D3 and E3 permits this formula to be copied down to D15. Double clicking on the fill handle of D10 is the quickest way to copy it.

(d) The formula in E10 is a little more complicated: =IF(C10>=$D$5, B10*$E$5, IF(C10>=$D$4, B10*$E$4, 0)). One may read this as: if the sales figure (C10) is greater than or equal to D5, then the increase is found using B10*E5; otherwise test the sales figure again and if it is greater than or equal to D4 the raise is B10*E4 but the increase is zero if the sales figure is less than D4. Copy the formula down to E15.

(e) In D16 and E16 we sum the column above them using =SUM(D10:D15) and =SUM(E10:E15), respectively.

(f) In D17 use =IF(D16>$D$6,"High","OK") and copy it to E17. This tests if the total increases in the two plans exceed the available budget increase.

(g) Save the worksheet.

Note how we have put the values of the manager's plan into cells. Had we omitted them and, for example, coded D10 as =IF(C10>=250000,B10*5%,0), then we could not play what-if games to see the effects of other break points or percentages. You should experiment.

Exercise 3: Logical Functions

At the start of this chapter, some examples of IF formulas using NOT, AND and OR are listed. These terms are the logical, or Boolean, functions. They return the values TRUE or FALSE.

(a) On Sheet3 of CHAP5.XLS, construct a worksheet with the values and formulas as shown in Figure 5.4 and note the values returned. B1 will display TRUE; you may accidentally get this (or FALSE) when you mistakenly type an equal sign rather than a plus sign within a formula.

(b) The logical functions may be combined to make more complex tests. You should be very careful when doing this because (i) you must understand the following order of precedence: NOT followed by AND then OR; and (ii) in everyday language we frequently say 'and' where 'or' is what is meant logically. Logically, it is meaningless to say 'This is a list of my friends who live in Canada and USA' because it is unlikely that any friend has a residence in both countries. If in doubt use two or more cells to make complex logic tests.

	A	B	C
1	10	=A1=10	=AND(A1>5, A2>5)
2	20	=A3>20	=OR(A1>15, A2>15)
3	30	=NOT(A1=10)	=A3=A1-A2

Figure 5.4

There are some common combinations that are useful to know. In the following table, *X* and *Y* may be expressions or references to cells containing the values TRUE or FALSE.

Name	**Formula**	**TRUE returned if**
NAND	=NOT(AND(X, Y))	*Not both* true
NOR	=NOT(OR(X, Y))	*Neither* is true
XOR	=OR(AND(X, NOT(Y)), AND(Y,NOT(X)))	*Only one* is true

(c) On the worksheet, construct formulas to test the above. Show that the statement 'Not both true' is *not* equivalent to 'Both are false.'

Note. A cell may be given the value TRUE (or FALSE) by typing (i) TRUE, (ii) =TRUE, or (iii) =TRUE(). Use the last form if it is likely that your work needs to be compatible with other spreadsheet applications such as Lotus 1-2-3 or Quattro Pro.

Table Lookup Functions

Table lookup functions have a range of uses. Whenever you find yourself composing a multi-nested IF function you should consider whether a lookup function would be more appropriate.

A worksheet table is simply a range of values. The difference between vertical and horizontal tables is shown in Figure 5.5.

Sales	Base	%
0	0	6%
1,000	60	8%
2,000	140	10%
3,000	240	12%

Vertical table

Sales	0	1,000	2,000	3,000
Base	0	60	140	240
%	6%	8%	10%	12%

Horizontal table

Figure 5.5

We could use either table to look up the parameters needed to calculate a salesperson's bonus based on sales. With the vertical table, we would search the first column while with the horizontal table we would search the first row. The choice between vertical or horizontal is yours; one has no advantage over the other. The data in the first column of a vertical table, or the first row of a horizontal table, must be in ascending order. The command Data|Sort may be used to order your table. Use the Option button to specify a sort by column or by row.

A table may contain textual data. The horizontal table in Figure 5.6 could be used to look up a department and find the manager or the number of employees.

The two functions VLOOKUP and HLOOKUP have similar syntax:

VLOOKUP(lookup_value, table_array, column_index_num, range_lookup)

HLOOKUP(lookup_value, table_array, row_index_num, range_lookup)

Dept	Accounts	Sales	Service	Shipping
Manager	Jo Lorkins	Tim Turner	Nicky Fowler	Simon Dennis
Phone	555-2345	555-3456	555-4678	555-6782
Employees	6	12	6	8

Figure 5.6

Lookup_value Is the value to be located in the first column of a vertical table (or the first row of a horizontal table). *Lookup_value* may be either a numeric or text value or a cell reference.

Table_array Is the range reference or name of the table.

Column_index_num (*row_index_num*)
Is the column (or row) of the table from which the value is to be returned.

Range_lookup Is a logical value (TRUE or FALSE) specifying whether you want an approximate or an exact match. If range_lookup is TRUE or omitted, and there is no exact match, then the function returns the next largest value that is less than the lookup value. If FALSE and no exact match is found, the function will return the error value #NA. If lookup_value is less than the lowest value in the first column (first row with HLOOKUP), the function returns the #NA error value.

Exercise 4: Using VLOOKUP

In this exercise we use the VLOOKUP function. The scenario is: you have a list of salespersons and their monthly sales figures. You need to compute the commission for each person. We will begin with a simple bonus scheme and move to something more complicated.

	A	B	C	D	E	F
1	**Bonus Scheme**			**Salesperson**	**Sales**	**Bonus**
2	**Sales**	**Bonus**		Mary	500	0
3	0	0		Jack	1200	60
4	1000	60		George	3000	240
5	2000	140		Karen	5500	500
6	3000	240		Fred	2250	140
7	4000	360		TOTAL	12450	940
8	5000	500				

Figure 5.7

(a) In Sheet4 of CHAP5.XLS enter the table shown in A1:B8 of Figure 5.7. A person selling from $0 to $999 earns no bonus, when the sales amount is from $1,000 to $1,999 the bonus is $60, etc. Note that there are steps in the bonus values. A bonus of $60 is earned on $1,100 and on $1,500. In the next stage we will introduce a 'smooth' scheme.

(b) Enter the labels in D1:F1 and the data in D2:E6.

(c) In F2 enter the formula =VLOOKUP(E2, $A$3:$B$8, 2). We want to lookup the sale values from E2 in the first column of the table A3:B8 and we wish to have the corresponding value in column 2 of the table returned by the function into cell F2. Copy the formula down to F6. The absolute reference $A$3:$B$8 ensures that the reference to the table is unchanged when the formula is copied. Note how the VLOOKUP function matches the value in column E with the value in column A that is either equal to the E value or is the largest A value that is less than the E value.

(d) Use the AutoSum tool to insert the SUM formulas in E7 and F7. Save the workbook.

Now we will make the bonus scheme more comprehensive. A person with a sales figure of $2,200 will get a larger bonus than one with \$2,000. From the table in Figure 5.7 we see that this person will get \$140 for the first \$2,000 of the sales and 10% for the balance.

(e) Enter the bonus scheme table as shown in H1:J8 of Figure 5.8. We shall be making reference to this table a number of times so it will be convenient to name it. Select H3:J8 and use the menu command Insert|Name|Define and name this table scheme.

	H	I	J	K	L	M	N
1		**Bonus Scheme**			**Salesperson**	**Sales**	**Bonus**
2	**Sales**	**Base**	**Percent**		Mary	500	30
3	0	0	6%		Jack	1200	76
4	1000	60	8%		George	3000	240
5	2000	140	10%		Karen	5500	575
6	3000	240	12%		Fred	2250	165
7	4000	360	14%		TOTAL	12450	1086
8	5000	500	15%				

Figure 5.8

(f) Enter the labels in L1:N1 and the data in L2:M6 — you could copy this from D2:E6.

(g) The formula to enter in N2 is:
=VLOOKUP(M2,scheme, 2)
+(M2-VLOOKUP(M2,scheme, 1))*(VLOOKUP(M2,scheme, 3))

Copy this formula down to N6.

(h) Complete the worksheet with the AutoSum tool and save the workbook.

The formula in column N looks complex but when analysed it is straightforward. Let us see how it works to compute Jack's bonus on a sales figure of \$1,200. The first term, VLOOKUP(M2, scheme, 2), returns the value from column 2 of the *scheme* table. Thus, it returns the base amount (\$60) of the bonus scheme for a sales figure of \$1,000. To complete the calculation, we need to add 8% of the balance. The term M2 – VLOOKUP(M2, scheme, 1) will compute the balance and the 8% figure is returned by VLOOKUP(M2, scheme, 3).

Exercise 5: Another VLOOKUP example

In this exercise we use the VLOOKUP to locate a textual item in a table. Your company, located in Nova Scotia, Canada, uses one of four couriers to deliver parcels to customers. You need a method of looking up which courier to use and calculating the cost of shipping.

(a) On Sheet5 on CHAP5.XLS enter the data shown in Figure 5.9. Select G1:M14 and use the command Insert|Name|Define to name the table (without the headings) as *shipping*.

As an example of the use of this table we see that a parcel with an Alberta address will be shipped by UPS. If the package weighs less than 5 kg it will cost $5, if it weighs from 5 to 10 kg the cost is $10, after that the cost is $20 for the first 10 kg and $2 for every kilogram thereafter.

(b) Enter the text in A1:A9 and the values in B4:B5 of Figure 5.10.

(c) The purpose of B7 is to validate the entry in A4. We need a formula that will return the name of the province having the abbreviation entered in B4. The required formula is =VLOOKUP(B4,shipping,2,FALSE). By including the last argument with a value FALSE we require the VLOOKUP function to find an exact match. If one is not found, the function returns the error value #N/A.

Note that table lookup functions are not case sensitive. Thus an exact match will occur if the user enters *AB*, *Ab* or *ab*.

(d) The formula =VLOOKUP(B4,shipping,3) in B8 returns the courier's name.

(e) The shipping costs may be computed by using an IF formula. Perhaps this is not the best way but it is one the reader who has followed this text will understand. We need to test if the weight is (i) greater than or equal to 10, (ii) between 5 and 10, or (iii) less than 5. One way to do this is with:
=IF(B5>=L1, VLOOKUP(B4, shipping,6) + (B5-L1) * VLOOKUP(B4, shipping,7), IF(B5 >= K1, VLOOKUP(B4, shipping,5),VLOOKUP(B4, shipping,4))).
Enter different values in B4 and B5 for the province abbreviation and for the weight to test your formulas.

(f) You may wish to prevent yourself from inadvertently typing over the formulas in B7:B9. Begin by selecting B4:B5, use the command Format|Cells|Protection and remove the check mark in the *locked* box. This will let you change the values in these two cells after we have protected the worksheet. Now use Tools|Protection|Protect Sheet. Do not add a password — our purpose is merely to prevent accidents and a forgotten password is a true headache! Check that cells B4 and B5 can still be changed but that no other cell can be altered.Save the workbook.

	G	H	I	J	K	L	M
1	Code	Province	Carrier	0	5	10	extra
2	AB	Alberta	UPS	5	10	20	2
3	BC	British Columbia	UPS	5	10	20	2
4	MN	Manitoba	Purolator	4	6	15	2
5	NB	New Brunswick	Purolator	3	5	10	1
6	NF	Newfoundland	Purolator	4	7	12	1
7	NS	Nova Scotia	Purolator	3	5	10	1
8	NU	Nunavut	FedEx	8	12	25	4
9	NW	North West Territories	FedEx	8	10	22	4
10	ON	Ontario	UPS	4	6	12	2
11	PE	Prince Edward Island	Purolator	3	5	10	1
12	PQ	Quebec	UPS	4	6	12	2
13	SK	Saskatchewan	FedEx	5	7	11	2
14	YK	Yukon	FedEx	8	11	24	4

Figure 5.9

	A	B
1		
2	**Shipping Costs**	
3		
4	Destination	nf
5	Weight	5
6		
7	Province	Newfoundland
8	Carrier	Purolator
9	Cost	7

Figure 5.10

The HLOOKUP function is the same as VLOOKUP but is used when the table is constructed horizontally rater than vertically.

Exercise 6: Using INDEX and MATCH

The INDEX function is used to return a value from a table. Unlike VLOOKUP and HLOOKUP, this function does not search a table. Rather, it is given the row and column numbers of the table and returns the value at the intersection of these. The syntax is INDEX(array, row_num, column_num). Thus =INDEX(A1:C10, 2, 3) returns the value at the intersection of row 2 and column 3 of the table A1:C10. In this example, it returns the value from cell C2.

The MATCH function does perform a search but rather than returning a value from a table, it returns the position within the table where the match was found. Its syntax is MATCH(lookup_value, lookup_array, match_type), where *lookup_value* is the value you wish to match, *lookup_array* is the table to be searched, and *match_type* specifies how the match is to be performed. When match_type is 0, an exact match is required; when it is -1 the function finds the smallest value that is greater than or equal to lookup_value, and when it is +1 (or omitted) it finds the largest value that is less than or equal to lookup_value.

Clearly, a combination of INDEX and MATCH can be useful. MATCH can locate the position of a lookup_value within a table, and INDEX can return the actual value of another row or column in that table.

(a) We begin by making a copy of Sheet4 in CHAP5.XLS. Hold down the Ctrl key and drag the Sheet4 tab to the right. When you release the key you will have a copy of the sheet and it will be called Sheet4(2).

(b) Delete the formulas in F2:F6. In F2 enter:
=INDEX($A$3:$B$8,MATCH(E2,$A$3:$A$8),2).
Copy this down to F6. The results should be the same as before.

In the formula in F2, MATCH(E2, $A$3:$A$8) tries to match the value in E2 with the values in A3:A8. Since there is no exact match it returns the row number (in this case 1) of the value in the array that is less than E2 since we have omitted the third argument of MATCH.

The INDEX function is given the reference of an array together with a row and a column number, and returns the value of that element of the array. The MATCH part of the formula serves as the second argument of the INDEX function — the row of the table. INDEX returns the array element at the intersection of the specified row and column. In the example, the array is A3:B8 while the row we want is the one returned by the MATCH function and the column is 2 since this is where the bonus values are.

Here the VLOOKUP function seems somewhat simpler than the combination of the INDEX and MATCH functions. However, at other times the combination method is preferred because the combination can give more options. For example, the MATCH function can be used to find an exact, a lesser or a greater match. Furthermore, with a very large worksheet the INDEX/MATCH combination is generally faster than a lookup function.

The CHOOSE function is somewhat similar to the INDEX function. The syntax is =CHOOSE(index-value, value1, value2, ... value29). Thus if D5 has a value of 3, then =CHOOSE(D5, A1, A2, A3, A4, A5) will return the value in A3. Should D5 be less than 1 or more than 5 in this example, the error value #VALUE! would be returned. The values may be cell references as in the example, or actual values as in =CHOOSE(D5, 10%, 15%, 30%, 35%, 50%). If the value in D5 represented a student's grade, we could use the formula =CHOOSE(INT(D5/10)+1,"F","F","F", "F","F","D","C","C","B","A","A") to return a letter grade.

Exercise 7: Conditional Counting and Summing

Figure 5.11 shows a worksheet in which a series of phone calls has been analysed in two ways. The exercise would perhaps be more meaningful if the lists in columns A and B were longer but the methodology is the same regardless of the number of calls.

(a) Begin this exercise on Sheet6 of CHAP5.XLS by entering the data shown in A1:B16 of Figure 5.11.

(b) Select A1:A16 and use the command Insert|Name|Create to name the two columns. Note that you must remove the check mark in the *Left Column* item of the dialog box — we do not wish to use the employee names for cell names!

In the first table (D1:F7) we analyse the data by employee. We will use COUNTIF and SUMIF in this exercise. In a later chapter we explore the topic of Pivot Tables which may be used for similar analyses.

(c) Enter the text in D1:F1 and in D2:D7.

(d) The formula in E2 =COUNTIF(Caller, D2) counts Agatha's

calls. This means: count every cell in the Caller range (A2:A16) which has a value equal to that in D2.

	A	B	C	D	E	F
1	Caller	Jan Cost		Caller	Count	Cost
2	Fred	1.50		Agatha	3	4.47
3	Charlie	2.00		Carol	2	8.21
4	Agatha	0.76		Charlie	3	3.5
5	Carol	3.65		Fred	4	8.56
6	Charlie	0.85		Susan	3	5.22
7	Fred	3.21		Total	15	29.96
8	Susan	1.92				
9	Fred	0.85				
10	Susan	0.85		Range	Count	Cost
11	Agatha	2.96		1.00	6	4.71
12	Agatha	0.75		1.50	1	1.50
13	Carol	4.56		2.00	2	3.92
14	Charlie	0.65		2.50	1	2.45
15	Fred	3.00		3.00	2	5.96
16	Susan	2.45		more	3	11.42
17				Total	15	29.96

Figure 5.11

(e) To sum the calls made by Agatha in F2 use =SUMIF(Caller, D2, Jan_Cost). Note the underline in *Jan_Cost*. A range name cannot contain a space, so Microsoft Excel added the underline during the naming process in step (b). Read this formula as: test every cell in the Caller range, if it equals the value in D2 then sum the corresponding cell in the Jan_Cost range.

(f) Copy E2:F2 down to row 6. The references to D2 will be changed as the formulas are copied but the range names will not. Had we not used range names, we would have needed absolute references for the ranges. Thus E2 would have read =COUNT($A$2:$A$16, D2).

(g) Use the AutoSum tool to get the total in E7 and F7. Save the worksheet.

Perhaps this analysis is being performed daily throughout January adding data to columns A and B. Do we have to update the formulas every time? We could rename the new ranges each day, but this is extra work. Alternatively, from the start of the project, we could name the range A2:A400 as Caller and the range B2:B400 as Jan_Cost — there is no reason why a named range

B2:B400 as Jan_Cost — there is no reason why a named range cannot contain empty cells. If we want to play safe there are two more or less equivalent ways to proceed.

(h) Replace the formula in E2 by =COUNTIF(A:A, D2). We have replaced the range name by A:A which means all the cells in column A. Similarly, in F2 enter =SUMIF(A:A, D2, B:B). Copy E2:F2 down to row 6. Is the data the same as before? Add some new data starting wherever you wish, say A20. Is the new data included in the analysis? Close the workbook without saving it as we are about to try another experiment and we want the original formulas in E2 and F2.

(i) Reopen CHAP5.XLS and go to Sheet6. We are going to combine the use of a range name and the reference to an entire column. Use Insert|Name|Define, select the Caller name and in the Refers To box enter =$A:$A. Click the OK button. Excel will append the sheet number to the reference — see Figure 5.12. Repeat this to make Jan_Cost refer to $B:$B. Be careful not to use the arrow keys when the Define Name dialog box is open but move round with the mouse. Your result should not change until you add new data in columns A and B below the existing data.

Figure 5.12

The syntax of the COUNTIF function is COUNTIF(range, criteria) and for SUMIF it is SUMIF(range, criteria, sum_range). In the examples above, our criteria were simple references to cells. At other times one could use criteria such as "apples" or ">54". These must be entered with the quotation marks. How then can we have a criterion that means, for example, 'greater than the value in D11'? We answer this in the next analysis.

In D10:F17 the phone call data is analysed to show how many calls had a cost of up to $1.00, how many from $1.00 up to $1.50, etc.

Please note that this part of the exercise is designed to explore the COUNTIF and SUMIF functions. The results we get could be found more readily using the FREQUENCY function which we look at in a later chapter.

(j) Enter the values in D11:D16.

(k) In E11, enter the formula =COUNTIF(Jan_Cost,"<="&D11). We have constructed the criteria from three parts: (i) "<=" meaning greater or equal to, (ii) the concatenation operator, &, which adds text items, and (iii) the cell reference, D11. So our criteria is greater than or equal to the value in D11. Similarly the formula in F11 is =SUMIF(Jan_Cost,"<="&D11). Note that we have omitted the third argument since it is the same as the search range specified in the first argument.

(l) We cannot make compound criteria in this way. So to find in E12 the number of calls from 1.00 to 1.50, we use =COUNTIF(Jan_Cost,"<="&D12) - E11. This finds all calls under 1.50 and subtracts the cell above which equals the number of calls up to 1.00. Having seen this somewhat cumbersome method, you will appreciate the FREQUENCY function when we introduce it later. The formulas to complete this analysis are:
E12: =COUNTIF(Jan_Cost,"<="&D12) - E11
E13: =COUNTIF(Jan_Cost,"<="&D13) - (E11 + E12)
E14: =COUNTIF(Jan_Cost,"<="&D14) - (E11 + E12 + E13)
E15: =COUNTIF(Jan_Cost,"<="&D15) - SUM(E11:E14)
E16: =COUNTIF(Jan_Cost,">"&D15)
E17: =SUM(E11:E16)
F12: =SUMIF(Jan_Cost,"<="&D12) - F11
F13: =SUMIF(Jan_Cost,"<="&D13) - (F11 + F12)
F14: =SUMIF(Jan_Cost,"<="&D14) - (F11 + F12 + F13)
F15: =SUMIF(Jan_Cost,"<="&D15) - SUM(F11:F14)
F16: =SUMIF(Jan_Cost,">"&D15)
F17: =SUM(F11:F16)

(m) Save the workbook.

Summary

The IF function provides the easiest way to handle alternative situations. More complex tests may be constructed by nesting IF statements to a maximum of seven levels.

You should be careful with your choice of comparison operators. For example, you may be tempted to use greater than (>) when, in fact, greater than or equal to (>=) would be more appropriate. Likewise be very careful to use the logic meaning of AND and OR rather than the colloquial use they can have in English.

When you find that your IF statement is getting too long it is time to consider the use of a table with a VLOOKUP or HLOOKUP function. It is advisable, and mandatory when doing an approximate lookup, to have the table sorted by the search field. If an exact lookup is specified but no match is found, the lookup functions return #N/A.

The functions INDEX, MATCH and CHOOSE, either singularly or in combination, provide alternative means of extracting information from a table. The table may be part of the function as in =MATCH(A2, {"A", "B", "C", "D", "E"}, 0). In this example, the value 1 is returned if A2 contains *A* or *a*, 2 if it contains *B* or *b*, etc.

Conditional counting and summation are possible using the COUNTIF and SUMIF functions.

Problems

1)* Employees at the Fringe Telemarketing company are given a rating based on daily sales according to the table below. A sales figure of 5,000 or more earns an A rating, 4,000 or more a B, etc. Less than 2,000 merits an E.

Sales	5,000	4,000	3,000	2,000	less
Rating	A	B	C	D	E

Assuming the sales figure is in A2, write an IF formula to return the rating in B2.

2.* You have a worksheet in which B2:B22 contains the salaries of a group of workers. The values range from 12,000 to 45,000. You wish to find salaries that will result when a 10% raise is given to those currently earning 20,000 or less but no raise is to be given to others. What formula will you use in C2 and copy down to C22?

3) Replace the formula with the VLOOKUP function in step (g) of Exercise 4 by using a combination of the MATCH and INDEX functions.

4.* Redo Problem 1 using INDEX and MATCH without composing a table on the worksheet. Your formula will have the form:
=INDEX(★★★★★, MATCH(★★★★★)).

6

Printing a Worksheet

Objectives

In this chapter we learn:

- how to specify the area of the worksheet to be printed;
- how to preview the printed document;
- about various options such as margins, gridlines, etc.;
- how to add headers and footers;
- how to make a worksheet fit on a specified number of sheets of paper.

Exercise 1: A Quick Way to Print

Shortcuts: To get to A1 use Ctrl+Home .To get to the bottom of a column use Ctrl+End.

Printer tool

(a) To begin this exercise, open CHAP5.XLS (or any file which was saved in a previous chapter) and use the first Sheet.

(b) If you are working in a network environment you may need a means of identifying your work. Go to the bottom of column A and type your name.

(c) Click on the Print button on the standard toolbar and retrieve your printout. Note that the printed area is just large enough to include all the cells containing entries. By default your printout will not show the gridlines of the worksheet. We can change this later when we experiment with Page Setup.

(d) Inspect your worksheet screen. There will be vertical and horizontal dotted lines. The exact positions depend on the margin setting and font size. Generally, the first vertical line will be near column H and the first horizontal one near row 50. These lines show you what data will fit on a single page.

Exercise 2: Another Way to Print

Shortcut: Use Ctrl+ P to open the Print dialog box.

This exercise uses the menu to print a worksheet. To demonstrate how this is more versatile than the Print button, we will print just a part of the worksheet.

(a) Select the range from A1 to the bottom of column A.

(b) From the menu select File|Print to open the dialog box shown in Figure 6.1. In the *Print What* area, click the *Selection* radio button to specify that we wish to print only the selected area.

(c) To save both time and paper, and to demonstrate another feature, we will not click the OK button to start the printing process. Rather, click the Preview button. The screen will show how your printed page(s) will look. At the top there are various buttons which access other menus. At this point you may wish to experiment with Zoom before selecting Close.

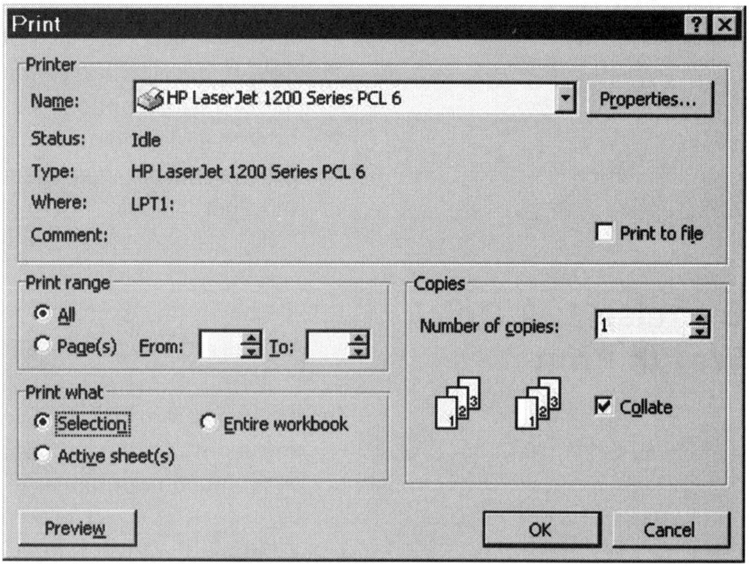

Figure 6.1

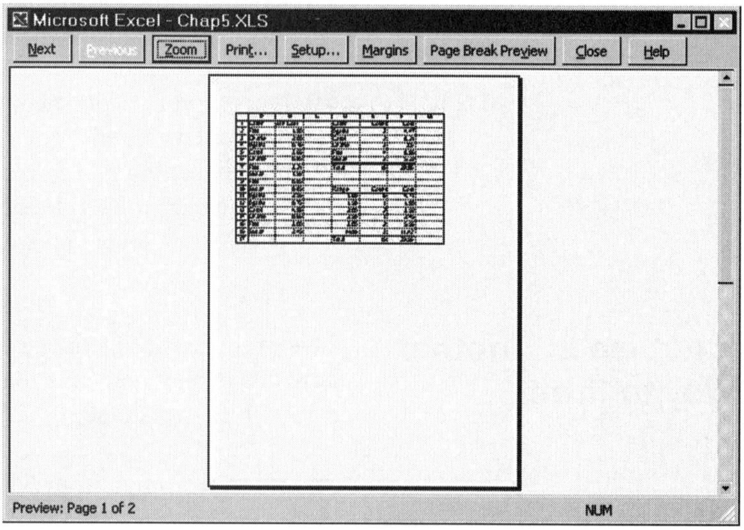

Figure 6.2

Exercise 3: Page Setup

The Page Setup and the Preview dialog boxes are intimately related. We may access Page Setup from using either File|Page Setup or we may use File|Print Preview and press the Setup button. Either way, we are presented with a Page Setup dialog box similar to that in Figure 6.3. From here we may make many changes that affect the way our work appears on paper.

(a) Before we experiment with Page Setup, go to cell P1 and type Test. Now use File|Print Preview and, with the Next and Previous buttons, convince yourself that the worksheet will require two pages. Click on the Setup button in Preview.

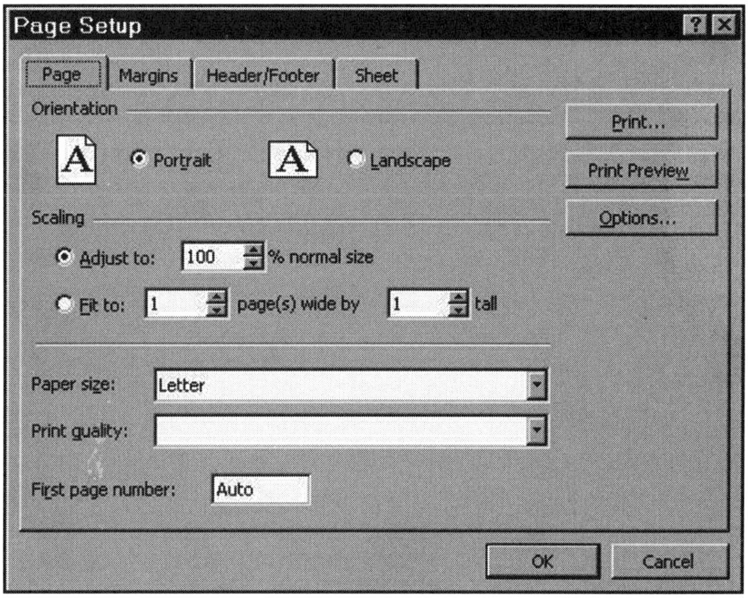

Figure 6.3

(b) Click on the Page tab if it is not the active item. In the Scaling area, click the Fit To radio button and leave the values in the two boxes at 1. This will cause Excel to shrink the font size such that your work will fit on one page. Fit To does not enlarge, it only shrinks.

(c) Click on the Preview button on the right of the dialog box. You will now find that the worksheet can be printed on one page.

(d) Did you also note that in the Page Setup it is possible to change the page layout from portrait to landscape? Experiment with changing this setting and previewing how the worksheet would be printed.

Exercise 4: Changing Margins

(a) With your work showing in Print Preview, experiment with changing the margins by clicking the Margins button. Six dotted lines appear to show the margin positions. The mouse pointer shape changes to a magnifying glass until it crosses one of the margins when it takes on a ✛ shape. When it has this shape, hold down the mouse button and drag one of the margins to a new position.

(b) Click again on the Margins button to remove the margins from the view.

Note that there are six margins: left and right, top and bottom, one for the header and one for the footer. You must be careful not to make the last two so small that the data in the worksheet overlaps the header or footer.

(c) While the method above is useful for a 'quick-and-dirty' fix, it is generally better to set the margins to defined values. Go to the Page Setup dialog box and click the Margins tab.

(d) You can set each margin by either typing a new value in the appropriate box or by clicking the spinners. Set each margin to 1 inch (or 2.5 cm) and preview your document.

(e) Did you notice the two radio buttons on the Margins tab of the Page Setup dialog box which allow you to centre the worksheet data on the page? Experiment with setting these and preview the result.

Exercise 5: Header and Footer

For course work it is often convenient for the instructor to have the student's name in the header. Many users like to have the file name and the printing date in the printout. Let's see how we do this. Remember you can use Preview at any time to see the results.

(a) Access the Page Setup dialog box and activate the Header/Footer tab to obtain a dialog box similar to that in Figure 6.4. The objective is to have your name as the header. If you click the [↓] near the mouse pointer in the figure, you may find your name there. However, if you are using Excel on a network, extra steps are required.

(b) Clicking the Custom Header button will open a dialog box as shown in Figure 6.5.Select the text in the Center section and delete it. Type your name in this section and click OK.

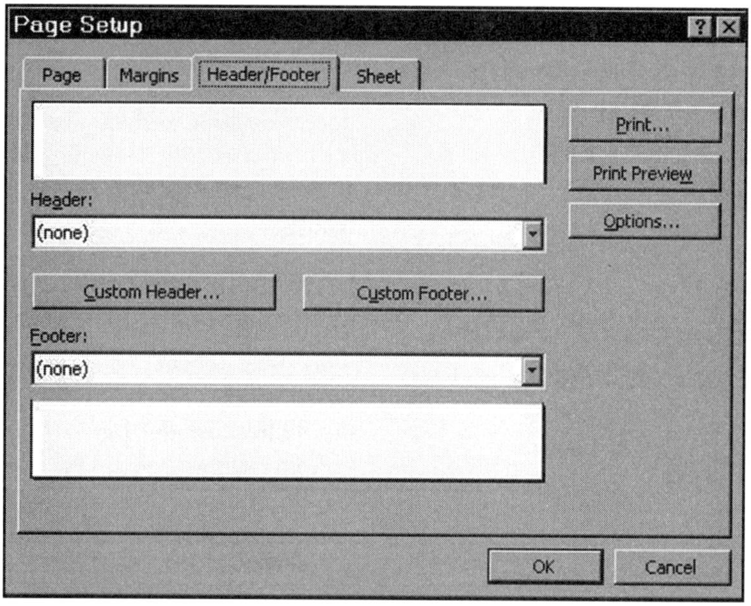

Figure 6.4

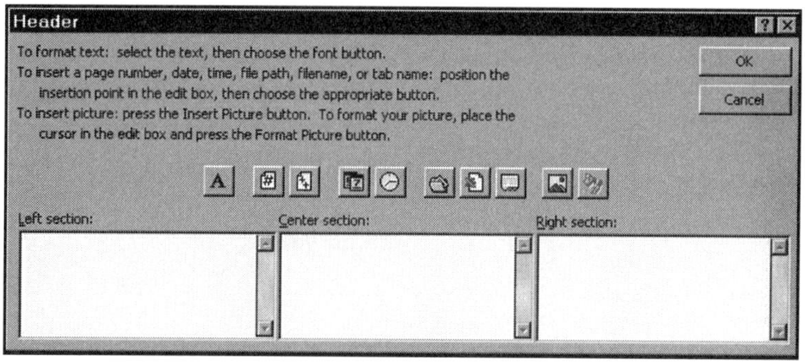

Figure 6.5

(c) Now click the Custom Footer button. The resulting dialog box will be similar to Figure 6.5 except it will have Footer as its title. The insertion marker will be in the Left section. Click the Date icon (it is in the centre and represents an open desk calendar) and the text &[Date] will appear in the section.

(d) Click the Right section to move the insertion marker. Click the File icon (it has an Excel X on it) and the text &[File] appears in the section. You may wish to experiment with the other icons. Delete any text you do not need afterwards.

(e) Now preview the worksheet. Return to step (a) if the results are not satisfactory.

Exercise 6: Gridlines and Row/Column Headings

There are times when a printed worksheet looks better without the gridlines. Sometimes we would like to have a printout in which the row and column headings are displayed; this is useful for documentation and for instructors marking papers. You will find the options for these on the Sheet tab of the Page Setup dialog box. You are encouraged to experiment with these and to preview the results.

Exercise 7: Setting the Print Area

In Exercise 2 we saw one method of printing only a part of a worksheet. There is a better way which involves setting the Print Area. An area (or a *range*) in Microsoft Excel is defined by typing the address of the top left cell, a colon and the address of the bottom right cell. From the File menu, go to Page Setup and select the Sheet tab. In the box entitled Print Area, type A3:C5. Now preview the result.

Note that when Page Setup is accessed from Preview, the text *Print Area* shows in light text, meaning that this option is currently inaccessible.

Customizing: You can add more buttons to either of the toolbars. If it would be useful, go to Help and find how to add a Print Preview or a Print Area button to the standard toolbar.

You may also set (and unset) the print area from the Print Area command on the File menu after selecting the required area with the mouse. Alternatively, you may wish to use Help to learn how to add a Print Area button to the standard toolbar. Unfortunately, this may have to be done for each new Excel session if you are on a network.

Exercise 8: Printing Formulas

When a cell in a worksheet contains a formula, its value is displayed on the screen and on the printed page. We can always see the formulas by looking in the formula bar but sometimes we would like a printout showing the formulas for documentation.

(a) Create a simple worksheet with a few formulas such as Exercise 2 in Chapter 1.

(b) We can have Excel display formulas by setting the appropriate option in the View tab of Tools|Options but the simplest way is to press Ctrl+` where the ` is the key next to the 1 on the top row of the 'typewriter' keys. Your worksheet will resemble Figure 6.6 and will show the formulas.

(c) Note that we can no longer see all the text in A1 since it overflows into B1. If the formulas are long, they also may be truncated. In which case, select the appropriate column heading and use Format|Columns|AutoFit to have Excel adjust the column widths.

(d) Print or preview the worksheet. Press Ctrl+` to return to the normal view. Readjust the column widths if needed.

	A	B	C	D
1	Office furniture calcula			
2	Item	Cost	Quantity	Extension
3	Desk	234.56	2	=B3*C3
4	Chair	75.43	6	=B4*C4
5	Coat rack	45.67	1	=B5*C5
6	Total		=SUM(Quantity)	=D3+D4+D5

Figure 6.6

Exercise 9: Printing a Large Worksheet

If the worksheet contains a large amount of data, it may not be possible to print it on one page. Microsoft Excel generally looks after this but there are occasions when the user may wish to intervene. In this exercise we see how to insert page breaks and how to use the same column headings on every page. To save time and paper we use Preview rather than Print.

(a) We start by making a large worksheet. Open a new workbook and on Sheet1 enter the data shown in Figure 6.7.

	A	B	C	D	E
1	No	Employee	SIN	Rate/Hr	Tax Rate
2	1	John	123456	12.25	15%
3	2	Mary	234567	14.75	17%

Figure 6.7

(b) We really do not want to spend our time making a lot of data so copy A2:D3 down to row 100 by selecting the range and dragging the fill handle. It does not matter that Excel has tried to make a series from the numeric data and has generated meaningless values! Note that you are not copying the column heading in row 1.

Caution: The Page Setup dialog can be reached either (i) from the File menu or (ii) from the Print Preview menu. However, when method (ii) is used both the Print Area and the Print Titles areas are greyed out.

(c) We wish to have the column heading in row 1 repeated on every printed page. Use File|Page Setup and on the Sheet tab locate the box labelled *Rows to repeat at top*. Type 1:1 in the box — Excel will change it to \$1:\$1.

(d) For this demonstration, let us say we require the data for 30 employees on each page. Move to row 31 (30 employees plus

1 for the headings) and use the command Insert|Page Break. A horizontal dotted line will appear. Repeat at lines 61 and 91. A misplaced horizontal page break can be removed by moving to a cell just under the break and issuing the command Insert|Remove Page Break.

Vertical page breaks are added in a similar way by first selecting a column heading.

(a) Use Print Preview to see that Excel needs another page to print this worksheet.

(b) You can view the worksheet in a way that clearly indicates the pages with the command View|Page Break Preview. The worksheet will be displayed with watermarks reading Page 1, Page 2, etc. With this view it is possible to relocate page breaks by dragging them with the mouse. Generally, one would not wish to edit a worksheet in this view as the cells are very small. Return to the regular view using View|Normal.

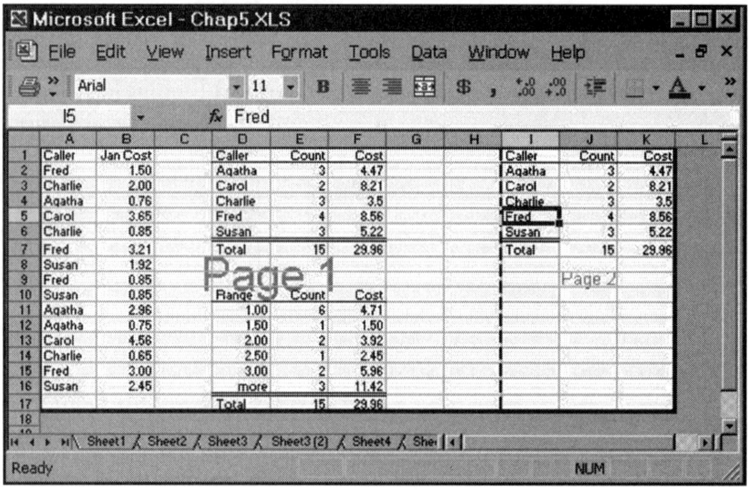

Figure 6.8

Summary

We have seen that many of the commands in the File menu are interrelated in that we can go from one to another. Figure 6.9 shows this graphically.

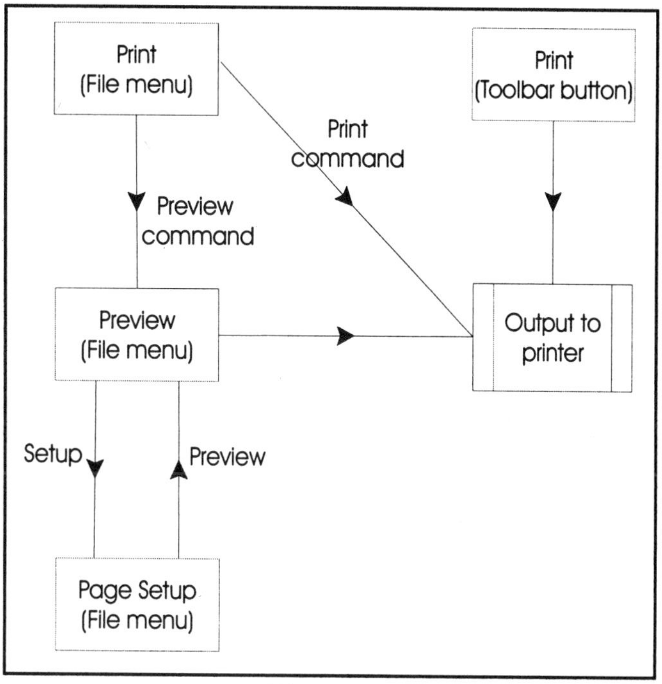

Figure 6.9

We set various options using the Page Setup dialog box. On the Page tab we may:

(i) change between portrait and landscape paper orientation;

(ii) specify what size paper is being used;

(iii) either enlarge the worksheet or reduce it to fit a specified number of pages.

On the Margins tab we may:

(i) specify the top, bottom, left and right margins independently. We may also change the size of the area for headers and footers;

(ii) arrange that the worksheet is centred horizontally and/or vertically on the printed page.

The Header/Footer tab has provisions for:

(i) selecting an existing style for a header and/or a footer; or

(ii) generating a custom header and/or footer.

The Sheet tab has a large number of options including:

(i) setting the Print Area. This can also be done with the command File|Print Area;

(ii) specifying the rows and columns to be repeated on each printed page;

(iii)stipulating whether (1) gridlines and/or row and column headings are to be printed, (2) the printing is to be in black and white when printed on a printer with colour capability, (3) comments are to be printed and, if so, where;

(iv)selecting how a large worksheet will be paginated: either down and over, or over and down.

7
Charts

Objectives

Upon completion of this chapter, you will:

- be familiar with the different types of charts available in Microsoft Excel;.
- be able to use the Chart Wizard to construct a chart;
- be able to change the appearance of a chart to suit your need;
- know how to add error bars;
- know how to handle missing data;
- be familiar with the use of drawing tools to add documentation to a chart;
- be able to add new data to an existing chart;
- know how to construct a dynamic chart which adds new data automatically.

Types of Charts

Microsoft Excel has an excellent chart drawing facility. The major types of charts are: Pie, Bar, Column, Line, XY and Radar. Associated with each type are a number of subtypes. The user can change the appearance of nearly every chart feature.

The data in Figure 7.1 was used to make the charts shown in Figure 7.2. The data in B1:E1 is called the *category data*. We have two *data series* in the table: one in row 2, the other in row 3.

	Brand A	Brand B	Brand C	Brand D
Series 1	1,255	1,000	750	600
Series 2	600	800	500	300

Figure 7.1

Both data series were used for the sample column chart but only the first data series was used for the other sample charts. In the bar chart, note how the rectangles are placed horizontally with the category values along the y-axis. In the column chart the rectangles are upright. Many people call this type of chart a 'bar chart' but Excel uses the term 'column chart'. In the column and line charts, the category data is on the x-axis and the data values are on the y-axis.

The pie chart shown in Figure 7.2 uses a 3D visual effect and has one part of the pie 'exploded'.

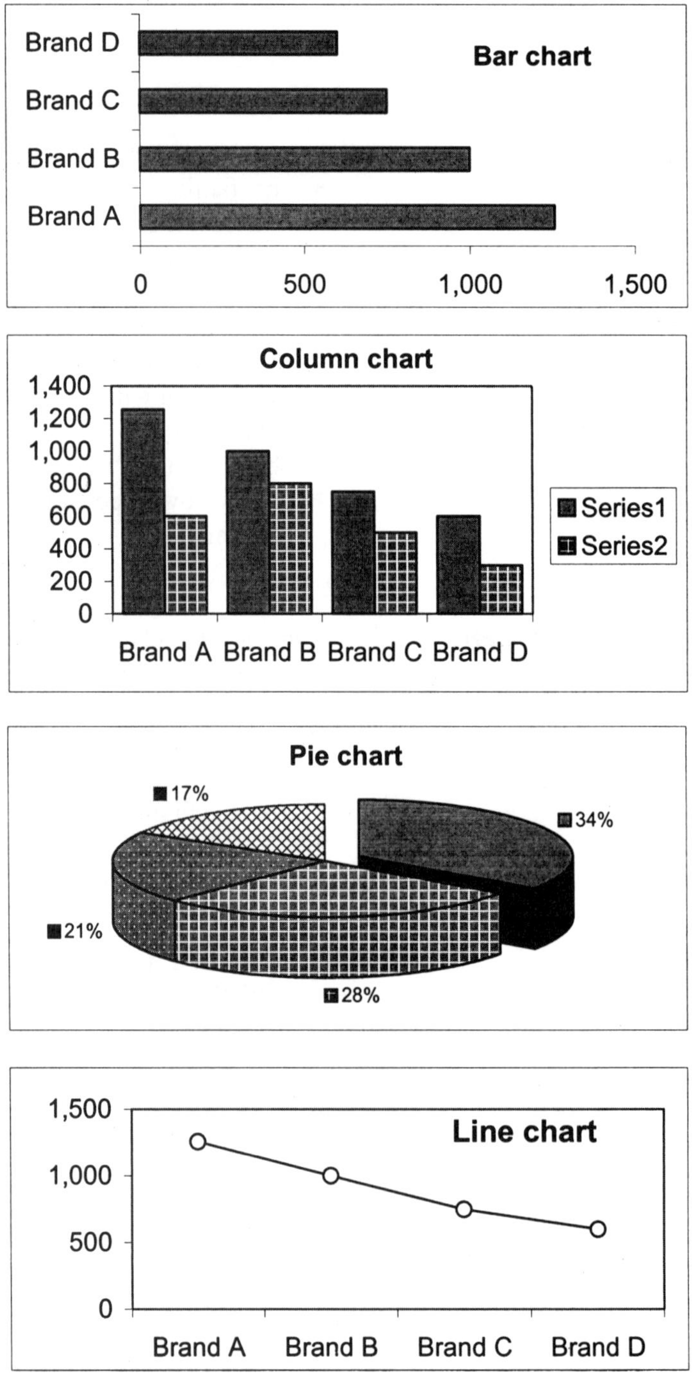

Figure 7.2

The category data (values for the x-axis) for XY charts must be numeric. This type of chart is what is called a *graph* in high school mathematics and science courses.

Anatomy of a Chart

The components of a chart are technically called *objects*. Figure 7.3 identifies many of these objects. You can *format* every object; that is to say, you can change the appearance of an object.

The *chart area* encompasses the entire chart. The border may be removed or given a different colour, and the space inside may be given a colour and/or a pattern or texture.

The *plot area* encompasses everything other than the titles and legend. In the figure, the plot area has a pattern. If you do not need the pattern, you set pattern to 'None', as is explained in a later exercise.

Gridlines are optional; you may include vertical and/or horizontal gridlines at the minor or major levels.

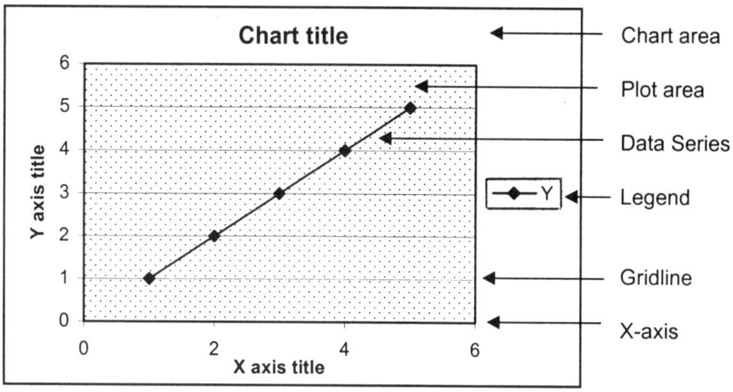

Figure 7.3

The chart has one *data series*. Each item in the series is called a *data point*. This chart has been drawn with both *markers* (in this case, the dots) and a *line* which joins the markers. You may opt to have one or both of these. You can also specify none for both; in which case the data disappears! The colour of each may be specified separately. There are a number of styles (e.g. solid or dotted) and width options for the line. Similarly, the shape of the markers may be changed.

The scale (maximum and minimum values) of each axis may be changed, and there are options to change the number and placement of the *tick marks* on each axis, the font, etc.

One of the options for changing the appearance of an XY chart is *smoothing*. When this option is selected the line joining the data points will be smooth (made mathematically continuous). Otherwise it will consist of a series of straigh- line segments. It is appropriate to use smoothing when the data is known to obey a mathematical function. Smoothing can give unsatisfactory results when plotting data subject to experimental errors.

X- and Y-values

The data used to create a chart may be in rows as in Figure 7.1 or in columns as in Figure 7.4. There is no advantage to using one rather than the other but most people design worksheets such that data is in column form.

The data to be used on the x-axis (the horizontal axis) of column and line charts, or for the y-axis on a bar chart, is called the x-category data. This can be text or numbers. In Figure 7.1 the x-category data is in row 1, while in Figure 7.4 it is in column A.

The data to be charted is called a data series. A chart may have more than one data series. Only one data series was used for the bar, pie and line charts shown in Figure 7.2 but two were used for the column chart.

The y-values may include a name. In Figure 7.1 the cell A2 contains the name for the data in B2:E2. Similarly, cell B1 of Figure 7.4 contains the name for the data in B2:B13. If I select A1:C13 (that is, if I select both the names and the data) then the data series B2:B13 will be given the name in B1 (in this case the name will be *A*). The name is used in the chart's legend. If the data selected for a chart does not include names then Excel assigns the names Series 1, Series 2, etc.

The x-category data is optional. If it is omitted, Excel uses the numbers 1, 2, 3, etc. for the x-category data. This can give rise to a problem: if your x-category values are numeric, Excel will mistakenly take them for y-values and chart them as such using 1, 2, 3, etc. for the x-category values. Problem 1 at the end of the chapter will help you solve this.

Embedded Charts and Chart Sheets

A chart may be created either on a worksheet or on a separate sheet that contains only that chart. In the former case we say the chart is *embedded.* In the second case the chart is said to be on a chart sheet as opposed to a worksheet. We shall make all our charts embedded since it is then easier to see how the chart changes when the data is altered. The steps for creating and modifying a chart in its own sheet are the same as for an embedded chart.

Exercise 1: Column Chart

For the purpose of this exercise we will assume that your company sells two products and that you wish to prepare a chart to show how the sales of product A are seasonal while the sales of B are apparently independent of the time of year. We will create the column chart shown in Figure 7.4.

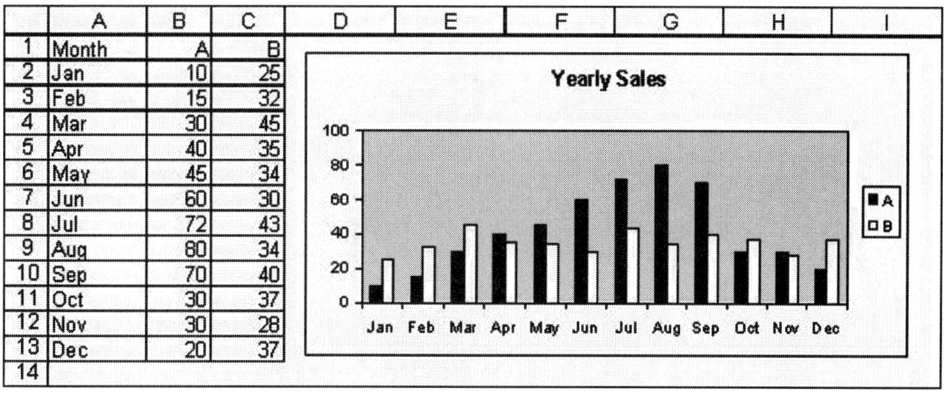

Figure 7.4

(a) Start a new workbook. In the range A1:C13 type the data shown in Figure 7.4. You can use the Auto Fill feature for the month names.

Chart Wizard tool

(b) Select the range A1:C13. If you wish to make a chart on its own sheet, press F11 to create a chart sheet. Otherwise, click the Chart Wizard icon; it is on the standard toolbar.

(c) The first of four Chart Wizard dialog boxes appears — Figure 7.5. Using the *Standard Types* tab, we will select the type of chart from the lefthand menu and the subtype from the icons on the right. We need a Column chart in which the columns are displayed side by side — not stacked. Choose the first one in the second or third row.

Note the button labelled *Press and hold to view sample*. This can be helpful when making a chart type selection. Press the Next button when you are ready.

(d) The dialog box for step 2 is shown in Figure 7.6. Microsoft Excel has correctly deduced that the data is in columns so there is no need to change anything. Press the Next button.

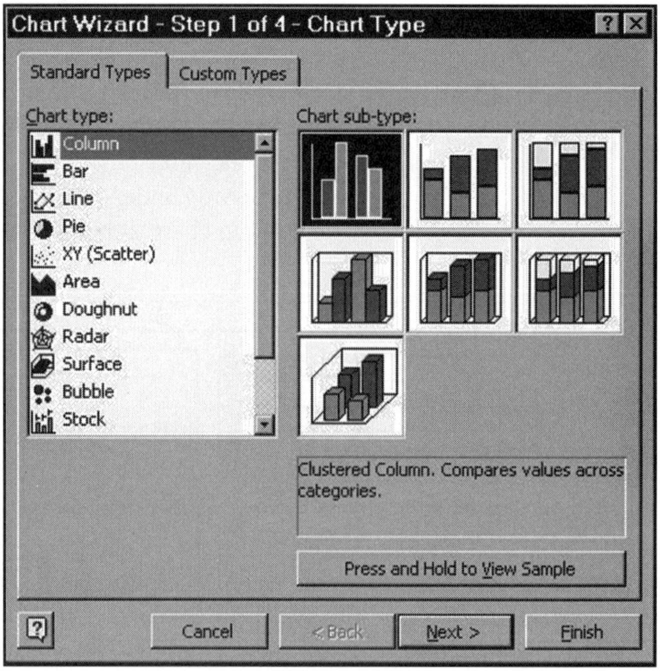

Figure 7.5

(e) In Step 3 (see Figure 7.7) we have the opportunity to make some adjustments to the chart. On the Titles tab we can enter the title for the chart (Yearly Sales) and for the two axes (leave blank). On the Gridlines tab we can decide which, if any, gridlines are to be displayed. In the example all options were de-selected. The Legend tab allows us to choose the position for the legend or to opt for no legend.

(f) In the final step, we have the option to place the chart on the current (or any other) worksheet or place it on a chart sheet — Figure 7.8. Press the Finish button when ready.

(g) It is unlikely that you will be pleased with the size or position of the chart but we will correct this later. Save the workbook as CHAP7.XLS.

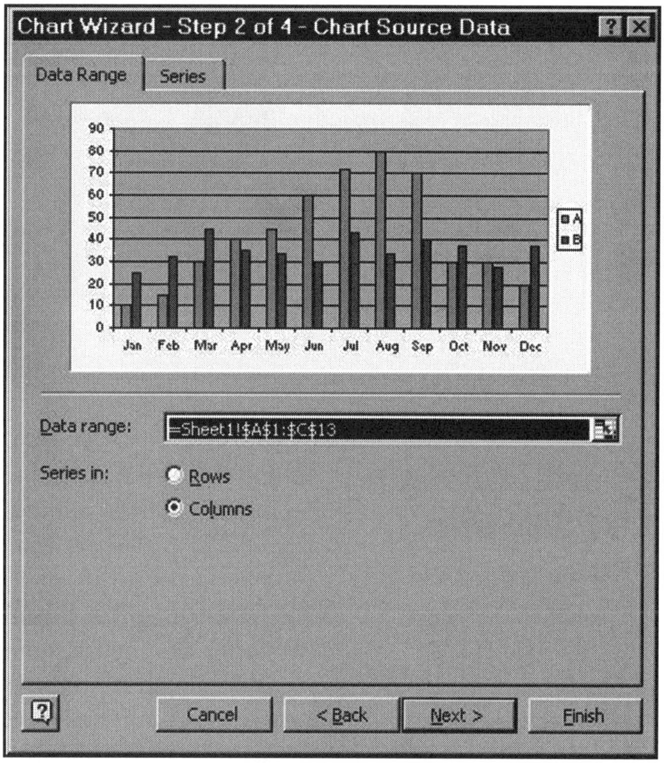

Figure 7.6

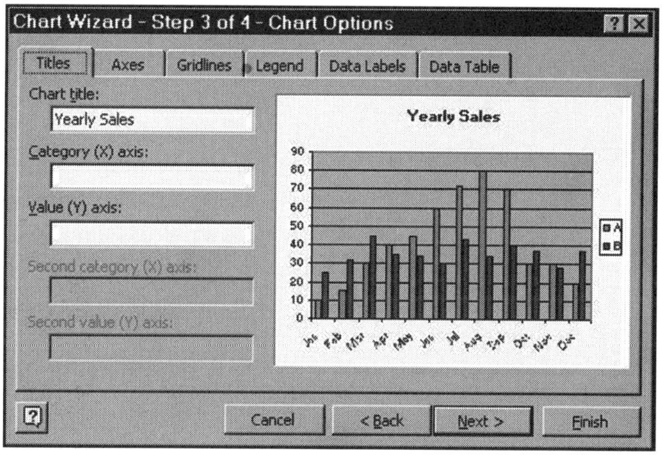

Figure 7.7

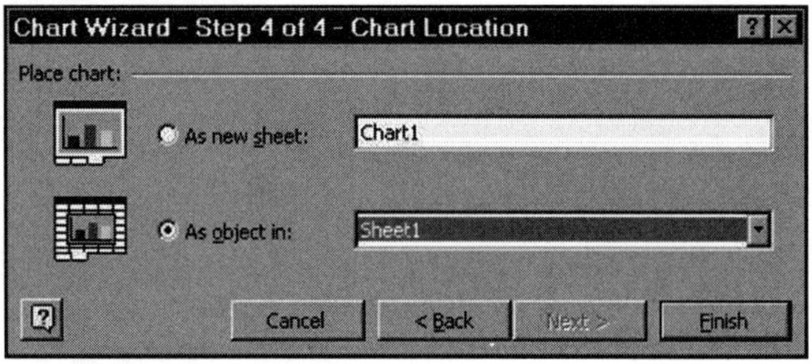

Figure 7.8

Exercise 2: Changing a Chart Size and Position

In this exercise we will change the size and position of the chart produced in the previous exercise. Open the workbook CHAP7.XLS at Sheet1 and do the following.

1. Changing the position and size of the chart

(a) Move the mouse pointer just inside the chart and left click. You should see eight small solid squares called *handles* around the chart border. The chart is now said to be selected. If the handles are on the inner box, the plot area, click again closer to the outer border. If in doubt, let the pointer linger until a screen tip appears displaying *Chart Area.*

> **Reminder:** If you make a mistake undo it with Ctrl+Z or the Undo tool.

(b) Hold down the left mouse button and drag to change the position of the chart on the worksheet.

(c) Move the mouse pointer to one of these handles. When it is over a handle, the pointer shape changes to a double headed arrow. Press and hold down the left mouse button while dragging the mouse. The chart size will alter. Experiment with a handle in the centre of a side and with one at a corner.

(d) Do with same with the plot area, experimenting with moving and resizing it.

(e) Click outside the chart to deselect it.

2. Moving the chart to a new location

We wish to experiment with moving the chart to a chart sheet but still want to keep a chart on the worksheet. We will first make a copy of the chart and then move the copy to a new location. We shall use the pop-up menu rather than the Copy and Paste tools to show the convenience of the menu.

(a) Right click on the chart area, remembering to look for handles on the outer border, and use the Copy item from the menu. Right click on an empty cell below the chart and use the Paste item. Now we have two charts.

Shortcut: You can right click anything (cell, chart, drawing, etc.) on a worksheet and use the Copy item to place it on the Clipboard — this is standard Windows practice.

(b) Right click on the second chart to display a pop-up menu. Select the Location item and specify Chart Sheet. Locate the new tab to left of the Sheet1 tab and open it to view the chart.

Exercise 3: Modifying a Chart

In this exercise we will make a number of changes to the chart created in the first exercise. Every object in a chart may be modified. Some objects may be added or deleted. We will explore a few of the possibilities in this exercise.

1. Format the Plot Area

By default, Excel gives the plot area a shaded background. While this looks fine on the screen, generally it is less pleasing on a printed page. In this exercise we will remove the pattern but the same technique may be used to change its appearance.

(a) Open Sheet1 of CHAP7.XLS where the chart was made in Exercise 1. Click on the plot area; the Chart toolbar appears — Figure 7.9. If you missed the plot area, select it from the option list that opens when the down arrow is pressed.

Note: If the Chart toolbar does not appear, use View|Toolbars and check the Chart toolbar. It will now automatically appear and disappear as a chart is selected and unselected. If you close the toolbar with the × on its title bar you will need to repeat the first step in this note.

Figure 7.9

(b) The icon on the Chart toolbar next to the text box opens the Format Plot Area dialog — Figure 7.10. In the Area box, click the None button to specify that no fill is required in the plot area. Note that you could decide to replace the grey fill with a coloured one and that the same dialog box allows you to change the weight, style and colour of the plot area border. Close the dialog box with the OK button.

Tip: Sometimes it is difficult to click on exactly the correct object. When the chart is activated by clicking on it, the four navigation keys may be used to select individual objects.

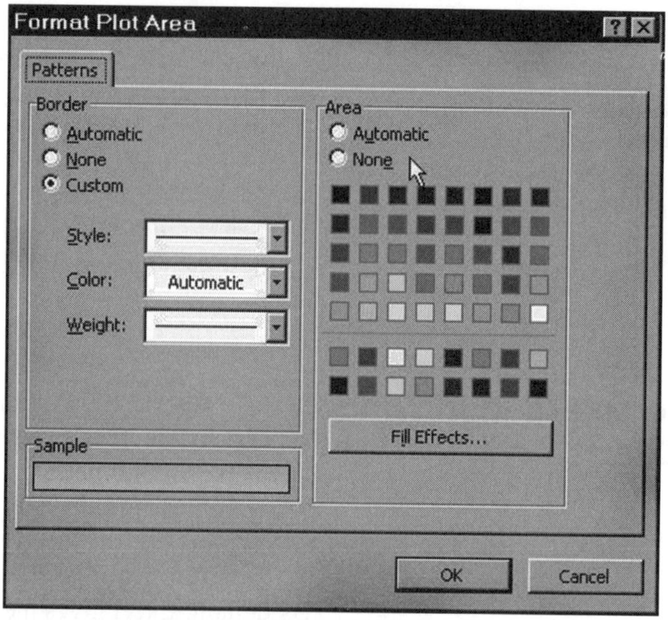

Figure 7.10

2. Format Data Series

You may prefer your columns to have patterns rather than solid colours. Perhaps you wish to change the colour of a column.

(a) Rather than use the Chart toolbar for this operation, we will open the pop-up menu by right clicking on one of the columns — Figure 7.11. The list of items in the pop-up menu varies with the object which is right-clicked but it will always have a formatting option. Select the Format Data Series item.

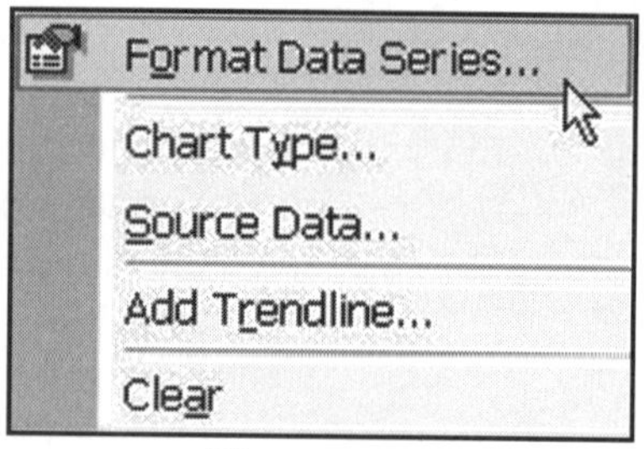

Figure 7.11

(b) The resulting Format Data Series dialog box (Figure 7.12) has a number of tabs. On the Pattern tab there is a region for the Border and one for the Area within it. Using the Fill Effect option give the data series a pattern and another colour.

Tip: If you select a data series in a chart and then click again on a column or marker, you can format a single data point.

3. Changing a column separation

You may wish to make the columns wider and/or have them overlap.

(a) Open the Format Data Series dialog as before but go to the Options tab. Experiment with the two controls and observe the effect in the preview window. If you decide you do not wish to make a change press the Cancel button.

(b) Open the Series Order tab and experiment.

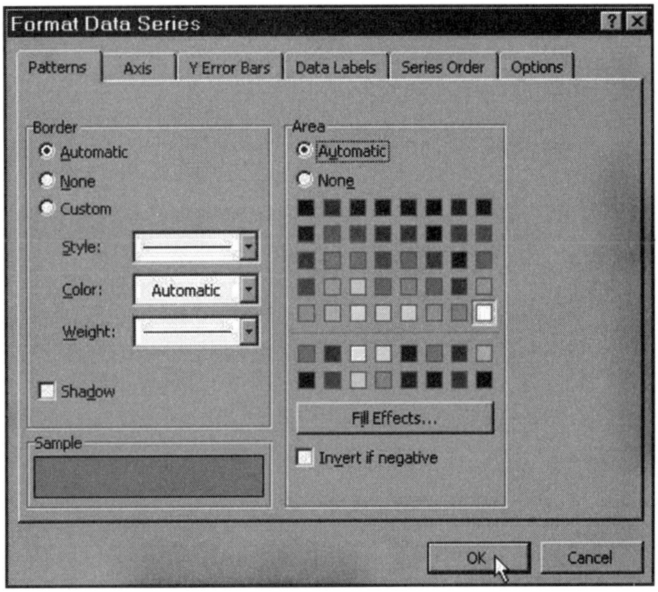

Figure 7.12

4. Format other objects

Using the same basic steps as above you may wish to experiment with:

i) altering the font of the title;

ii) changing the scale of the y-axis; and

iii) adding gridlines.

You can also experiment with right clicking on the chart and selecting the menu item Chart Options.

Exercise 4: A Combination Chart with Two Y-axes

When a chart has two data series with very different numerical ranges it may be advisable to use two y-axes. If the data series represent items that are also qualitatively different, you may wish to plot one as columns and the other as a line. This is called a combination chart.

Here is the scenario for this exercise. Your company is downsizing its workforce. A serious morale problem has arisen. You wish to demonstrate graphically how the downsizing has affected days lost through sickness. The number of workers ranges from a high of 195 to a low of 108, while days lost range from 5 to 15. If we charted the two on the same scale, the sick days would be 'lost' along the x-axis.

(a) On Sheet2 of CHAP7.XLS enter the data shown in Figure 7.13 and construct a chart similar to the one in the figure.

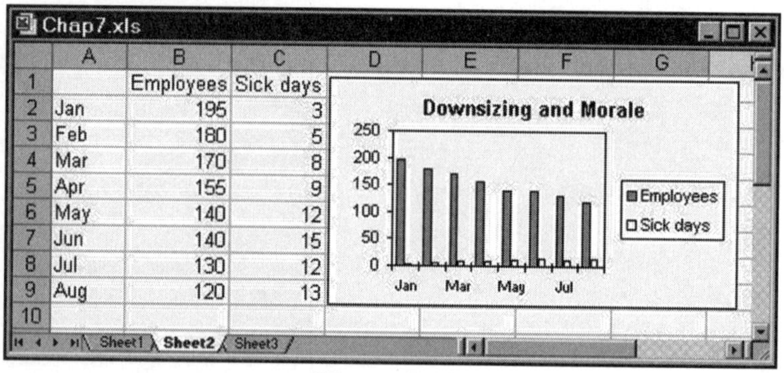

Figure 7.13

(b) The next step is to have sick days charted as a line rather than as columns. Right click on one of the sick day columns and select Chart Type from the pop-up menu. From the dialog box (Figure 7.14) select the Line type and the subtype from the first item in row 2. Experiment with the preview to convince yourself that the other subtypes are inappropriate. Note that we are changing the chart type of only the selected data series, namely the sick days data.

(c) The sick day line is barely clear of the x-axis so we will chart it with its own y-axis. Right click on the line and from the pop-up menus choose Format Data Series. In the dialog box (Figure 7.15) select the Axis tab. Locate the area that reads *Plot series on* and click in the *Secondary axis* box.

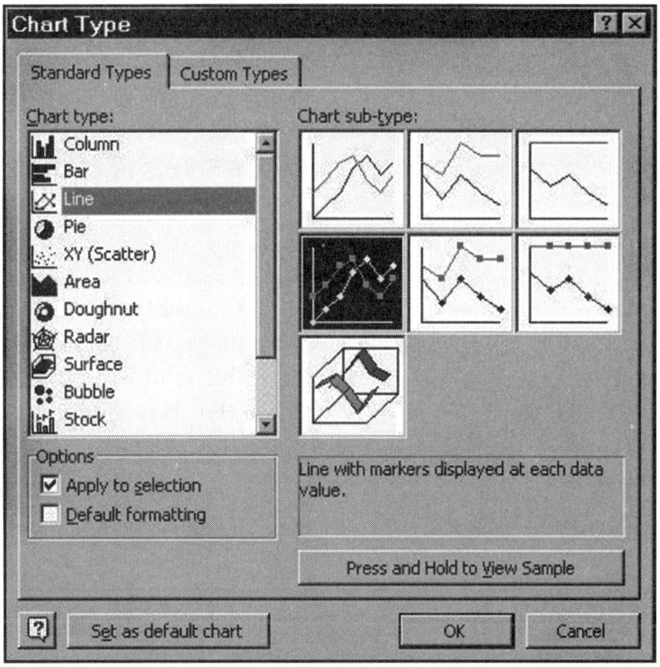

Figure 7.14

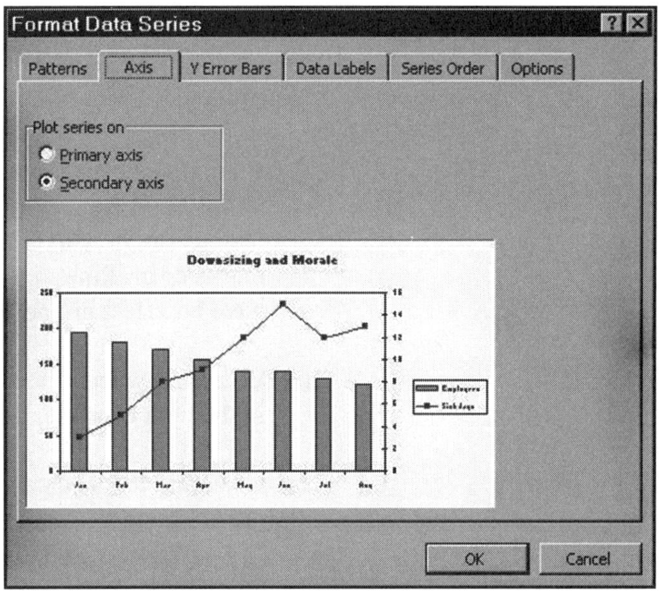

Figure 7.15

(d) We complete the chart by giving titles to the two y-axes. Right click on the chart area, select Chart Options and locate the Titles tab. Type in appropriate titles for each y-axis.

Exercise 5: Changing the Scale

In this exercise we show how to change the scale on an axis. On an XY chart the scale of either axis may be changed but on other charts only the scales for the y-values may be altered.

(a) On Sheet3 of CHAP7.XLS, create the chart shown to the left in Figure 7.16.

(b) To change the scale of an axis, open the Format Axis dialog box. Use the Scale tab to change the maximum values for the axis to 200 — see Figure 7.17. Note that when you enter a value in any of the text boxes, Excel removes the check mark in the corresponding Auto box.

Mon	110
Tue	120
Wed	150
Thu	140
Fri	170
Sat	90
Sun	120

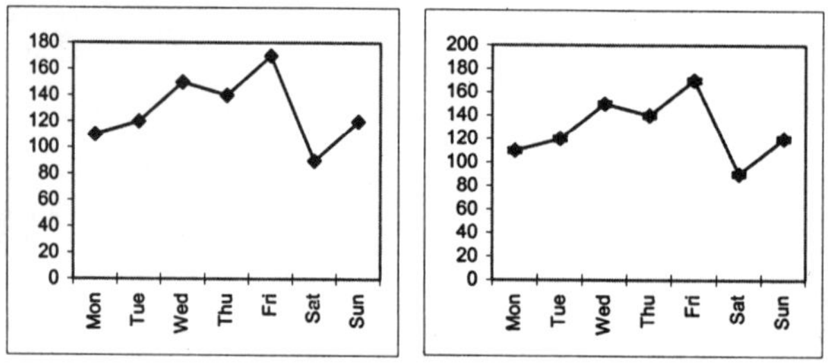

Figure 7.16

This dialog box may also be used to make a variety of changes including:

i) Changing the major and minor units. Changing the major units in this chart from 20 to 40 will give tick marks labelled 0, 40, 80, etc. on the y-axis. Since we are not displaying minor tick marks or gridlines, changing the value of this parameter will have no effect on the appearance.

ii) Changing where the x-axis crosses the y-axis; we look at this in the next exercise, and

iii) Changing the y-scale from normal to logarithmic.

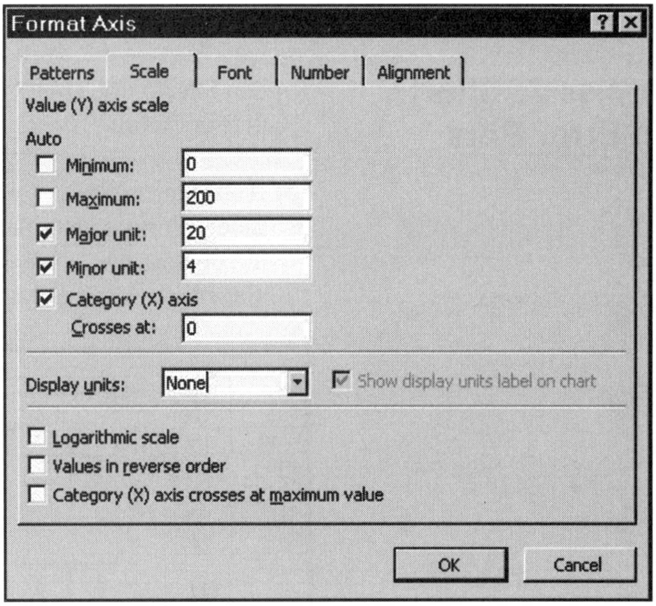

Figure 7.17

Exercise 6: Changing Axis Crossings

There are times when we wish to change where one axis crosses the other. In Figure 7.18 we have plotted a series of negative y-values. The default for a Microsoft Excel chart is for the x-axis to cross the y-axis as shown in the lefthand chart. Most of us would prefer the righthand chart.

(a) On Sheet4 of CHAP7.XLS, create the chart shown to the left of Figure 7.18.

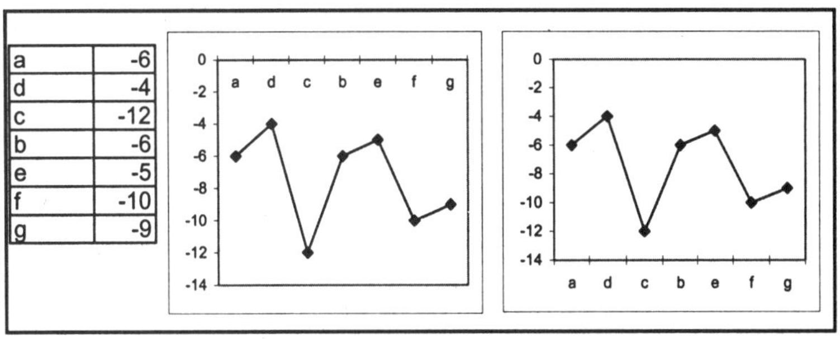

a	-6
d	-4
c	-12
b	-6
e	-5
f	-10
g	-9

Figure 7.18

(b) To change where the x-axis crosses the y-axis, right click on the y-axis and select Format Axis from the pop-up menu. In the *Scale* tab (Figure 7.17) enter your value in Category X Axis

Crosses At box. A value of – 14 was used in the example.

Exercise 7: Chart with Error Bars

(a) On Sheet5 of CHAP7.XLS, create the line chart shown on the left in Figure 7.19.

(b) To add error bars, right click on one item in the data series and select Format Data Series from the pop-up menu. Use the Y Error Bars tab to specify the type and value of the error bars. Save the workbook.

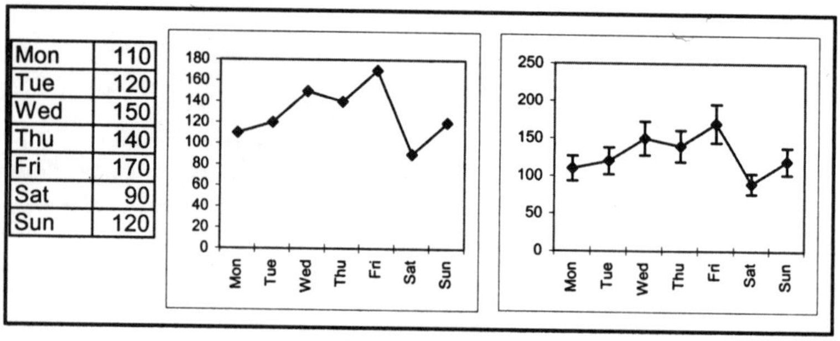

Figure 7.19

Note that High-Low charts are one of the types that can be chosen with the Chart Wizard.

Exercise 8: Blank Cells in the Y Range

We may find that our data has one or more missing Y-values, as in Figure 7.20. How do we wish our chart to appear? Do we want a gap at the missing point or not?

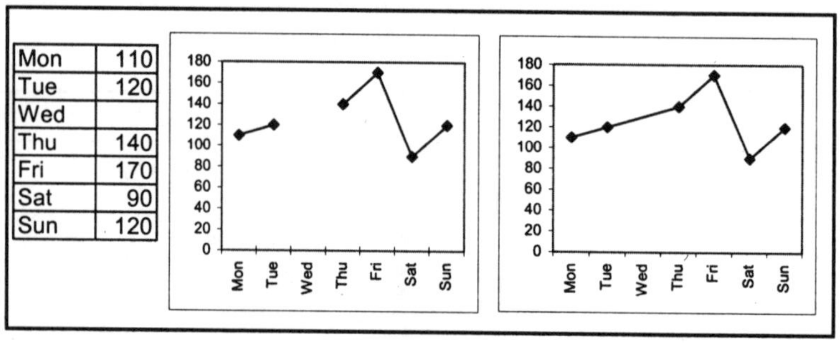

Figure 7.20

(a) On Sheet6 of CHAP7.XLS, create the line chart shown to the left in Figure 7.20.

(b) If we wish to join the Tuesday and Wednesday data, as in the righthand chart, we need to add the formula =NA() to the empty

Wednesday data cell. This will display as #N/A.

There is also an Option in the Tools menu for making charts with empty cells plot in this manner. However, this will affect all future charts opened in Microsoft Excel until you reset the option.

Exercise 9: Exploding a Pie Chart

Pie charts are most appropriate when the number of data points is small and you wish to demonstrate their size relationship. To accentuate one piece of data we often explode the pie as in Figure 7.21.

Food	100
Rent	300
Fares	50
Extra	100

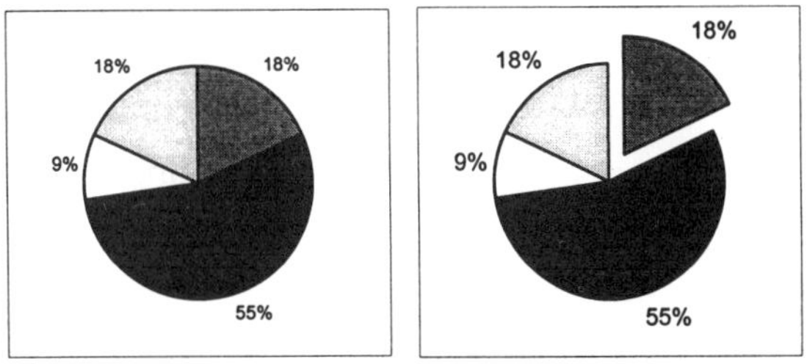

Figure 7.21

(a) On Sheet7 of CHAP7.XLS, create the pie chart as shown in the lefthand chart of Figure 7.21.

(b) We wish to explode one of the slices to accentuate it. Click once on the pie. Now click again on the slice to be exploded. This is not a double click but two separate clicks. Drag the slice as required; the data label will move with the slice. If you drag before the second click, the entire pie will explode. Remember, if at first you do not succeed you can use Undo.

(c) The data labels are very small. Format them to make them more readable.

Exercise 10: Selecting Non-adjacent Data

In the exercises above, the x- and y- values have been in neighbouring columns or rows. Often the data we wish to plot is not adjacent on the worksheet. There are two ways to select such data.

(a) Set up a worksheet on Sheet8 of CHAP7.XLS as shown in Figure 7.22. For the purpose of this exercise, we will pretend we need a chart showing sales by day.

	A	B	C
1	Day	Visitors	Sales
2	Mon	1000	100
3	Tue	1245	125
4	Wed	1567	162
5	Thu	890	99
6	Fri	1305	105
7	Sat	700	86

Figure 7.22

(b) The first way of selecting the two ranges is as follows. Select the first range A1:A7. While holding down the [Ctrl], select the second range (C1:C7) using click and drag. Use this method and create a line chart from the data.

(c) The second way looks more complicated but is often the best method. From the Edit menu choose the Go To command. In the Reference box type the two ranges, separated by a comma. In this case type A1:A7, C1:C7. Click the OK button. Create a bar chart with the selected data. Save the workbook.

Exercise 11: Annotating a Chart

Microsoft Excel charts may be annotated with text, shapes, arrows, etc. using the Drawing toolbar. The chart in Figure 7.23 was created from the data in Problem 2 of Chapter 3.

(a) Begin on Sheet9 of CHAP7.XLS by creating an XY chart of the data in A10:D22. You may specify no legend while creating the chart or you may delete the legend later.

(b) Using the instructions in Exercise 6, format the x-axis to make the maximum 28. This gives some space to enter the text A, B and C.

(c) To enter the text click on the chart, type the text required and either hit [Enter↵] or use the green check mark in the formula bar to complete the entry. What you have typed appears on the chart in a Text box which can be moved to its required position using the mouse, when a four arrowed cursor is displayed.

 Draw Arrow tool

 Draw Line tool

(d) We are now ready to enter the lines. Use the menu command View|Toolbars and put a check mark against *Drawing*. Lines may be drawn by selecting the line or the arrow tool on the Drawing toolbar. To make a straight line, hold down [⇧Shift] while dragging the mouse. Lines may be formatted by right clicking on them and selecting Format Autoshape. Formatting includes changing the style (solid or dotted line) and adding arrow heads at one or both ends. The length of the lines may be adjusted by right clicking and selecting Edit Points.

(e) Save the workbook.

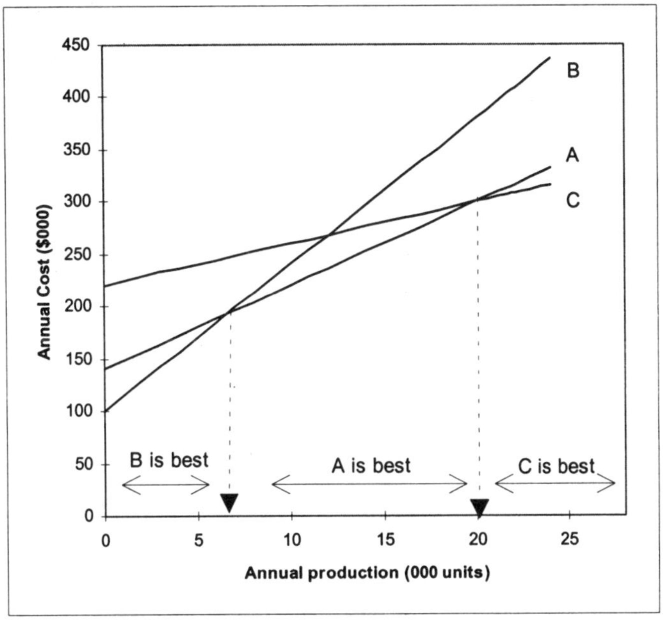

Figure 7.23

Note that the text is part of the chart, so if the chart is moved the text will go with it. However, the lines are overlays and are totally separate from the chart.

Exercise 12: Using Pictures as Markers or Columns

Charts can be made more interesting by replacing the columns, bar or markers with small graphics, as in Figures 7.24 and 7.25. Such charts are, of course, more impressive in colour.

(a) For the first chart, on Sheet10 of CHAP7.XLS, construct a column chart from the data in the normal way.

(b) Right click on a column, open the Format Data Series dialog box and, on the Patterns tab, click the Fill Effects button. When this opens, click the Picture tab (see Figure 7.26) and press the Select Picture button.

You now need to browse through your computer to find the folder in which you keep your pictures. Select one of them. Do not be overly concerned by the quality of the picture in the main viewing area; it is more important that it is fairly crisp in the *Sample* area.

Quarter	Profits
q1	10
q2	15
q3	20
q4	22

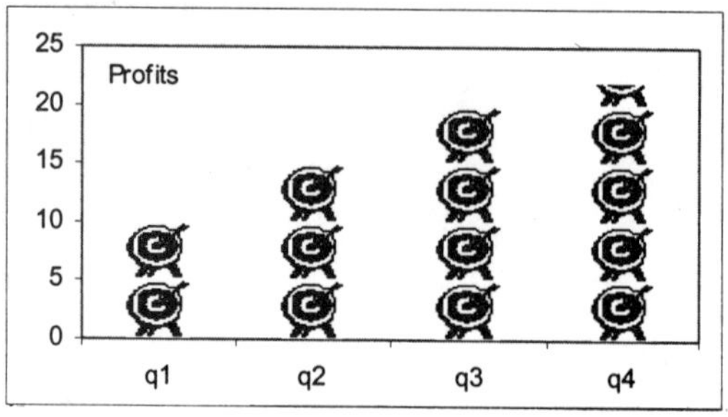

Figure 7.24

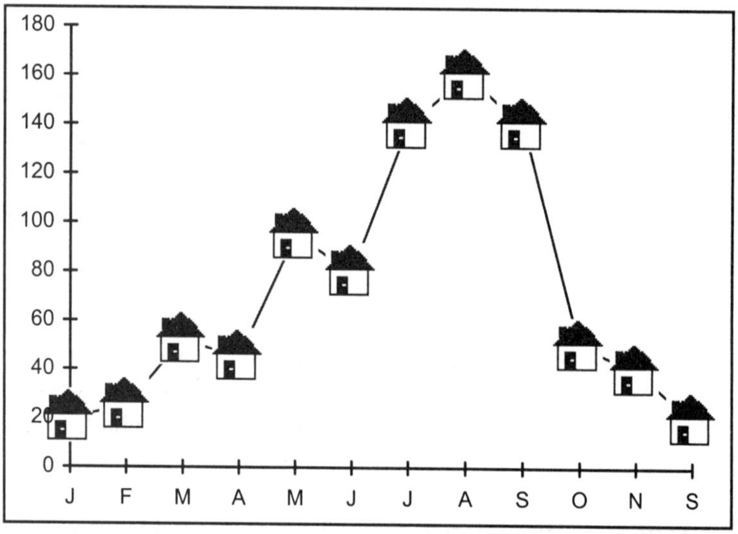

Figure 7.25

Return to the Fill Effects dialog box. Click the *Stack and scale* radio button and enter a value of 5 in the Units box. Close the dialog boxes using the OK buttons to return to the chart. You may wish to reformat the chart and experiment with the stretch or stack and scale formats in the Fill Effects dialog box.

Figure 7.26

(c) The second chart is slightly more difficult to make. One method is to begin with a column chart and add the picture as above. Then right click the chart and use Chart Type to convert it to a Line chart. The second method starts with a Line chart. Use Insert|Picture (ClipArt or From File) to place a picture on an empty space on the worksheet. Format the picture to give it a height of approximately 1½ rows. Place the picture on the Clipboard with the Copy tool, right click on the data series and use the Paste tool. The markers on the Line chart will be replaced by the picture. The original picture may be deleted when you are satisfied with the chart.

(d) The border of the plot area has been removed in this chart. To compensate, the weights of the lines for the two axes have been increased.

Exercise 13: Data Added Automatically

You have collected the data in the table below and have made a chart. You require any new data that gets added to the table to be automatically included in the chart.

Tip: By selecting the A header, the cells in column A have been given a Custom format of d-mmm.

	A	B
1	date	sales
2	1-Jun	10
3	8-Jun	29
4	15-Jun	39
5	22-Jun	25
6	29-Jun	22

Figure 7.27

Important: When definitions like this are used it is essential that there are no extraneous entries in columns A and B.

Tip: This method works well when data will be added on a frequent basis. For a one-time expansion of the series used by a chart: click on the data series and pull down the coloured ranger finders around the X and Y ranges.

(a) Create a Line or Column chart in the normal way on Sheet11 using the data in Figure 7.27.

(b) Use the menu command Insert|Name|Define. We will create two names: one for the x-axis values and one for the y-axis values. For the first name, in the Names in Workbook box type the name Date. In the Refers to box enter the formula =OFFSET(Sheet10!$A$2, 0, 0, COUNTA(Sheet10!$A:$A)-1). Click the Add button. For the second name use Sales and =OFFSET(Sheet10!$B$2, 0, 0, COUNTA(Sheet10!$B:$B)-1). Click Add then close the dialog box.

(c) Right click on the chart area and open the Source Data dialog box. In the *Value* text box type =Chap7.xls!Sales and in the *Category (X) axis labels* text box type =Chap7.xls!Date.

(d) Add some data to your table and watch the chart automatically expand. Save the workbook.

Exercise 14: Adding a New Data Series

There are times when we create a chart and later wish we had used more than one data series. Of course, we could delete the existing chart and start again but this can waste time especially if we have done a lot of customization. Here is a better way.

(a) As the business manager of a small museum, you wish to prepare a chart showing last week's attendance figures. On Sheet12 of CHAP7.XLS, make the chart shown in Figure 7.28 from the data in A1:G2.

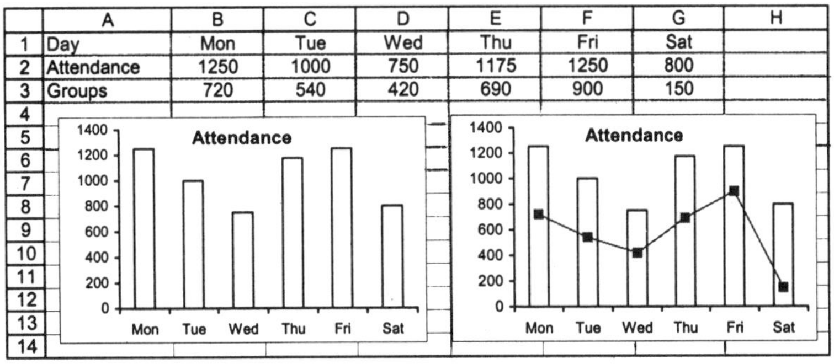

Figure 7.28

(b) You now wish you had included the data in the third row. Select A3:G3 and copy the data to the Clipboard with the Copy tool. Click on the chart. Use the menu command Edit|Paste Special to bring up the dialog box shown in Figure 7.29.

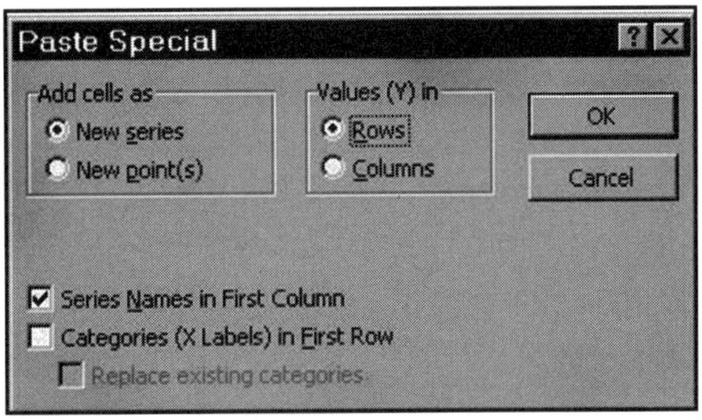

Figure 7.29

(c) We are pasting a new series copied from a row; the data included the name of the series in A3 but we have not copied x-category data. Select the elements in the dialog box to reflect these facts and click the OK button.

(d) You may wish to change the new data to line form. Your final chart will resemble that in the second chart of Figure 7.29.

Exercise 15: Drawing Lines

In Exercise 11 we saw how the drawing tool may be used to add lines and text to a chart. Another method of adding lines uses the Copy and Paste Special technique from the previous exercise. The advantage of this method is that the line can be exactly placed and moved at will by changing values in the worksheet. We will demonstrate this by constructing the chart in Figure 7.30.

(a) On Sheet13 of CHAP7.XLS, enter the data shown in A1:B19 and construct an XY chart from the data in A1:B12.

(b) To add the vertical line begin by selecting A15:B16 and click the Copy button. Open the chart by clicking on it. Use the command Edit|Paste Special. The dialog box shown in Figure 7.29 appears. Check the appropriate boxes to indicate you are adding a new series from data in columns which do not include names in the first row but the data does have category values in the first column. Click the OK button.

(c) You will need to format the new data series to display a line with no markers. You may wish to change its colour.

	A	B
1	x	y
2	0	24
3	1	31
4	2	38
5	3	45
6	4	52
7	5	59
8	6	66
9	7	73
10	8	80
11	9	87
12	10	94
13		
14	Vertical line	
15	4	0
16	4	52
17	Horizontal line	
18	0	52
19	4	52

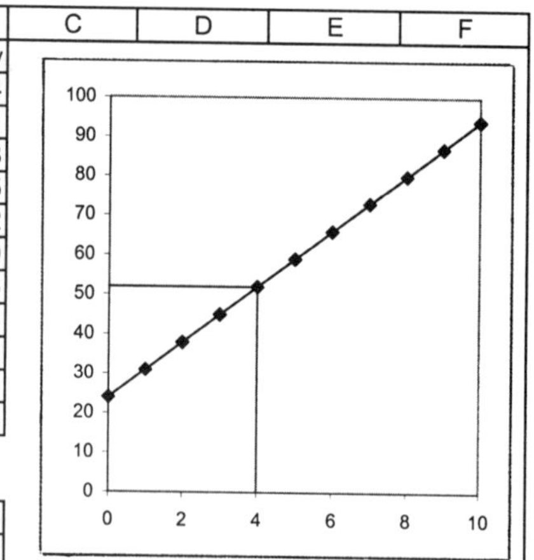

Figure 7.30

(d) Repeat step (b) using the data in A18:B19 to add the horizontal line. Format this line to display just a line.

(e) Save the workbook.

Exercise 16: Gantt Charts

The Gantt chart is useful when planning and scheduling simple projects. To make a Gantt chart with Microsoft Excel we start with a stacked bar chart with two data series and then hide one of the series.

(a) On Sheet14 of CHAP7.XLS, enter the data and text shown in A1:C8 of Figure 7.31. Construct a stacked bar chart as shown in the lower left corner of the figure. Do not be concerned that the x-axis values run from 0 to 50.

(b) The first task is to correct the x-axis values by having separate axes for the two data series. Right click on the 'start' series (the lighter one in the figure) and select Format Data Series. Open the Axis tab and put a check mark in the Secondary axis box. The top x-axis now has a scale of 0 to 20.

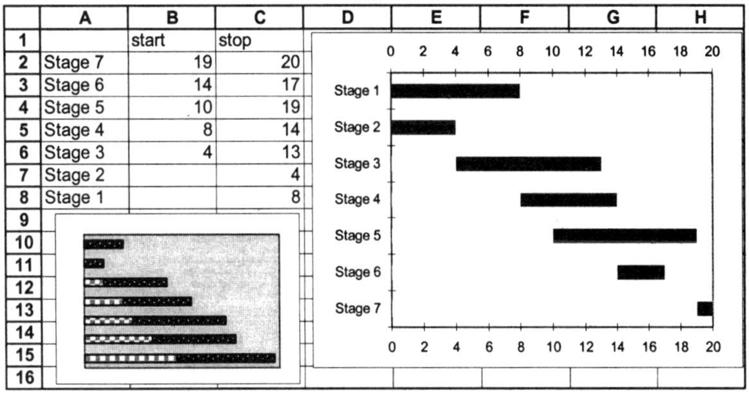

Figure 7.31

(c) Right click on the lower x-axis and give it the same scale (0 to 20) as the upper x-axis.

(d) To hide the 'start' bars open the Format Data Series dialog box again and open the Patterns tab. Set the Area colour to white (or some other colour) and the Line option to None. Click OK. Open the Format Plot Area dialog box and set the Area colour to white (or to the colour chosen for the 'hidden' bars).

(e) The final stage is optional unless you plan to print your Gantt chart. Open the format dialog box for the visible bars and set the *Border* to *None.* For some mysterious reason, if you fail to do this lines appear linking the visible bars with the y-axis when the chart is printed.

Unfortunately, we cannot display the x-axis gridlines on this chart since the hidden bars will cause the gridlines to appear broken.

Summary

We have seen the main types of charts that can be drawn in Microsoft Excel: bar, column, line, XY and pie. We have not looked at area, surface or 3D charts. The reader is encouraged to experiment with these. Excel also provides some specialized charts which are accessed at step 1 of the Chart Wizard by opening the Custom Types tab.

A chart is composed of a number of objects such as: chart area, plot area, data series, x- and y-axes, gridlines, etc. Objects can be formatted to change their appearance. The quickest way to format an object is to right click on it and use Format in the pop-up menu.

Some features (titles, for example) of a chart can be altered by using the Chart Option item in the pop-up menu when the chart area is right clicked.

If some y-values are missing, entering the formula =NA() in the empty cells generally results in a better chart.

The drawing tools can be used to annotate a chart. Data can be added to an existing chart using Copy followed by Paste Special. Titles and text boxes can be linked to cells using formulas in the form =[FileName.xls]Sheet1!$A$1.

Microsoft Excel provides many formats for charts. Always aim for clarity when designing a chart. Just because you can make a bar chart with three-dimensional bars does not mean that this is necessarily the best choice. Does the third dimension mean anything? Does it make the chart more interesting or does it merely confuse the viewer? Very often the simplest design is the optimum one.

Problems

1. Nova Manufacturing makes hammers which it sells for $22. Each hammer cost $15 in labour and materials. The daily fixed manufacturing cost is $1,000. Make a table as shown in Figure 7.32 giving the cost and revenue data for the production of up to 200 hammers. Make an XY chart to show that Nova Manufacturing should make about 140 or more hammers a day to be profitable.

	A	B	C
1	**Break Even Scenario**		
2			
3	Fixed costs	1,000	
4	Selling price	22	
5	Unit cost	15	
6			
7			
8	Units	Costs	Revenue
9	0	1,000	0
10	10	1,150	220
11	20	1,300	440
12	30	1,450	660
13	40	1,600	880
14	48	1,720	1056
15	60	1,900	1320
16	70	2,050	1540
17	80	2,200	1760
18	90	2,350	1980
19	100	2,500	2200

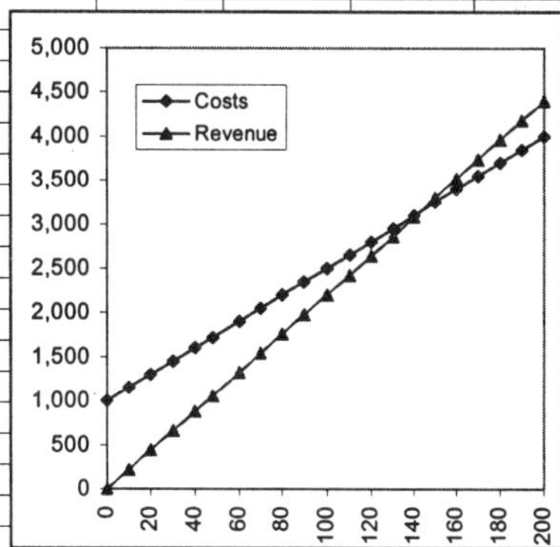

Figure 7.32

2. Construct the chart shown in Figure 7.33. It is a stacked column chart. The numeric x-category data will confuse Excel; you will need to adjust the series in Step 2 of Chart Wizard. The columns have been formatted — look in the Options tab. Do you understand the difference between the two charts?

College population

Year	1980	1985	1990	1995	2000
Males	2,000	2,790	3,000	2,750	2,500
Females	500	700	1,250	1,500	2,000

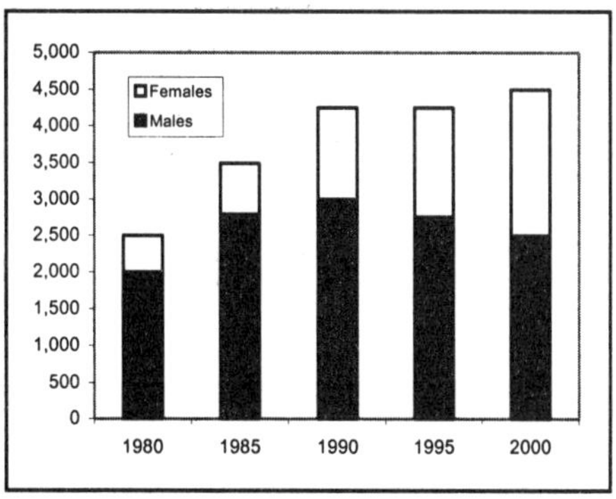

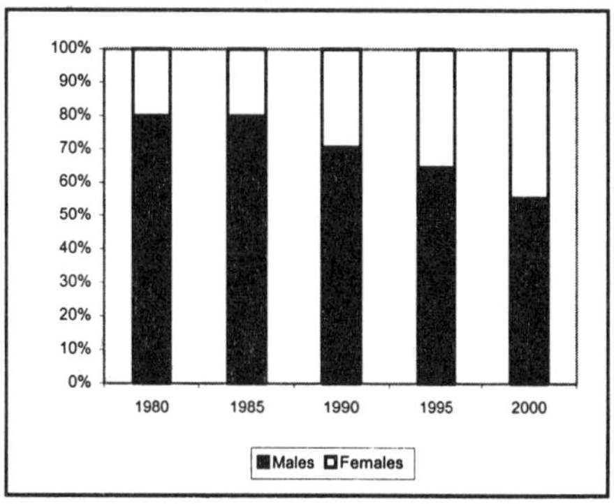

Figure 7.33

8 Modelling

Objectives

The purpose of this chapter is to consolidate the material covered so far. A few new features will be introduced:

- copying a worksheet from one workbook to another;
- creating a Line chart with numeric x-category values;
- giving a name to a formula;
- hiding zeros;
- using the depreciation functions (SLN, DDB, SYD);
- working with the net present value (NPV) and the internal rate of return (IRR) functions.

Exercise 1: Repaying a Loan

In Exercise 10 of Chapter 4 we developed a worksheet to show a loan amortization. Bearing in mind the old adage that a picture is worth a thousand words, in this exercise we will construct two charts that graphically illustrate a loan amortization. These charts show that the early loan repayments mainly pay off interest and that the principal does not decline significantly until later in the repayment schedule. The first chart in Figure 8.1 shows how the IPMT and the PPMT values vary with time, while the second chart shows the cumulative values.

It is convenient to copy the worksheet developed earlier rather than design a new one. Since the two data series have 120 values, we will need to make some modifications to the chart that were not covered in Chapter 7.

(a) Open CHAP4.XLS and move to Sheet7. Select the range A1:F122 and click the Copy button to place the selected material on the Clipboard.

New File icon

(b) Open a new workbook by clicking the first button on the standard toolbar or using File|New. Click on A1 to make it the active cell. Click on the Paste button to copy the contents of the Clipboard.

(c) Now for some housekeeping. Delete A8:A10 and increase the width of column B to allow the value in B6 to be seen.

(d) We would like to be able to change some of the parameters of the loan (i.e. the rate, the period or the principal) and see the effects on the charts. We need to make room for the charts. Click on the column C heading and drag the mouse to the G column heading. The five column headings will be shaded. Click the right mouse button and use the Insert item in the pop-up menu.

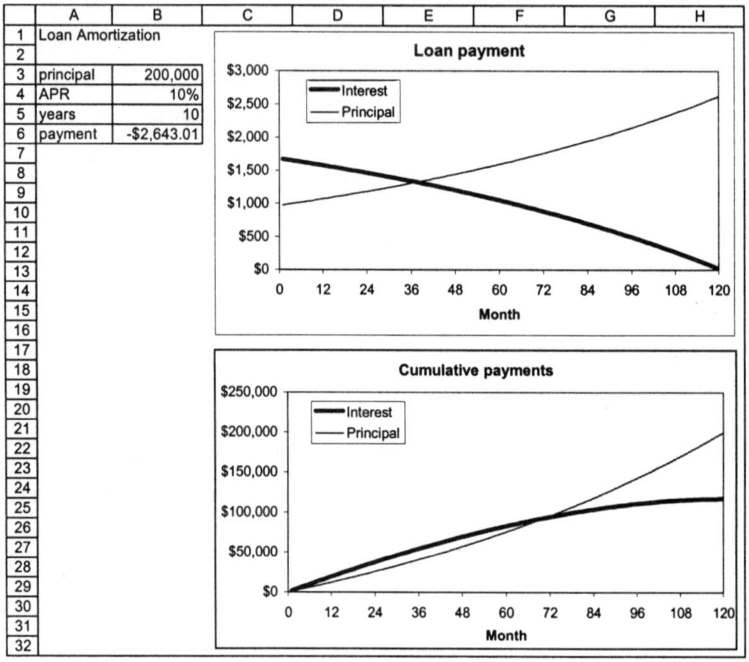

Figure 8.1

(e) Select I2:K122 and construct an XY chart.

(f) The resulting chart will not be satisfactory until you have done some work on it. With this large number of data points, the markers overlap. We begin by formatting the two data series to show only lines. The x-axis needs formatting because of the 120 data points. On the *Scale* tab, set the minimum and maximum to 0 and 120, respectively, and set the major unit value to 12.

Next delete the gridlines and format the Plot Area to have a white area. You may need to adjust the font size used for the titles and axis labels after resizing the plot area.

Next, we need to generate the data for the second chart to show the cumulative payments.

(g) Copy the text in J2:K2 to L2:M2. In L3 enter the formula =J3 and in L4 enter the formula =L3+J4, giving the cumulative values of the interest payments for months 1 and 2, respectively. Format these to show only dollar values and copy them to M3:M4. Select L4:M4 and copy this down to row 122.

(h) The next step is a little tricky since we will be working with non-continuous ranges. We need data from column I for the x-values and from columns L and M for the data series values. With I2 as the active cell, use [⇧ Shift]+[End]+[↓] to select I2:I122. Release all keys and while holding down the [Ctrl] key select L2:M122 — this is most readily done with the mouse.

Should this technique prove too frustrating, select I2:M122 and begin the Chart Wizard process. In step 2, open the *Series* tab and use the *Remove* button to delete the unwanted data series coming from columns J and K.

Format the new chart as before.

(i) Save the workbook as CHAP8.XLS.

You can now experiment with various values for the principal, rate and term of the loan. Of course, if the term is greater than 10 years our charts will cover only a portion of the repayment schedule unless you adjust the maximum for the x-axis scale.

Exercise 2: Whose Rule?

Consider the case where a person borrows money for a short period of time and makes partial payments before the final due date. Historically, there have been two common ways to compute the final balance. They differ in the way in which the interest on the payments is handled.

Under the Merchants' Rule the debt and each partial payment accumulate interest until the final settlement date. The balance due is the difference between the accumulated value of the debt and the accumulated value of the partial payments on that date.

Under the United States Rule the interest on the outstanding debt is computed each time a partial payment is made. If the payment is greater than the interest the difference is used to reduce the principal. If the payment is less than the interest it is held, without interest, until another partial payment is made.

In this exercise we will develop models for the two sets of rules. It is important to note that our purpose in doing so is to practise model development rather than to learn about these two different rules. So, for us, it is immaterial that the governments of some countries have made the Merchants' Rule illegal. We will be content to develop simple models in which repayments are assumed to be made at the end of a month. We compare the results of the two rules when $1,000 is borrowed for a 12-month period at 6% pa with simple interest. Two partial payments will be made: one of $300 at the end of the fourth month and another of $200 at the end of the tenth month. However, one does not develop a worksheet for a single problem. We usually make a worksheet general enough to cover a range of similar problems. Our completed worksheet should be able to compute the balance owing for the stated problem and for other partial payment scenarios.

We will start with the Merchants' Rule. We will make a spreadsheet to compute the balance due for any debt at a specific rate of interest with partial payments at the end of any month. The key to this model is knowing that the debt and the payments are treated the same: we need to calculate the accumulated value of each on the due date. For a simple interest problem the accumulated value of a principal P after m months when the annual rate is r is given by $P(1+rm/12)$. The direction of flow of cash for the debt and for the payments is, of course, different. We will recognize this by making the debt a positive value and the payments negative.

(a) On Sheet2 of CHAP8.XLS, enter the values shown in A1:C8 of Figure 8.2. In A9:A21 enter the series 0 to 12. To wrap the text in cell C8, use Alt+Enter↵ between the two words.

(b) Select A3:B4 and, using Insert|Name, give B3 the name *Rate* and B4 the name *Loan*.

(c) In B9 enter the formula =Loan. In C9 enter =B9*(1+Rate*(12 - A9)/12). This computes the accumulated value of the original debt for the 12-month term of the loan using simple interest. Since the loan is for a year, we could have entered =B9*(1+rate) but the more complex form allows us to copy it.

(d) Copy B9:C9 down to row 21. Our spreadsheet now contains a large number of zero values which distract us from the real data. We can avoid this by altering the formula in C9 to read =IF(B9=0," ",=B9*(1+Rate*(12- A9)/12)) and copy this down to C21. Remember the quick way to do this is to double click on the fill handle of cell C9.

	A	B	C	D	E	F	G	H
1			Paying off a short term loan					
2								
3	Rate	6%						
4	Loan	1000.00						
5								
6		Merchants' Rule				United States Rule		
7								
8	Month	Cash flow	Accumulated value		Month	Interest	Payment	Balance
9	0	1000.00	1060.00		0			1000.00
10	1				1	5.00		1005.00
11	2				2	5.00		1010.00
12	3				3	5.00		1015.00
13	4	-300.00	-312.00		4	5.00	300.00	720.00
14	5				5	3.60		723.60
15	6				6	3.60		727.20
16	7				7	3.60		730.80
17	8				8	3.60		734.40
18	9				9	3.60		738.00
19	10	-200.00	-202.00		10	3.60	200.00	541.60
20	11				11	2.71		544.31
21	12				12	2.71		547.02
22		Balance	546.00				Balance	547.02

Figure 8.2

(e) In B13 enter −300, this being the first partial payment, and in B19 enter −200, the second partial payment. The accumulated values of these on the due date are displayed in column C.

(f) The formula we need in C22 is =SUM(C9:C21).

Surprisingly, the United States Rule is somewhat more difficult to model. The best way to develop a model is to write out some results with pencil and paper and ask 'How can I get Excel to generate these values?' Imagine that you had generated E6:H22 of Figure 8.2 using pencil and paper.

The major problem here is the interest calculation. Remember, we are computing simple interest. Note that until a payment is made, the interest is computed for the principal value in H9. In the fifth month, the interest is computed on the principal value in H13. It is not immediately obvious how to tell Excel what to do. Then we note that the Balance value dips to a local minimum in cell H13.

We see the same thing in cell H19 when the second payment is made. This suggests that the MIN function could be used. And, indeed, that is what we will use.

If you test your finished worksheet, you will find that this approach fails when the interest rate is very high. As long as you are paying interest and not usury, the model works, but do not use your worksheet if you borrow from a loan shark who charges 75% interest! Also note that we have assumed that any partial payment will be large enough to cover the accrued interest. The model will be inaccurate for small payments.

Do not be too concerned that your model does not work when stretched to the limit. After all, scientists still use Newton's laws which are not accurate for objects smaller than atoms or for velocities near the speed of light but are just fine for everyday problems.

(g) Enter the text in E6:H8 and the series 0-12 in E9:E21.

(h) Enter the formula =Loan in H9.

(i) The formula in F10 is =MIN($H$9:H9)*Rate/12 and the formula in H10 is =H9+F10-G10. Select F10:H10 and copy the range down to row 21. The final balance in H22 is found with the formula =H21. If the formula in F10 seems strange, move to any month below (say month 5) and note how the formula correctly selects the minimum value from the Balance column using a range that starts at the top and ends with the Balance for the preceding month.

(j) To allow for the partial payments, enter the value 300 in G13 and 200 in G19. Note that because of the way we have designed this part of the model, positive values are to be used for payments.

(k) Save the workbook.

One test of the model would be to enter values equal to the projected balances ($546.00 and $547.02) as payments in the last month. Your new balances should be zero. You can also experiment with the model to see how final balances for the two rules differ with other interest rates and/or payment schedules.

Exercise 3: Depreciation Models

Note: The functions SLN, DDB and SYD could be used for these calculations, but we will learn more here using our own formulas.

All tangible assets have a finite lifetime. Machines, for example, either wear out or become obsolete. The values of these assets decline over their lifetime. This loss in value is called depreciation and is treated as a business expense. In this exercise we will model three commonly used methods of computing annual depreciation: the straight-line, the double declining balance and the sum-of-years' digits methods.

Before looking at the models we need to define some terms. *Cost* is the money spent to acquire the machine, *Lifetime* is the useful life in years, *Residual* or *Salvage value* is value at the end of the lifetime, and *Book* or *Carrying value* is the value at which the asset is shown in the company's accounting records. In the first year the book value is equal to the cost; in year two it is the cost less the first year's depreciation.

The taxation authority of a country generally specifies the lifetime of categories of assets and other rules about depreciation allowances. We will construct a worksheet allowing for lifetimes up to 10 years. These models would be suitable for most types of machinery but not for buildings or assets (such as aircraft and ships) that have longer lifetimes.

Straight-line (SL) method

This is the simplest method of computing depreciation. In this method an equal portion of the cost of the asset is allocated to each period. For example, a company buys a new truck for £32,000 and expects to keep it for 5 years when it hopes to get £6,000 for the used vehicle. The depreciable cost is £26,000 (32,000 less 6,000) which divided by 5 gives £5,200 as the annual depreciation.

This is relatively easy to model and the result is shown in Figure 8.3. We have a model that can be used for lifetimes up to 10 years, but we need some way of terminating the calculations when the lifetime is less than 10. We do this with IF worksheet functions which return blanks when no calculation is needed. In a later model we will use functions that return zeros and we will hide the zeros.

(a) On Sheet3 of CHAP8.XLS, enter the text shown in A1:D10 of Figure 8.3. Enter the series in A11:A21.

(b) Use Insert|Name|Create to name the cells B3:B5.

(c) The formula in D11 is =Cost. Format the cell as Currency with zero decimals and no symbol.

(d) Enter these formulas:
B12: =IF(A12>Lifetime, " ", (Cost - Residual)/Lifetime)
C12: =IF(A12>Lifetime, " ", C11 + B12)
D12: =IF(A12>Lifetime, " ", Cost - C12)
You may use no space or one space between the quotations.

(e) Select B12:D12 and give the range the format Currency, with zero decimals and no symbol. Copy the range down to row 21.

(f) Save the workbook.

	A	B	C	D
1	**Depreciation Models**			
2				
3	Cost	32,000		
4	Residual	6,000		
5	Lifetime	5		
6				
7				
8		**Straight line depreciation schedule**		
9				
10	Year	Depreciation	Accumulated depreciation	Book Value
11	0			32,000
12	1	5,200	5,200	26,800
13	2	5,200	10,400	21,600
14	3	5,200	15,600	16,400
15	4	5,200	20,800	11,200
16	5	5,200	26,000	6,000
17	6			
18	7			
19	8			
20	9			
21	10			

Figure 8.3

Double declining balance (DDB) method

In the straight-line method, when the lifetime is 5 years, we depreciate the asset by one-fifth of the depreciable cost each year. Alternatively, we could say we used a depreciation equal to 20% of the cost. In the double declining method we double the rate obtained by the straight-line method. So if the lifetime is 5 years, the rate for the double declining method is 40%. If the lifetime is 3 years then the rate is 66%. Note that the simplest way to compute the rate is with the formula *2/Lifetime*. There are other declining methods. For example the 150% method uses 1.5 times the straight-line rate. An important difference is that this rate is applied not to the initial cost as in the SL method but to the current book value.

Figure 8.4 shows the worksheet we are about to develop. We are still working on Sheet3 so the named cells in rows 3 to 5 are available to us.

To help us to see how this worksheet was developed, imagine it was the result of pencil and paper calculations. Why is there no depreciation value after row 31? Clearly, there should be no values after line 32 since the 5-year lifetime is up. Now look at the value in B31— is this 40% of the previous year's book value? Clearly not. Had we used such a value, the book value would have fallen below the residual value. The minimum book value is the residual value. So we limited the depreciation to 912 (book value in year 3 less residual value) in year 4. In year 5 we can have no depreciation since the asset is already valued at the residual value.

	A	B	C	D
24	**Double declining balance schedule**			
25				
26	Year	Depreciation	Accumulated depreciation	Book Value
27	0			32,000
28	1	12,800	12,800	19,200
29	2	7,680	20,480	11,520
30	3	4,608	25,088	6,912
31	4	912	26,000	6,000
32	5	-	26,000	6,000
33	6	-	-	-
34	7	-	-	-
35	8	-	-	-
36	9	-	-	-
37	10	-	-	-

Figure 8.4

If we were doing this calculation by hand we would impose two rules on ourselves: (i) there can be no depreciation after the useful lifetime, and (ii) the depreciation can never be such that the book value becomes less than the residual value. We can incorporate these rules in our worksheet by using nested IF statements as will be seen in step (d) below.

(a) In this model we shall need to refer to the quantity 2/Lifetime in a number of formulas. We could place this in a named cell but, since we do not want the user to be able to change it, we will use a different method. Use Insert|Name|Define to open the dialog box shown in Figure 8.5.

In the Names in workbook box enter the name Double. In the Refers to box enter the formula =2/Lifetime. Click the OK button.

We now have a *named formula*.

(b) In A24 of Sheet3 enter the text as shown in Figure 8.4. Centre this across columns A:D.

(c) You may wish to copy A10:D21 to A26 and then delete B28:D37 as a quick way to get started. Note that D27 contains the formula =Cost.

Figure 8.5

(d) Enter these formulas:
B28: =IF(A28>Lifetime, 0, IF(D27 - Double * D27 > Residual, Double * D27, D27 - Residual))
Read this formula as: if the lifetime has been passed, the depreciation is zero. Otherwise, test if the double declining rate will give a book value less than the residual value. If not then use the double declining rate to compute the depreciation. Otherwise, the depreciation is whatever is needed to make the book value equal the residual value.
C28: =IF(A28>Lifetime, 0, C27 + B28)
D28: =IF(A28>Lifetime, 0, Cost - C28)

(e) Select B28:D28 and format the range as Accounting with zero decimals and no symbol. This will hide the zeros. Cells with zeros will display a simple hyphen which is far less distracting than a table full of zeros. Alternatively, format the range using Number with zero decimals but with *Use 1000 Separator* checked. Use the command Tools|Options, move to the View tab and remove the check mark in the Zero Values box. The last step will affect all cells in the current worksheet.

(f) Copy B28:D28 down to row 37 and save the workbook.

You may wish to experiment with other costs and residual values. For example, when the cost is 17,000 with a residual value of 2,000 and a lifetime of 5 years then each of the 5 years has a depreciation greater than zero. Note that the double declining balance method can never bring the book value to zero since the annual depreciation is a percentage of the previous book value. When the residual value is zero, most companies switch to the straight-line method after a number of years, as you will see in Problem 2.

In the straight-line model we used IF formulas that returned either a value or blank. Why, in the DDB model, did we use IF formulas that returned either a value or 0s? Formulas such as =C27+B28 return a #VALUE error if either of the cells contains a blank so we resorted to using the second type of IF formula. This problem did not arise in the first model, so we could use either type of IF formula.

Sum-of-years'-digits (SYD) method

This method is best explained with an example. Let an asset have an initial cost of 10,000 and a residual value of 2,000 after 5 years. We begin by summing 1 + 2 + 3 + 4 + 5 to get 15. The first year's depreciation is 5/15 of the depreciable value, i.e. (5/15) × (10,000 – 2,000) or 2,667. In the next year it is (4/5) × (10,000 – 2,000) or 2,133. See Figure 8.6.

	A	B	C	D
40		Sum of the Year's Digits		
41				
42	Year	Depreciation	Accumulated depreciation	Book Value
43				32,000
44	1	8,667	8,667	23,333
45	2	6,933	15,600	16,400
46	3	5,200	20,800	11,200
47	4	3,467	24,267	7,733
48	5	1,733	26,000	6,000
49	6	-	-	-
50	7	-	-	-
51	8	-	-	-
52	9	-	-	-
53	10	-	-	-

Figure 8.6

(a) We need a formula to compute 1 + 2 + 3 … + n where n equals the Lifetime value. It can be shown that this is given by $n(n+1)/2$. Create a formula named SumDigits which refers to =Lifetime*(Lifetime+1)/2 as in step (a) above.

(b) In A40 of Sheet3 enter the text as shown in Figure 8.6, and centre it across columns A:D.

(c) You may wish to copy A10:D21 to A42 and then delete B43:D53 as a quick way to get started. Note that D43 contains the formula =Cost.

(d) Enter these formulas:
B44: =IF(A44>Lifetime, 0, (Cost - Residual) * (Lifetime - A43) / SumDigits)
C44: =IF(A44>Lifetime, 0, C43 + B44)
D44: =IF(A44>Lifetime, 0, Cost - C44).
Give B44:D44 Accounting format (no currency symbol, zero decimals) and copy the cells down to row 53.

(e) Save the workbook.

Exercise 4: To Buy Or Not To Buy?

Gourmet Catering is considering purchasing some new machinery for £45,000 which they expect to have a scrap value of £9,000 after 3 years. It is anticipated that this machinery will generate an extra £18,000 of income after deducting operating costs. The management committee needs to know if this is a viable project. Other factors to consider are the prevailing interest rate (8%) and the company's tax rate (25%). We will look at two possible calculations (the net present value and the internal rate of return) to help the committee. Our complete worksheet will resemble Figure 8.7.

	A	B	C	D	E	F	G	H
1	Capital Expenditure Decision							
2								
3	Cost	Scrap	NetIncome	InterestRate	TaxRate	Depreciation method		
4	45,000	9,000	18,000	8%	25%	SLN		
5								
6								
7	Cash Flow and Net Present Worth							
8								
9	Year	Net pretax income	Depreciation	Taxable Income	After tax Income	Scrap value	Cash flow	Present value
10	0						-45,000	-45,000
11	1	18,000	12,000	6,000	4,500		16,500	15,278
12	2	18,000	12,000	6,000	4,500		16,500	14,146
13	3	18,000	12,000	6,000	4,500	9,000	25,500	20,243
14						NPV	4,667	4,667
15							Proceed	Proceed
16								
17	Internal Rate of Return					IRR	13%	Proceed

Figure 8.7

We will begin by setting out the various parameters of the problem.

(a) On Sheet4 of CHAP8.XLS, enter the text and values shown in A1:F4. Remember that text wrapping is done with [Alt]+[Enter ↵]. You will also need to adjust some column widths.

(b) Select A3:E4 and use Insert|Name|Create to name the cells A4:E4. Note that F4 need not be named.

The next step is to generate the project's cash flow for the 3 years. The machinery is purchased in year zero. An additional £18,000 of income is generated each year. This income less the depreciation allowance is, of course, subject to tax. We subtracted the depreciation to compute the after tax income since depreciation is an allowable expense. However, unlike expenses such as material and labour costs, the company does not write a cheque to cover depreciation so we must add it back to the after tax income to produce the cash flow. We must also allow for the scrap value of the machinery in the final year of its lifetime.

(c) Enter the text in A7:G9 and the series in A10:A13.

(d) Enter the formulas:
G10: =-Cost (The cash flow in year zero)
B11: =NetIncome
C11: =SLN(Cost, Scrap, 3)
D11: =B11-C11
E11: =D11*(1-TaxRate)
G11: =C11+E11+F11 (The cash flow in year 1)

(e) Format B10:G11 as Currency with no symbol and zero decimals.

(f) Copy B11:G11 down to row 13.

(g) Enter =Scrap in F13. Remember the quick way to do this is to type the equal sign and click on cell B4 which is named *Scrap*.

We now have the cash flow data for the 4 years. We will find the net present value using a long-winded method and then show a simpler way. We need to discount the cash flow of each year to the reference year (year zero). Clearly, no discount is needed for year zero's cash flow value. For other years, the present value (*pv*) of cash flow (*cf*) values are found using $pv = cf/(1+rate)^{year}$. We can add these discounted values to get the net present value. A project is generally considered viable if the net present value is positive.

(h) Enter the title in H9 and =-Cost in H10. In H11 enter the formula =G11/(1+InterestRate)^A11. Copy H11 to H12 and H13.

(i) Use the AutoSum tool to enter the formula =SUM(H10:H13) in cell H14.

(j) In H15 enter =IF(H14>0, "Proceed", "No go").

We now understand the concept of net present value and can use Help to see if Microsoft Excel provides a function to compute it. We find the function NPV has the syntax ***=NPV(rate, value1,*** *value2,...)*. If we jump the gun and enter in G14 =NPV(InterestRate, H10:H13) the resulting value is slightly less than our longer method yielded. If we carefully read the specifications for the NPV function, we find that it assumes that *value1* is received after 1 year but the cash flow value in H10 is for the end of year 0 (or the start of year 1). As we have seen, this value does not need to be discounted.

(k) In G14 enter =G10 + NPV(InterestRate, G11:G13). This gives the same result as in H14.

(l) Copy the formula from H15 to G15. This cell displays *Proceed* since the NPV for the project is greater than 0.

You will see that the NPV function is similar to the PV except that the PV function can be used only when cash flow values are constant over the period.

Financial analysts prefer to talk about rates of return rather than dollar values. If the cash flow values after year zero were constant, we could use the RATE function but for variable cash flow values we use the IRR function which has the syntax =**IRR(values,** guess). The IRR function finds its result by a recursive process — more on this in the next chapter — which may be helped by providing a value for the optional *guess* argument. IRR uses a value of 10% if the argument is omitted. Should IRR not be able to find a solution it returns the #NUM! error value. When this happens you should provide a *guess* value to assist the function.

Each company has a minimum required rate of return. For a small business this may be related to the bank lending rate. Larger corporations use a value related to their net income as a percentage of equity which can be significantly higher than the bank rate. For the purpose of this exercise we will use the bank lending rate as the minimum acceptable rate of return.

(m) Enter the text in A17 and F17. Enter the formulas
G17: =IRR(G10:G13)
H17: =IF(G17>InterestRate,"Proceed","No go")

From a mathematical point of view IRR is the interest rate corresponding to a zero NPV. This topic is investigated in Problem 5. The IRR function can, of course, return only one value. Mathematically, the maximum number of possible IRR values equals the number of times there is a change in the sign of the cash flow values. The sign of the cash flow changes only once in the period of our project. In other cases one may make a chart to check the IRR value — see Problem 5.

The model is now complete and the committee can use it for 'what-if' analysis. For example, what if the scrap value is only £1,000? The model can be used to do a sensitivity analysis. By keeping all but one parameter constant, we can see how sensitive the estimated NPV is to changes in that parameter. We have assumed that the net income will be the same in each year. You can override this assumption by simply entering values in B11:B13.

Exercise 5: Cost of Inventory: FIFO and LIFO

Bradshaw Hardware began in July 1999 with an inventory of six SuperBQs purchased in May and 12 in June. In July, they accepted a shipment of 40 more units. During the month of July they sold 50 SuperBQs. We wish to calculate the cost of goods and the change in the value of inventory for the income statement for July.

There is a complication: the unit cost to Bradshaw's for the items was not the same for the three shipments. Which of these purchases represents the cost of the items remaining in inventory at the end of the accounting period? There are four accounting practices that cover this situation. They are called *specific identification*, *average cost*, *first-in-first-out (FIFO)* and *last-in-first-out (LIFO)*. We will design a worksheet to calculate the Cost of Goods using the FIFO and LIFO methods. It is beyond the scope of this book to comment on the appropriateness of the methods but our worksheet will show that quite different results may be obtained when the cost of items vary with the time of purchase. At the conclusion of the exercise, our worksheet will resemble that in Figure 8.8.

In the FIFO model it is assumed that the items purchased first are the first to be sold. The inventory at the end of the period consists therefore of the items most recently purchased.

The worksheet has three areas.

(i) The starting inventory data for the accounting month is recorded in A3:C8.

(ii) A11:D17 is used to enter the quantity sold in the month and to perform the FIFO or LIFO calculations. The Cost of Goods (COG) is computed in C16.

(iii)E3:H9 reports the end-of-month inventory data and computes the COG in H9 as a check on the value in C16.

The Sorting tools on the Standard toolbar are useful for sorting a single column of data. We learn more sorting tables in Chapter 10.

Sort Descending tool

Sort Ascending tool

	A	B	C	D	E	F	G	H
1	FIFO and LIFO methods to compute Cost of Goods							
2								
3	Units available in accounting month				Starting and Ending Inventory values			
4	Purchase date	Starting quantity	Unit cost		Starting quantity	Starting value	Ending quantity	Ending value
5	1-May	6	$ 125.00		6	$ 750.00	0	$ -
6	2-Jun	12	$ 145.00		12	$ 1,740.00	0	$ -
7	5-Jul	40	$ 160.00		40	$ 6,400.00	8	$ 1,280.00
8	Total	58			58	$ 8,890.00	8	$ 1,280.00
9							Cost FIFO	$ 7,610.00
10								
11	Total Units sold			50				
12		Units sold	Cost of Goods	Units to allocate		For FIFO model sort A5:A7 ascending		
13	1-May	6	$ 750.00	44		For LIFO model sort A5:A7 descending		
14	2-Jun	12	$ 1,740.00	32				
15	5-Jul	32	$ 5,120.00	0				
16	Total	50	$ 7,610.00					
17			Cost FIFO					

Figure 8.8

We begin a new workbook by entering the start-of-month inventory data in A3:C8.

(a) On Sheet5 of CHAP8.XLS, enter the test and values shown in A1:C7. The title in A1 is centred across A1:H1 with the Merge and Center tool. To wrap the text in a cell, use Alt+Enter between the words that split the entry. Enter the dates in the form 1-May and format the cells to displays the dates as shown in the figure. Apply the currency format to the range C5:C7 using the Currency tool.

(b) Add the word Total to A8 and use the AutoSum tool to enter =SUM(B5:B7) in B8.

(c) Use the Border tool to add the borders. Save the workbook.

In the next area of the worksheet we apportion the sold items to the three sets of inventory — the May, June and July purchases. For the FIFO method, we use the May units first and the July units last.

(d) Enter the text shown in A11:D16. Put in the borders for this area of the workbook.

(e) We need to record the total units sold in the accounting month. In D11, enter the value 50; the number of SuperBQs Bradshaw's sold in July. To ensure that this value does not exceed the total number available, in C11 enter the formula =IF(D11>B8,"Error"," ").

(f) In A13, enter =A5 to duplicate the first date from the start-of-month inventory data. Copy this down to A15.

(g) Now we get to the nub of the problem — how many of the May units did we sell? Since the total number sold (50) exceeded the May inventory (6) we must have sold all of them. Had the total number sold been a smaller value, say 4, we would have sold only 4 from the May inventory. This calls for an IF construct. The formula in B13 is =IF(B5>=D11,D11,B5).

(h) In C13 we compute the cost of the units taken from the May inventory with the formula =B13*C5. Format this cell with the Currency tool.

(i) Having calculated the number of units sold from the May inventory, we need to compute the number of sold units that have yet to be accounted for. The formula for this (in D13) is =D11-B13.

(j) We compute the number to be apportioned to the June inventory using the same logic as in step (g). However, we now examine not the total 50 units sold (from cell D11) but the 44 units (from cell D13) left to be apportioned. So in B14 we enter =IF(B6>=D13,D13,B6).

(k) The cost of the units apportioned to June's inventory is computed the same way as in step (j). The simplest thing to do is copy the formula in C13 to C14.

(l) How many units remain to be apportioned? The formula for this is =D13-B14 which we enter in D14.

(m)The calculations for July are identical to those for June, so copy B14:D14 down one row.

(n) Use the AutoSum tool in B16 and C16. Construct the borders as shown. We will add the entry in C17 later. Save the workbook.

A visual check of the worksheet seems to indicate we have the correct answer. We have apportioned 6, 12 and 32 units to the May, June and July inventories, respectively. The sum of these figures agrees with the value for the total units sold in the accounting period. We have exhausted the May inventory before using the June, and the June before using the July — we have followed the FIFO model.

If we were constructing a complete accounting package we would need to know the end-of-month value of the inventory. We will perform the required calculations in the last area of the worksheet. While we do this, we also calculate the Cost of Goods in a slightly different way. Internal consistency (getting the same answer two ways) within a model is often used to check the calculations.

(o) Enter the text shown in E1:D4 of the figure.

(p) Enter the formulas:
E5: =B5
F5: =B5*C5
G5: =B5-B13
H5: =G5*C5
Copy E5:H5 down two rows.

(q) Compute the total in row 8 using the AutoSum tool. Compute the Cost of Goods as the difference between the start and the end values, =F8-H8.

(r) Save the workbook.

The second calculation of COG (cell H9) agrees with the first (cell C16); this enhances our confidence in the model we have constructed.

Having developed a model for the FIFO method, can we make a new one for the LIFO method? Let us pause before hitting that keyboard! After a moment's reflection we should see that all that is needed is a slight modification to the FIFO model. In the Inventory area (A3:C7) we have the earliest data first and the sold units are apportioned 'downwards' — first in first out. If we list the inventory with the last purchases at the top, our model will apportion the newest ones first. This is the LIFO — last in first out — model. We can rearrange the inventory using the Sort command or tools.

(s) Select the range A5:C7. Click the Sort Descending tool on the Standard toolbar. The data is now sorted in descending order with July at the top and May at the bottom. Note that we now apportion the first 40 units sold to the July inventory and the balance to the June inventory. None of May's inventory is used. This agrees with the LIFO model. The COG in C16 is now $7,850.00.

(t) Select the range A5:C7. Click on the Sort Ascending tool. The data is now sorted once more in ascending order — the FIFO model.

(u) It would be useful to be able to see more quickly which model is being used. In cell C17 enter =IF(A5>A6,"Cost LIFO","Cost FIFO"). In G9 enter =C17. Now as you click on the sort tools, C17 and G9 change to indicate the model in use. Save the workbook.

You can experiment with other values in the A5:C7 range and the total sales in D11.

Problems

1.* We try to design our worksheets to be as general as possible. The spreadsheet in Exercise 3 works quite well with any principal, rate and partial payment schedule when the loan is for a year. However, if one was given the problem of finding the payment for a debt which was due after 6 months, our worksheet would not correctly compute the answer. Assume that cell B2 is named *Term* and contains a value between 1 and 12, inclusive. What modifications are needed to the formulas in the worksheet? We cannot prevent a user entering a payment after the due date but can we indicate an error has occurred?

2. A chart is useful to compare various models. Make a chart showing how the book value varies over 5 years with each depreciation model — see Figure 8.9. Begin by selecting A10:A21 and D10:D21 of Sheet3 to construct a chart of the SL method. Remember that non-contiguous ranges may be selected by holding down the Ctrl key. Then use the procedure you learned in Exercise 14 of Chapter 7 to add new series to the chart. Tidy up the chart to produce an acceptable result.

3.* What would be the formulas in B12, B28 and B44 of the worksheet if we used the Microsoft Excel functions SL, DDB and SYD?

4. TJD Enterprises is considering two mutually exclusive projects which have the cash flows shown in the following table. Assuming an interest rate of 18%, compute the net present value of each project.

   Make a table (see Figure 8.9) showing the NPV of each project when the interest rate is 0%, 5%, 10% and 20%. Make an XY chart of the table. Which project has the more attractive NPV when the interest rate is 10%? The IRR of each project is the interest value when the line crosses the x-axis. Do the IRR estimates read from the chart agree with values found with the IRR function?

Year	Project A	Project B
0	-$10,000	-$12,000
1	8,000	4,000
2	4,000	4,000
3	1,000	4,000
4	-500	4,000

Figure 8.9

5.* When an asset has a zero residual value, the double declining balance method fails to bring the book value to zero at the end of the lifetime. Companies switch to the straight-line method at some point to allow for this. The worksheet in Figure 8.10 models this process. For this model, the straight-line depreciation is based on the previous year's book value and the remaining lifetime. With the values in the figure, the SL depreciation for year 1 is one-fifth of 10,000 while the second year's value is one-fourth of 6,000. The switch from DDB to SL occurs in the year when the SL annual depreciation exceeds the DDB value. Construct this worksheet and report the formulas used in cells B11:F11.

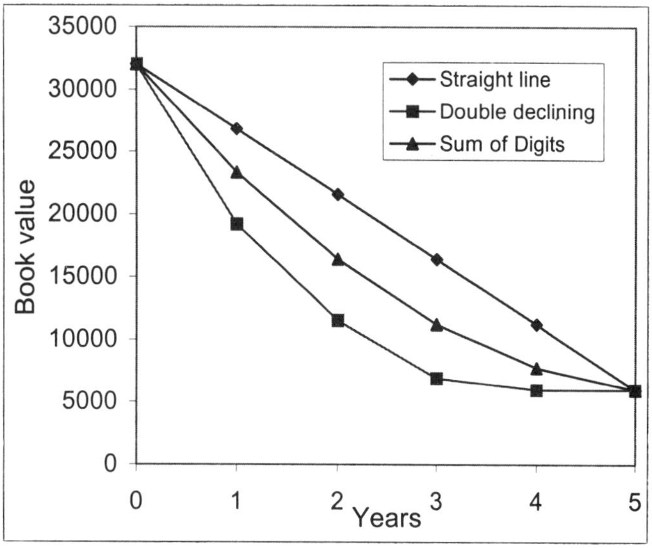

Figure 8.10

9
Goal Seek and Solver

Objectives

Upon completion of this chapter, you will be able to:

- use Goal Seek to change the value of an input cell so as to give the required result in a cell containing a formula;
- use Solver to change the value in one or more cells so as to give a desired value, or a maximum or minimum value in a cell containing a formula;
- add constraints to a Solver model;
- make adjustments to various Solver options;
- save the results of Solver as scenarios;
- use Solver for linear programming problems.

Exercise 1: Goal Seeking

A worksheet is set up in Figure 9.1 to solve three problems. They each have the characteristics that can enable us to find an answer with Goal Seeker. The questions are:

1. By what percentage must a $36,000 salary be raised to give $40,000?

2. What interest rate is required to double an investment in 5 years?

3. How long will it take a £1,000 deposit to be worth £5,000 when the interest rate is 5%?

In each case we have: (i) a cell containing a formula and we have a required value (goal) for this formula, and (ii) the goal can be obtained by changing a single variable. If the problem is more complex than this, Solver should be used.

Goal Seek does not add any new functionality to Microsoft Excel. The problems it solves could readily be solved by simple mathematical methods. Goal Seek relieves us of the burden of performing these mathematical operations.

For the first problem, we would like to know what percentage increase (value in C5) would change the current salary of 35,000 (value in B5) to the goal value of 40,000. We start with an arbitrary value in C5. Since *new salary = old salary × (1 + %increase)*, we could write *%increase = (new salary/old salary) - 1* and find the answer without Goal Seek. Alternatively, we could experiment with the value in C5 until D5 displayed a value of about 40,000. We can see that 5% is too low so we might try 10%, 15%, etc. until we overshoot the target value of 40,000 and then go back reducing C5 in smaller increments. This is essentially the same method that Goal Seek uses but its 'guesses' are computed using the method known as Newton's Method of Successive Approximations.

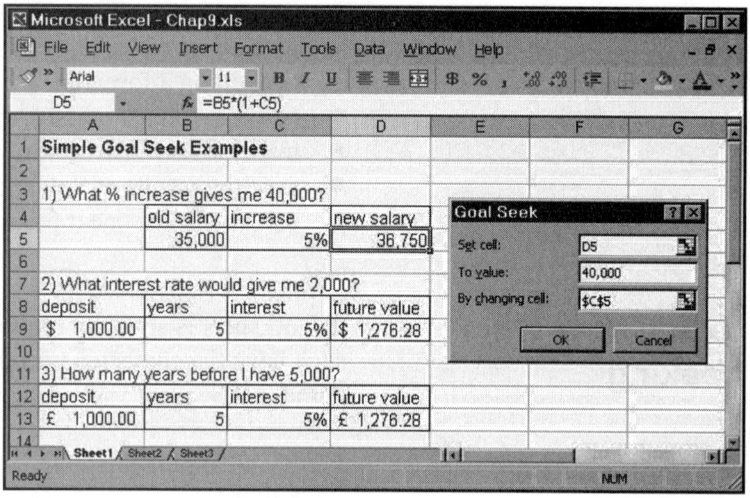

Figure 9.1

Note: There is no functional reason for entering 40,000 rather than 40000. The comma separator was used to make it easier to read.

(a) Open a new workbook and enter the text shown in rows 1 to 4 and the values shown in B and C5. In D5 enter the formula =B5*(1+C6) to compute the salary after the raise.

(b) We invoke Goal Seek from the Tools menu. In the dialog box (Figure 9.1), the *Set cell* is the cell (D5) in which we wish to have a specific value, the *To value* is the goal of 40,000 and the *By changing cell* is the cell (C5) to be changed to achieve this goal. You can type in the cell references without the $ symbols (i.e. as relative addresses) or you can click on the cell. In the latter case, Excel will display an absolute cell reference. When these entries have been made, click on the OK button.

(c) A second dialog box appears (Figure 9.2) and, as Goal Seek has found the required result, we are given the option of accepting the result. An increase of 14.3% gives the required result. You may need to use the Increase Decimal tool to display the answer to one decimal place.

(d) Enter the text shown in rows 7 and 8 and the values shown in A9:C9. In D9 enter the formula =A9 * (1 + C9) ^ B9. In this exercise we are compounding annually.

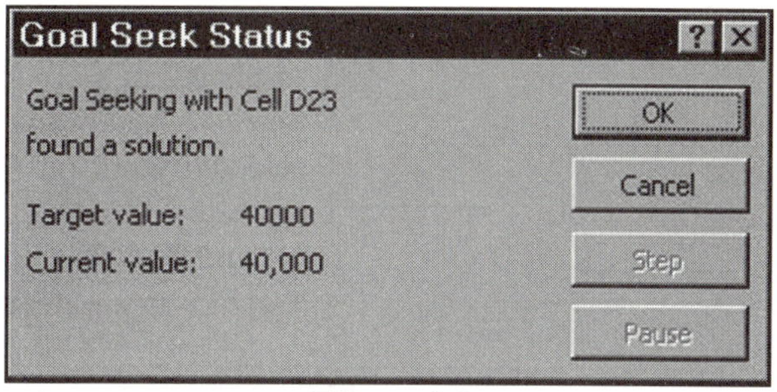

Figure 9.2

(e) Start the Goal Seek dialog using cell D9 as the Set Cell, 2,000 in the To value box and C9 as the By changing cell. You should get an interest rate of 14.9% as the required rate to earn 2,000 in 5 years.

(f) Enter the text shown in rows 11 and 12 and the values shown in A13:C13. In D13 enter the formula =A13 * (1 + C13) ^ B13 by copying the cell D9 to D13.

(g) Start the Goal Seek dialog using cell D13 as the Set Cell, 5,000 in the To value box and B13 as the By changing cell. You should find that about 33 years are required for a deposit of 1,000 to accrue to 5,000 at 5% interest. A good reason to start saving early for one's pension!

If Goal Seek fails to give a result, try some other starting value after you have checked the logic of your formula. Sometimes there are multiple solutions to a problem. For example, suppose A2 contains =A1^2 and you ask Goal Seek to find what value is needed in A1 to give A2 a value of 9. Clearly, the answer could be -3 or +3. Goal Seek will generally give the result which is closest to the starting value in A1.

Exercise 2: Another Goal

In Exercise 4 of Chapter 8 we computed the net present value of a possible capital project. We will use this model for another demonstration of Goal Seek.

For this exercise we would like the NPV value (G14) to increase to 6,000 by changing the value of NetIncome (C4). Unlike the example in the previous exercise we cannot use simple algebraic work to solve this problem. Nor is there a worksheet function that will do it. We have only trial and error or Goal Seek (or Solver once we have learnt how to use it!).

(a) We begin by copying the model to our new workbook. Move to Sheet2 of CHAP9.XLS and open CHAP8.XLS at Sheet4. Select A1:G15 and use the Copy tool to put a copy of the selected work on the Clipboard. Use the Window menu to activate CHAP9.XLS, move to cell A1 and use the Paste tool to copy from the Clipboard. Return to CHAP8.XLS and tap the Esc key to unselect the range. Go back to CHAP9.XLS.

(b) Use the Tools menu item to open the Goal Seek dialog box. The Set Cell is G14, the To value is 6,000 and the By changing cell is C4. Click the OK button.

(c) Goal Seek should inform you that it has found a solution. Click the OK button. The value in G14 is now 6,000. This was obtained by Goal Seek changing the value in C4 to 18,690.

(d) Return the value in C4 to the original 18,000 — you can use the Undo tool to accomplish this. Now have Goal Seek find what interest rate (value in D4) is required for the NPV value to be 6,000. The answer (to two decimal places) should be 6.65%.

(e) Save the workbook.

Exercise 3: Goal Seek and Charts

A single data point in a chart may be dragged to a new location. If the chart is an XY, Line, Bar, or Column chart and the value of the data point comes from a formula then the act of dragging the point invokes Goal Seek.

In Problem 1 of Chapter 7 we did a break-even analysis. We will use the same data to demonstrate the linkage between charts and Goal Seek. Nova Manufacturing would like the break-even point to be 80 hammers and we will use the chart dragging method to find the new selling price.

(a) Using the procedures outlined in (a) of Exercise 2 above, copy A1:C29 to Sheet3 of CHAP9.XLS. Do not copy the chart since the source of the data for a copied chart remains as the original data.

(b) Generate the break-even chart as shown in Figure 7.37. You may wish to enlarge the chart before proceeding.

(c) Select the Revenue data series. A change in the appearance of the markers will signal success. Pause and then click on the marker corresponding to 80 units. A helpful screen tip is displayed with the words *Series 'Revenue' Point '80 ' Value: 2000* and the cursor becomes a double headed up-down arrow.

(d) Drag the data point up towards the Cost line. We want the value of the data point to be about 2,200 so that the two lines cross at 80 units. Excel displays a screen tip showing the new value. With the earlier versions, you will need to do this by eye but there is also a sliding mark on the y-axis to help.

(e) When you release the mouse button the Goal Seek dialog box appears. The first two boxes already have values. The Set Cell box displays C17 while the To value box should display a value near 2,200. If it is too far from this, change it. All that remains is to tell Goal Seek the By changing cell is B4. Goal Seek should find a value of about 27.50 as the selling price that will make the new break-even point 80 units.

(f) Save the workbook.

Exercise 4: Introducing Solver

Note: Solver takes some time to open the first time in each work session. Do not get alarmed.

Solver can do everything that Goal Seek can do and much more. So why does Microsoft have both? Solver uses up resources such as memory and not everyone needs it. Those who need to keep their Excel slim and trim do not instal Solver. Before we begin, check that your PC has Solver installed. Use the menu command Tools and look for a Solver item on the drop-down menu. If you do not see Solver look in Appendix A.

To introduce Solver we will use it to solve the same problems as we used Goal Seek for in Exercise 1.

(a) In Sheet1 of CHAP9.XLS, reset the cells C5, C19 and B13 to their original values as shown in Figure 9.1.

(b) Use the command Tools|Solver to bring up the Solver Parameters dialog box — Figure 9.3. Enter D5 as the *Set Target Cell*, click on the *Value* radio button and enter 40,000 in its box and enter C5 in the *By changing cells* box. Click the *Solve* button.

> **Note:** You may type relative cell references in the parameter boxes. If you use the pointing method, Excel enters absolute cell references. In Solver, they function the same.

(c) Solver has no trouble finding a solution to the problem posed and the Solver Result dialog box (Figure 9.4) is displayed. As with Goal Seek we have the option of accepting the offered solution or reverting to the original values. Leave the Keep Solver Solution radio button selected and click the OK button.

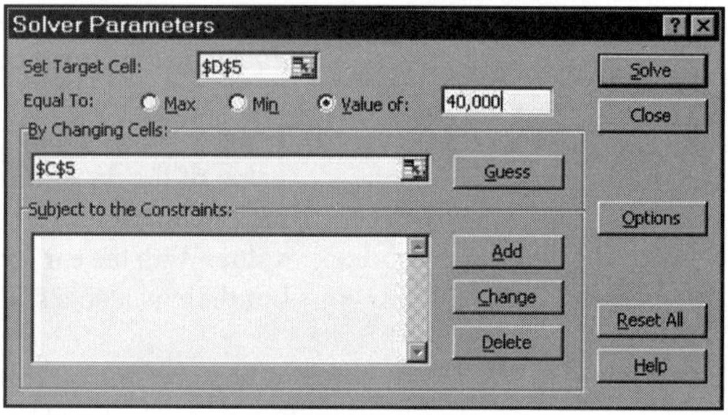

Figure 9.3

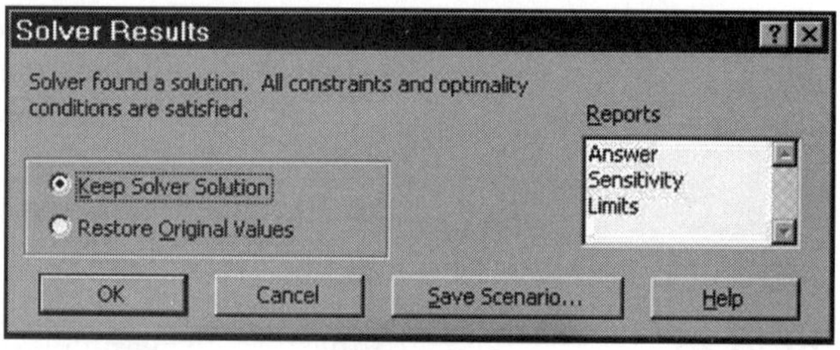

Figure 9.4

The value in C6 (to one decimal place) is now 14.3% while D6 displays the required 40,000. As expected, Solver returns the same increase rate in C6 as Goal Seek. You are now ready to use Solver for the other two problems on this sheet.

(d) Open the Solver Parameter dialog box with Tools|Solver. You will see that Solver has remembered the previous problem. Had you saved the workbook after step (c) and returned to it later, Solver would still have remembered the last problem. You can either overwrite each box one by one or empty all of them with the Reset button and start afresh. With D10 as the target cell and 2,000 as the required value, have Solver find what value is needed in C10 for the interest rate.

(e) Find what value is needed in B13 to result in D13 becoming 5,000. Save the workbook.

Exercise 5: Finding a Maximum

It is time to demonstrate features of Solver that Goal Seek lacks. In this exercise we will perform a very simple maximization analysis.

Midland Transport has determined that the cost of operating a truck (fuel, tyres and other maintenance costs) driven at an average speed of v miles/h is given by the formula $(30 + v/2)$ cents/mile. Midland pays its drivers $14/h. What is the optimum speed for a truck?

(a) Begin the work on Sheet4 of CHAP9.XLS, inserting a new sheet if required. Enter the text shown in column A of Figure 9.5.

(b) We need a starting value for the speed. A value of 10 has been used in B3 quite arbitrarily.

	A	B
1	**Trucking problem**	
2		
3	speed	10
4		
5	cost / mile	
6	truck	0.35
7	driver	1.4
8	total	$ 1.75

Figure 9.5

(c) Enter the formula =(30 + B3/2) / 100 in B6. The factor of 100 is used to convert the cost to dollars. The driver is paid $14/h. A truck travelling at v miles/h will take $1/v$ hours to travel a mile. So the driver will be earning $14(1/v)$ for each mile travelled at that speed. Enter the formula =14/B3 in B7 to compute the driver's earnings. The total cost for every mile is computed in B8 with the formula =B6+B7.

(d) Open the Solver Parameter dialog box. The target cell is B8 (the total cost). We want this to be a minimum so click on the Min radio button. Rather than typing B3 in the By changing cells box, this time click on the Guess button. Solver correctly identifies B3 as the value to be changed. Click on the Solve button.

(e) Solver reports it has found a solution. To the right of the Solver Report dialog box is a report section. Highlight the word Answer by clicking on it. Click on the OK button.

(f) The reported value is 53 miles/h as the optimum speed and this results in a cost of 83 cents/mile. Solver has added a sheet called *Answer Report 1* to the workbook. Open this and you will see that it reports the initial and final values of the target and changing cells as shown in Figure 9.6.

Solver reports: Solver offers three reports: Answer, Sensitivity and Limits. None is particularly informative for this very simple problem but we make one for practice.

The report heading reads *Microsoft Excel 10.0*. This is the internal name for Excel 2002.

Microsoft Excel 10.0 Answer Report
Worksheet: [Chap9.xls]Sheet4
Report Created: 03/11/2001 11:40:48 AM

Target Cell (Min)

Cell	Name	Original Value	Final Value
$B$8	total	$ 1.75	$ 0.83

Adjustable Cells

Cell	Name	Original Value	Final Value
$B$3	speed	10	53

Constraints
NONE

Figure 9.6

(g) Save the workbook.

You may wish to construct an XY chart plotting velocity against cost to confirm that Solver has obtained the correct result.

Exercise 6: Using Constraints

Consider the following types of problems: (i) To increase my profit I might increase the selling price of an item. But this will probably be offset by an increase in sales resistance (i.e. there is a relationship between the price and the quantity sold) so there is some optimum price that will maximize profits. (ii) The purpose of advertising is to increase profit by increasing sales. But advertising costs money. Furthermore, the relationship between expenditure on advertising and the sales figures is not a linear one. Again, there is some optimum amount to be spent on advertising. Solver can be used to find these optimum values provided one knows the mathematical relationship between the two competing quantities. Nova Manufacturing has purchased a new machine to make shovels. The machine is capable of making up to 200 shovels/h. However, the hourly cost of operating the machine increases with its rate of production. The relationship is given by the formula

Hourly cost = *Rate*^{2}/10. Regardless of the rate of production, the machine must be attended by workers whose total rate of pay is \$80/h and there is a fixed daily cost of \$200 associated with running the machine. The materials cost \$2 a shovel and the finished product sells for \$15. There are two parameters that can be adjusted in order to maximize the profit margin. They are: (i) the rate at which to run the machine, and (ii) how many hours during a normal 8-h working day to operate the machine.

In problems such as this it is helpful to separate the parameters (such as the machine's rate, the fixed costs, the selling price, etc.) from the calculated values (machine operating cost, wages, revenue, etc.). It is also helpful to separate the parameters into *constants* (values set by the problem which cannot be altered) and *variables* (values which may be changed). Figure 9.7 shows how we will set out the current problem. We start with arbitrary values for the *rate* and *hours*.

	A	B	C	D	E	F	G
1	**Factory Problem**						
2							
3		**Variables**				**Constants**	
4	Rate	10	units/hr		FixedCosts	200	$
5	Hours	1	hr		Wages	80	$/hr
6					Materials	2	$
7					SellPrice	15	$
8							
9				**Calculations**			
10	***Costs***			***Revenue***		***Profit***	
11	Machine	10		150		-160	
12	Wages	80					
13	Materials	20					
14	Fixed	200					
15	TotalCost	310					

Figure 9.7

(a) On Sheet5 of CHAP9.XLS, enter all the text shown in Figure 9.7.

(b) Enter the values shown in rows 4 through 7.

(c) Name the cells B4:B5 and F4:F7 with the text to the left of each of them.

(d) The formulas in the lower half of the worksheet are:
B11: =(Rate^2)/10 * Hours
B12: =Wages * Hours
B13: =Materials * Rate * Hours

B14: =FixedCosts
B15: =SUM(B11:B14)
D11: =SellPrice * Rate * Hours
F11: =D11 - B15

When the machine is run for 1 hour producing 10 units/h the company incurs a loss of $160. We need to maximize the profit value by changing the Rate and Hours parameters. There is a limit for each. The machine cannot make more than 200 units/h and the machine cannot be run for more than 8 h. Solver refers to conditions such as these as *constraints*. We will also inform Solver that the values for the Rate and Hours cannot be negative. You may wonder why we need to make such obvious statements but you should appreciate that Solver deals with mathematical rules not with the real world!

(e) Use Tools|Solver to bring up the Solver parameter dialog box (Figure 9.8). The *Set Target Cell* is F11. We wish to find a maximum by changing B4 and B5. Set the top part of the dialog box to reflect this. For the *By Changing Cells* you may enter B4:B5 or B4,B5. In the latter case, Solver will change the cell references to cell names.

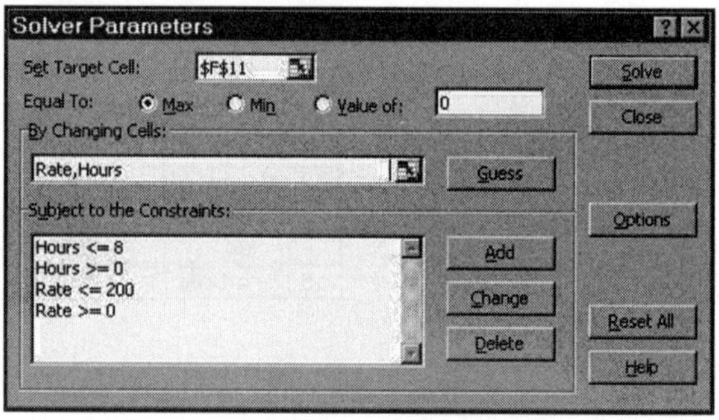

Figure 9.8

(f) Click on the Add button in the constraints area to bring up the *Add Constraint* dialog box — Figure 9.9. The first constraint will limit the rate to a maximum of 200.

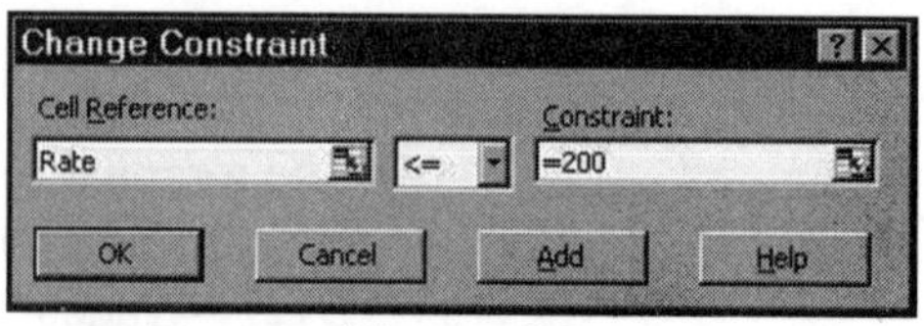

Figure 9.9

This is entered by setting the *Cell Reference* to Rate, click on the centre arrow to open the option list and select the <= condition (you can most likely skip this step since this is the default condition), and enter the value 200 in the *Constraint* box by typing. Since we have more constraints, click on the Add button.

Solver presents a new Add Constraint dialog box. We need Rate >= 0 to require the Rate parameter to have a non-negative value. Press the Add button again. The third and fourth constraints are Hours <= 8 and Hours >= 0, respectively. When the last constraint has been added, click on the OK button.

When you return to the Solver Parameters dialog box you will note that any cell references used in the constraints area have been replaced by cell names in alphabetical order.

Note: Since the non-negative constraint is a very common requirement, there is a quicker way to achieve this — see *Options in Solver* later in the chapter.

(g) Click on the Solve button. When the Solver Results dialog box appears, click on OK. Solver has found that the profit is maximized at $2,540 when the machinery is run at the rate of 65 units/h for 8 h.

(h) Save the workbook.

Exercise 7: Linear Programming

We have already seen a linear programming problem in Exercise 6. Many of the linear programming problems encountered in the business world could be categorized as 'product mix' problems. So we shall use this type of problem to continue our exploration of Solver.

Nova Manufacturing makes two models of workshop knifes, Alpha and Beta. Two machines are involved in the production, assembly and sharpening. The Alpha model takes 1.5 minutes of assembly time and 1.25 minutes of sharpening while the Beta model takes 1.75 and 0.5 minutes, respectively. In each shift, the machines and workers limit the capacity of the assembly machine to 8 h and the sharpening to 4 h. The Alpha model has a profit margin of £7.75 and the Beta a margin of £5.25. The sales manager has recommended that no more than 200 units of the Beta model be made. Our task is to find the product mix that maximizes the profit margin.

(a) On Sheet6 of CHAP9.XLS enter the text shown in Figure 9.10.

(b) Enter the values shown in B4:E5. This data represents all we know about the two products. The values of 1 in B4 and B5 are, of course, only starting values. Solver will be asked to change these.

(c) Enter the data in B7:D7. These are the constraint values. We will use B7 as the maximum value allowed for the number of Beta items to be produced. The values in C7 and D7 are computed by the formulas =8*60 and =4*60 since the machines can be used for 8 and 6 h respectively.

	A	B	C	D	E
1	**Product Mix**				
2					
3		Number	Assemble	Sharpen	Profit
4	Alpha	1	1.5	1.25	7.75
5	Beta	1	1.75	0.5	5.25
6					
7	Maxima	200	480	240	
8					
9	Total	2	3.25	1.75	13

Figure 9.10

(d) The formula in B9 is =B4+B5.

(e) We need to compute the total time each machine is used. In C9 we could use =B4*C4 + B5*C5 or =SUMPRODUCT(B4:B5, C4:C5). We will opt for the second formula but will enter it as =SUMPRODUCT($B$4:$B$5, C4:C5). Recall that the $ symbols, which can be entered with the F4 key, make the references absolute. This means they do not change when the formula is copied. Copy C7 to D7 and E7 to compute the usage of the Sharpener and the total contribution to the profit margin.

Note: Mathematicians speak of the *Objective* and the *Decision Variables*. In this Exercise the objective is to maximize the total profit. The decision variables are numbers of each product.

(f) Now we are ready to set up Solver. The value in the target cell E9 is to be maximized by changing B4 and B5. The constraints are listed below.

(i) The number of items produced cannot be negative: B4>=0 and B5>=0.
(ii) The number of Beta units must not exceed 200: B5<=B7.
(iii) The total times for each machine have a limit: C9<=C7 and D9<=D7.

Click the Solve button when the Solver Parameter dialog box has been completed.

(g) Solver finds a solution in which 125.22 Alpha units and 166.96 Beta units are produced. Clearly, the fractional parts of these numbers are meaningless in this example. The profit margin total is £1,847. Note that both the Assembler and the Sharpener are being used to the maximum capacity — C9 equals 480 and D9 equals 240.

We can do a sensitivity analysis with this model. Suppose the time to assemble a Beta unit is not 1.75 minutes but only 1.5 minutes. How will this effect the result?

(h) Enter the new value of 1.5 in C5 and have Solver redo the problem. All you need to do is open the Solver Parameter box and press the Solver button.

(i) The new result is 112 Alphas and 200 Betas. Note that the Assembler is not being used to full capacity. The limit on the number of Betas has kicked in this time. A 14% change in one parameter has made a large difference in the required product mix.

(j) Save the workbook.

Exercise 8: A More Complex Problem

Pauline runs Sandbaggers Inc. which purchases sand which it cleans and sells to computer chip manufacturers. Pauline has two plants with differing capacities and running costs. She purchases the raw materials from three suppliers: Wayne, George and Archie. Each Monday the suppliers inform Pauline how much sand they will be able to deliver the next week and the cost. The suppliers sell the sand for different prices and have an additional charge for transportation which depends on the plant to which the sand is sent. Pauline has to decide how much sand to purchase from each supplier for each plant.

(a) We will begin our spreadsheet on Sheet8 of CHAP9.XLS by entering the text and values shown in columns A:D of Figure 9.11. The input parameters include the selling price of the finished product, the two plants' capacities and operating cost, and the amount of material available from the three suppliers together with their selling prices and shipping costs.

In the righthand side we set up the operating plan for the week. We will use some arbitrary value (25) for the tons of sand to be purchased from each supplier for each of the two plants.

(b) Enter the text shown in F1:I11 and the value 25 in G7:H9. The remaining cells in this area have the formulas:
I7: =G7+H7. This is copied down to I9.
G10: =SUM(G7:G9). This is copied across to I10.

Next we calculate (in F12:I18) the expenses associated with this purchasing scenario. Starting with the first supplier and the first plant, we compute the cost of purchasing sand and having it delivered. The formula in G14 for this is =G7*(C15+B22), where G7 represents the tonnage value and C15 and B22 the material and shipping cost for a ton, respectively. We will use a slight modification of this so that we can copy it.

(c) Enter the text in F12:I18. In G14 enter =G7*($C15+B22). Copy this down to row 16 and across to column H. The operating cost in G17 is found using =G10*B11. Copy this to H17.

(d) Compute the column and row total using =G14+H14 in I14 which can be copied down to I17, and =SUM(G14:G17) in G18 which can be copied across to I17.

We complete the worksheet by computing revenue and profit.

(e) Enter the text in F20 and F22. The formula in G20 to compute the revenue is =I10*B6 while the profit is computed in G21 with =G20-I18.

Now it is time to have Solver maximize the profit value by varying the tons of sand purchased from each supplier for each plant. The *Target Cell* is G22 and the *By Changing Cells* is the range G7:H9 — note this is a range and so uses a colon separator. The constraints need to be carefully thought through.

(i) The values for the tons purchased must be non-negative. This can be entered as G7:H9>=0. Use the mouse to select the range when filling in the Solver dialog box.
(ii) The amount purchased from each supplier cannot exceed the amount available. This requires three entries: I7<=B15, I8<=B16 and I9<=B17.
(iii)The amount sent to each plant cannot exceed its capacity. The two constraints are G10<=B10 and H10<=C10.

	A	B	C	D	E	F	G	H	I
1	**Sandbaggers Inc.**								
2									
3		***Input parameters***					***Operating plan***		
4									
5	Product					Tons at each plant			
6	Sells for	50	$/ton				Plant A	Plant B	Total
7						Sam	25	25	50
8	Sandbaggers' two plants					George	25	25	50
9		Plant A	Plant B			Archie	25	25	50
10	capacity	450	550	tons		Total	75	75	150
11	operating costs	25	20	$/ton					
12						Expenses			
13	Suppliers information						Plant A	Plant B	Total
14		tons	cost/ton			Wayne	300.00	312.50	612.50
15	Wayne	200	10			George	250.00	262.50	512.50
16	George	300	9			Archie	325.00	275.00	600.00
17	Archie	400	8			Operating	1,875.00	1,500.00	3,375.00
18						Total	2,750.00	2,350.00	5,100.00
19									
20	Shipping costs (dollars/ton)					Revenue	7,500.00		
21		Plant A	Plant B						
22	Wayne	2	2.5			Profit	2,400.00		
23	George	1	1.5						
24	Archie	5	3						
25									

Figure 9.11

(f) Complete the Solver Parameter dialog box and click on the Solve button. Solver returns a value of $15,375 for the profit with quantities purchased as shown below.

	Plant A	Plant B	Total
Wayne	200	0	200
George	150	150	300
Archie	0	400	400
Total	350	550	900

(g) Save the workbook.

Options in Solver

Clicking on the Options button of the Solver Parameters dialog box brings up the Solver Options dialog shown in Figure 9.12.

The first item *Max Time* sets a limit on the time Solver may use to solve a problem. The default of 100 seconds is ample for a modern personal computer unless the problem is exceedingly complex. Similarly, most tractable problems can be solved with 100 iterations. The *Precision* value stipulates the tolerance for constraints. For example, with a *Precision* setting of 0.000001 and a constraint of A1>=0, Solver would consider an A1 value of –0.0000005 to satisfy the constraint. *Tolerance* sets the tolerance for integer constraints. Relaxing this value (i.e. making it larger) can help Solver find answers to integer problems. *Convergence* specifies how close the target value of successive trials solutions must be before Solver stops. The Assume Non-Negative box may be used when you wish to specify the constraint that all decision variables are zero or greater. The other options are beyond the scope of this book but a great deal of information can be found on the Web site of Frontline Systems Inc., the developers of Solver.

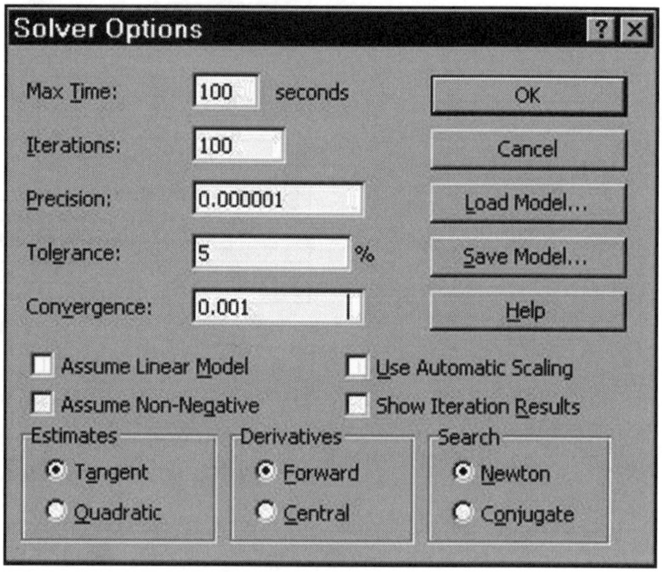

Figure 9.12

Summary

Goal Seek can be used to solve many numerical problems but Solver is far more powerful. Unless you have special needs and do not wish to load Solver, it may be used in place of Goal Seek.

Solver remembers the last problem it was used for on a worksheet. One can retain various Solver answers in Scenarios.

Solver can find maximum and minimum values when they exist. For these and other problems, if Solver fails to find an answer you can try with a different starting value. If that fails then look at the options discussed above.

Solver can be used for linear programming problems. It allows you to set constraints. Remember that it is often necessary to set a constraint such as NumberUse > 0 even when to the human user this is totally obvious!

Problems

1. How could Solver be used to find the selling price for a break-even of 80 units in Exercise 3?

2.* The relationship between a bond's value or price, face value, coupon value, maturity date and yield is given by the expression

$$Bond\ value = Coupon \times \frac{1 - 1/(1+r)^m}{r} + \frac{Face\ value}{(1+r)^m}$$

where the yield is presented by r, and the years to maturity by m.

Construct a worksheet similar to that in Figure 9.13. This shows that when the yield to maturity is 10%, then a 6-year, 8% coupon bond is worth £912.89. However, generally we know the value (or the price) and wish to know the yield. It is not easy to solve the expression such that the yield is computed. This is an ideal problem for Goal Seek or Solver. Find the yield if this bond is selling at £955.14. Compare your result with the approximation found in Problem 2 of Chapter 2.

	A	B	C	D	E
1	Yield to Maturity				
2					
3	Coupon	Face value	Value	Maturity	Yield
4	£80	£1,000	£912.89	6	10.00%

Figure 9.13

3. Gourmet Catering has purchased a large quantity of cherries and apricots with the view to making some tarts. They have on hand 2,000 kilograms of flour and 1,500 kilograms of sugar. Each batch of cherry tarts uses 6 kg of flour and 3 kg of sugar, while a batch of apricot tarts uses 4 kg of each. Cherry tarts give a profit of £5.50 a batch and apricot tarts £4.60 a batch. Assuming that there is an unlimited quantity of fruit for the project, find what mix of the two tarts maximizes the profit.

10
Working with Lists

Objectives

Upon completion of this chapter, you will:

- be familiar with the operations needed to sort a list;
- know how to use, and understand the results of, the FREQUENCY function;
- be familiar with the Histogram tool;
- be able to make test data using the RANDBETWEEN, INDEX and MROUND functions together with the Paste Special tool;
- have a working knowledge of the Microsoft Excel Pivot Table feature;
- be able to use the data filter features to select records from a list;
- know how to import data from a text file.

Exercise 1: Sorting a List

The data in Figure 10.1 is a list. Each row contains information about a single entity and that data is presented in columns. Each column contains data about a particular attribute of the entity. In this example, the entities are members of a class. The fields are the person's first name, last name and grade. Very often a list such as this comes from another source — from a company's mainframe computer, for example. In this exercise we learn how to sort a list. We shall use the menu command Data|Sort; the sort tools on the Standard toolbar are best used for sorting a single column of data.

(a) Open a new workbook and enter the data shown in Figure 10.1. It is not necessary to use exactly the same names or numeric values.

(b) Select A1:C21 (the entire list including the headings) and use the command Data|Sort. The Sort dialog box appears — see Figure 10.2.

We will begin by sorting the list alphabetically by both names. The items on which a list is sorted are called the keys. The most important of these (the key used for the major sort) is called the primary key. In our case the primary key is the last name. Microsoft Excel specifies the primary key first in the Sort dialog box.

	A	B	C
1	First Name	Last Name	Grade
2	George	O'Brien	75
3	Pauline	LeBlanc	29
4	Rebekah	Dennis	71
5	Bert	White	32
6	Paul	Chisholm	80
7	Joyce	James	35
8	Simon	Schwartz	55
9	Fred	Adams	66
10	Florence	Jones	50
11	Ethel	Jones	77
12	Peter	Macdonald	65
13	John	Adams	60
14	Nichola	Holland	58
15	Bernard	Holland	64
16	Nicolas	MacDonald	52
17	James	Cormier	88
18	Victoria	Dennis	55
19	Michael	Fox	25
20	Henry	Walsh	52
21	Mary	Smith	51

Figure 10.1

Figure 10.2

(c) Our list has a header row and Excel has recognized this as indicated by the selected radio button at the bottom of the dialog box. We can, therefore, specify our sort keys using the names in the header row. If there was no header row we would use column headers to indicate the position of the keys. Use the option lists in the Sort dialog box to specify the list is to be sorted first by Last Name, then by First Name. Leave the

Ascending radio buttons selected. Click on the OK button.

(d) Click outside the list when Excel has completed the sort.

We opted to sort on two keys (Last Name and First Name). Would it have made any difference if we had used Grade as the third key? If there had been two entries with the same last and first names, they would have appeared in the sort list in the same order as in the pre-sorted list when the sort used only the two keys. We would have specified the third key had we wanted people with the same name sorted by their grade.

Note how Microsoft Excel has sorted Nicholas MacDonald and Peter Macdonald. They have been sorted as if they had the same name. The sort has disregarded the fact that one has a capital D.

(e) Reselect the list and open the Sort dialog box. Click on the Option button and in the Option dialog box put a check mark in the *Case Sensitive* box then click OK to return to the Sort dialog box. Click OK.

(f) Now Peter Macdonald precedes Nicholas MacDonald. Click the Undo tool to cancel the last sort. Click Undo until the list is in the pre-sorted order. Do not be concerned if this is not possible, the rest of the exercise will still be useful.

It would clearly be a mistake to sort only column A of this list and Microsoft Excel warns you of the danger if you attempt to do so. The next step will demonstrate this.

(g) Select A1:A21 and open the Sort dialog box. A Sort Warning dialog box appears. With the Extend the Sections radio button selected, click on the Sort button. Proceed with sort operation.

Microsoft Excel is not infallible. It is the user's responsibility to use the sort operation with care. In the next step we select only two columns of our list.

(h) Use the Undo button to cancel the sort. Select A1:B21 and use Data|Sort. This time there is no warning but it would be a grave mistake to sort on these two columns since the grades would no longer be associated with their owners. Click on the cancel button.

Note: Of course, you may wish to use Last Name and First Name as the second and third key, respectively. In this way those with equal grades will be listed alphabetically.

Next we will sort the list using the grade key. We will use the result in the next exercise.

(i) Select the entire list (A1:C21) and, this time, sort with Grade as the only key. You may sort ascending or descending as you wish.

(j) Save the workbook as CHAP10.XLS.

Note: The Sort dialog has only three fields. If you wish to sort with more fields, do it in two stages, starting with the least important fields.

When you wish to sort a list by its first field, you can use one of the tools on the Standard toolbar. There is one for an ascending and another for a descending sort. But be warned: these tools do not prompt you when you mistakenly select only one column.

Exercise 2: The FREQUENCY function

A common way to summarize numerical data is with a frequency table. For example, with the data in Figure 10.1, we may wish to know how many students had grades of 10 or less, how many had grades in the 20s, 30s, etc. This exercise will show how to use the FREQUENCY function to obtain this data. In the next exercise we use the Histogram tool to generate the data and chart it.

The syntax of the FREQUENCY function is *=FREQUENCY(data_array, bins_array)*. Clearly, *data_array* is the raw data that needs to be summarized. A 'bin' is a container. If we were sorting potatoes by size, we might have a collection of bins in which to place them. In the syntax the *bin_array* is a list of values. Each value in the raw data is compared with the values in the bin-array and a count is maintained of how many match each bin value. We will generate the frequency count with two bins to explain more readily how the bin array is used.

Note: The text in boxes and the arrows were inserted using tools from the Draw toolbar to insert comments. This is not part of the exercise.

(a) Open CHAP10.XLS at Sheet1. Enter the text shown in rows 1 and 14 of Figure 10.3. Enter the series of values in F2:F12 and I2:I12. Remember the quick method: type 0 and 10, select the two cells and drag the fill handle.

(b) Select the range G2:G13 and use the Insert Function tool to enter the formula =FREQUENCY(C2:C21, F2:F12). This function is located in the Statistical category. The formula is an array formula and you must complete the entry using [Shift]+[Ctrl]+[Enter] and not the simple [Enter] key.

(c) In J2:J13 enter =FREQUENCY(C2:C21, I2:I12) using the same technique.

(d) To complete the worksheet use the AutoSum tool to add =SUM(G2:G13), and =SUM(J2:J13) in G14 and J14, respectively.

	F	G	H	I	J	K
1	Range	Freq		Range	Freq	
2	0	0		0	0	
3	10	0		9	0	
4	20	0		19	0	
5	30	2		29	2	
6	40	2		39	2	
7	50	1		49	0	
8	60	7		59	7	
9	70	3		69	4	
10	80	4		79	3	
11	90	1		89	2	
12	100	0		99	0	
13		0			0	
14	sum	20		sum	20	
15						
16	How many with			How many with		
17	grades in range			grades in range		
18	41 to 50 inclusive			50 to 59 inclusive		
19						

Figure 10.3

Your first question might be: why is the FREQUENCY function placed in 12 cells while there are only 11 values in the bin array? This is not required but it is often done just in case the data array contains values that exceed the largest value in the bin array. A non-zero value in the last cell of the FREQUENCY array will alert you to this fact.

To explain how the counting is done by the FREQUENCY function we will first look at the count in G7 which corresponds to the bin value in F7. The bin value in F7 is 50 and the preceding value in F6 is 40. The value in G7 is a count of the values in the array that are greater than the previous bin value (40), and less than or equal to the current bin value (50). It is, therefore, a count of the data array values that are in the inclusive range 41 to 50.

We now move to the second set of results and look at the count in J8. Since the bin value in I8 is 59 and the preceding bin value is 49 (in J7), the count in J8 is the number of data array values that are in the range 50 to 59, inclusive.

With a list as small as the one we are working with, you can confirm these facts manually. We sorted the list by Grade in the previous exercise to make this easier. Please note that it is not required to have a sorted list for the FREQUENCY function.

The data in G2:G13 and J2:J13 is *live* data. If you change a value in the data array (C2:C20) or in one of the bins, the FREQUENCY function will be recalculated.

Exercise 3: The Histogram Tool

A natural conclusion to Exercise 2 would be to construct a column chart of the frequency data. Such a chart is called a histogram. While we could readily do this using the Chart Wizard, we will obtain our histogram by investigating another feature of Microsoft Excel. Open the Tools menu and check that there is an item called Data Analysis. Refer to Appendix A if this is not available.

(a) Open CHAP10.XLS on Sheet1. Use the command Tools|Data Analysis to open the Data Analysis dialog box (Figure 10.4). Select Histogram and click on OK.

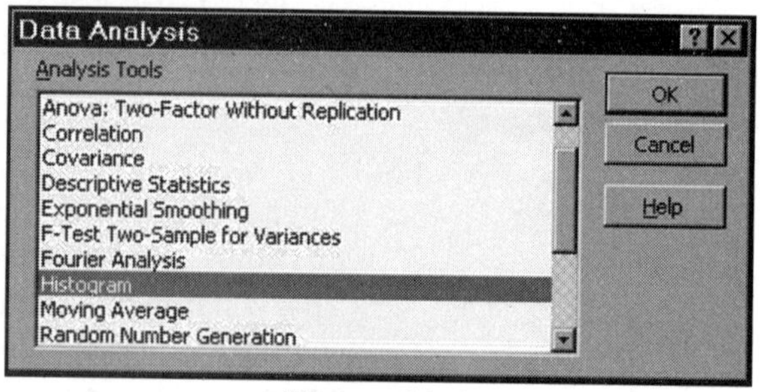

Figure 10.4

(b) In the Input area of the Histogram dialog box (Figure 10.5) enter C2:C21 for the Input Range and I2:I12 for the Bin Range. Leave the Labels box unchecked since we did not include the headings from row 1 in the two ranges. In the Output options specify that we wish the output to be on a new worksheet, and that we require the Cumulative Percentages and Chart Output. Click the OK button. A new sheet is produced.

(c) If your workbook had three sheets, the new Sheet4 (Figure 10.6) will be the active sheet. It will contain the frequency data, the cumulative frequency data and a histogram showing both sets of data. You will need to do some work on the chart (adjust its size, the font sizes, etc.) before it is acceptable.

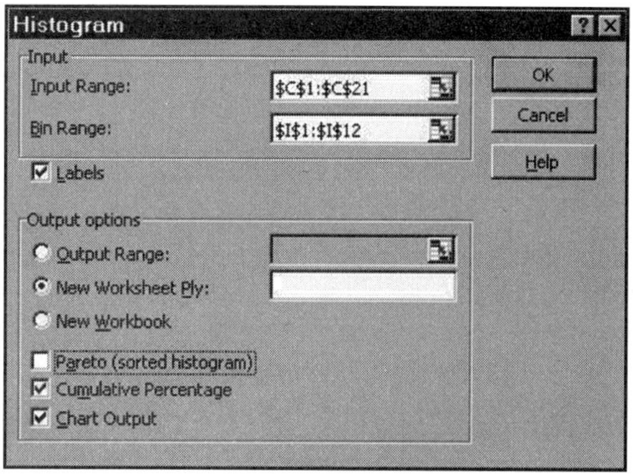

Figure 10.5

(d) Move to cell B2 of the new sheet. Note that it contains a value not a formula. The same is true of C2. The data on this sheet is static and does not respond to changes made in the originating data. You will need to re-run the Histogram tool if the values in C2:C20 are changed. However, the parameters in the Histogram dialog box will still be there when you reopen the workbook. Save the workbook.

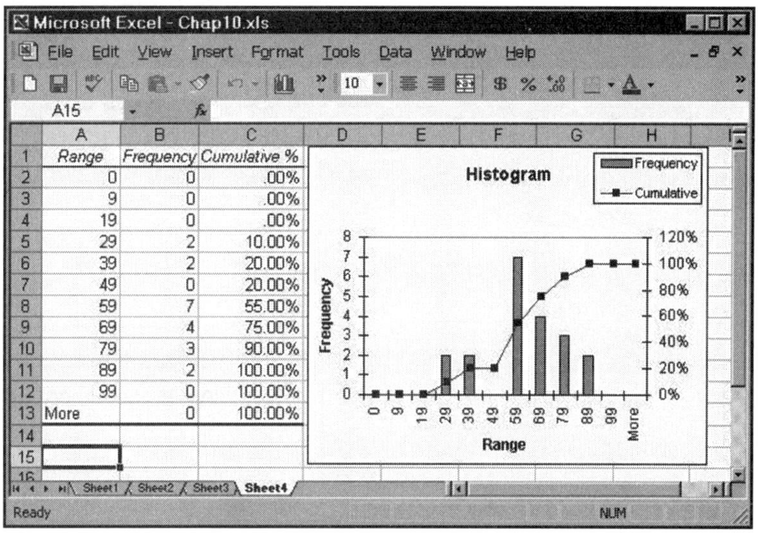

Figure 10.6

Exercise 4: Generating Data

> **Note:** The RANDBETWEEN and MROUND functions are available only if the Analysis ToolPak has been installed and added in — see Appendix A.

> **Note:** Dates are discussed in the next chapter

In Exercise 1 you were required to enter data into 60 cells to make a list so that we could demonstrate the Excel sort feature. There are times in the real world when the Microsoft Excel user needs to test a design before the actual data is available. It is time consuming to have to type test data manually so in this exercise we show the use of the functions RAND() and RANDBETWEEN() to generate some test data. We will use the data in subsequent exercises.

The RAND() function returns an evenly distributed random number that is greater than 0 and less than 1. If you enter the formula =RAND() in a cell the function will return a new value every time the worksheet is recalculated but we will find a way around this. The formula *=RAND()*(b−a)+a* will return a real number between *a* and *b*, while *=ROUND(RAND()*(b−a)+a, 0)* will return an integer value between *a* and *b*. A simpler way of getting the integer result is with the RANDBETWEEN function. The INDEX and MROUND functions were introduced in earlier chapters.

Exercise scenario: in our IT department, five staff members (Ture, Evelyn, Myrna, Stephen and George) provide support for the Microsoft Office Suite (Excel, Word, Access, PowerPoint) to three other departments (Sales, Manufacturing, Accounting). We would like to generate some test data in which each row contains a date, a department, a staff member, a product and the number of hours the staff person worked on the project. We will assume the data is for the first quarter of the year 2000 and that the hours are recorded in 15 minute increments with values from 0.25 to 25 hours.

(a) On Sheet5 of CHAP10.XLS enter the values shown in Figure 10.7.

	A	B	C	D	E
1	Start	End	Department	Staff	Product
2	01-Jan-2000	31-Mar-2000	Sales	Ture	Excel
3			Manufacturing	Evelyn	Word
4			Accounting	Myrna	Access
5				Stephen	Presentation
6				George	

Figure 10.7

(b) Using Insert|Name|Create name A2 as Start, B2 as End, C2:C4 as Department, D2:D6 as Staff and E2:E5 as Product.

(c) Starting in G1, enter the text shown in row 1 of Figure 10.8.

(d) The formulas in row 2 are:
G2: =RANDBETWEEN(Start, End)
H2: =INDEX(DEPARTMENT, RANDBETWEEN(1, 3), 1)
I2: =INDEX(STAFF, RANDBETWEEN(1, 5), 1)
J2: =INDEX(PRODUCT, RANDBETWEEN(1, 4), 1)
K2: =MROUND(RANDBETWEEN(15, 25*60),15) / 60

	G	H	I	J	K
1	Date	Dept	Staff	Product	Hours
2	February 20, 2000	Manufacturing	Ture	Presentation	5.50
3	January 30, 2000	Accounting	Myrna	Access	24.75
4	February 29, 2000	Manufacturing	Ture	Word	1.50

Figure 10.8

(e) Select G2:K2 and copy it down to row 201.

(f) Use Format|Cells|Number|Date on G2:G201 so that it displays a date in keeping with your regional settings. Format K2:K201 to display two decimal places.

(g) Select the column headings G to K and use Format|Column|Autofit selection. Your data should resemble that in Figure 10.8 but because we are using a random function it will not be exactly the same. Note that pressing [F9] will recalculate the fields in our table. In the next step we are going to freeze this data.

(h) Select G1:K201 and click on the Copy tool. The easiest way to select a range this large is to use the keyboard and not the mouse. With G1 as the active cell, hold down the [⇧ Shift] key and tap the [→] key four times. Still holding down the [⇧ Shift] key, use the keys [End] and [↓] to complete the selection.

(i) Move to Sheet6 and use the command Edit|Paste Special to bring up the dialog box shown in Figure 10.9. Click in the Values box and click the OK button to paste from the Clipboard. Note that we could have pasted right over the source data (G1:K201 of Sheet5) had we so wished.

(j) You will now note that your cells in Sheet6 no longer contain formulas. It will be necessary to adjust the column widths and to format column A as a date and column E to display two decimal places. To make the table more realistic you may wish to sort by the first column.

(k) Save the workbook.

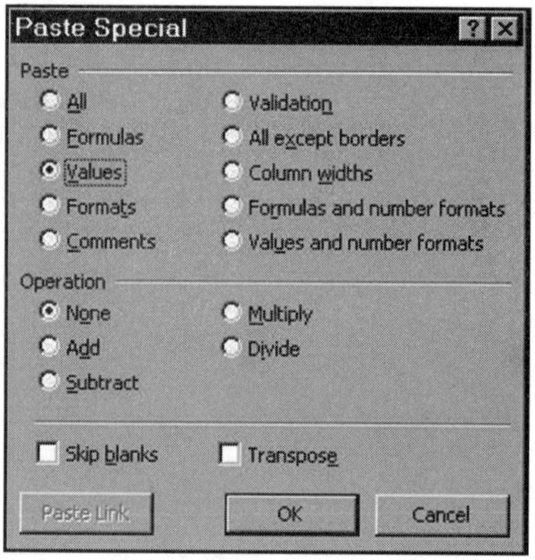

Figure 10.9

Exercise 5: Pivot Tables

A pivot table is a very useful way of summarizing tabular data. For example, the data we generated in the previous exercise could be summarized in a table showing the total hours of consulting time each IT staff member did for each of the company departments.

(a) Open Sheet6 of CHAP10.XLS and select A1:E201. Use the command Data|PivotTable... to bring up Step 1 of the PivotTable Wizard (Figure 10.10). Since we are analysing data from a Microsoft Excel list, make sure the first radio button is selected and click the Next button.

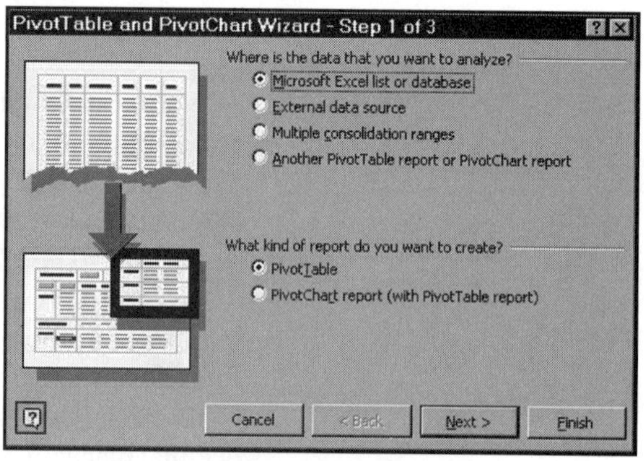

Figure 10.10

(b) Step 2 of the PivotTable dialog box appears (Figure 10.11). There should be no need to make any changes here so click the Next button.

Figure 10.11

(c) The Step 3 dialog box appears — Figure 10.12. We need to specify where we wish the pivot table to be constructed. Select the *Existing worksheet* option and enter G1 in the text box. We also need to design our pivot table so click the *Layout* button to open the Layout dialog box — Figure 10.13.

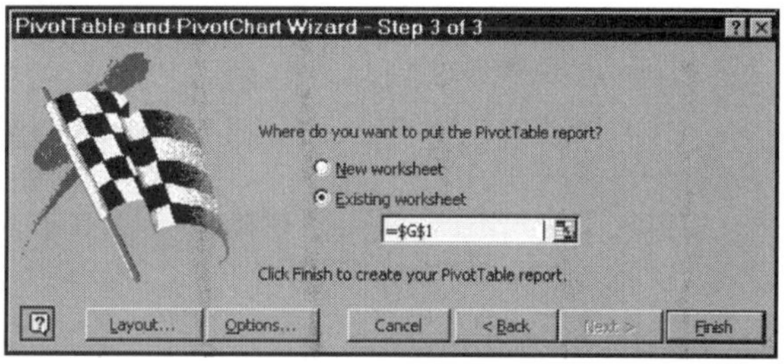

Figure 10.12

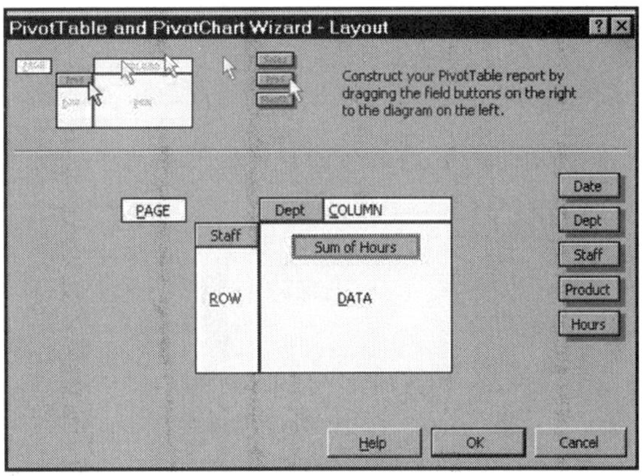

Figure 10.13

(d) To the right of this dialog box is a collection of field buttons; one for each of the column headings in our data. With the mouse drag the *Staff* field button into the *ROW* area, drag the *Dept* field button into the *COLUMN* area and drag the *Hours* field button into the *DATA* area. When you release the mouse this last button will change to *Sum of Hours*. The dialog box will now resemble that in Figure 10.13.

(e) Click the OK button to return to Step 3. We shall not explore the Options button, so click *Finish.*

(f) Figure 10.14 shows the resulting pivot table after formatting the values to display two decimal places. Note that your values will not be the same as shown since we generated the data with a random number function. The Pivot able Field List and the toolbar may be closed by clicking their close icons. You will want to format the data to show two decimal places in all cells. The pivot table we have generated summarizes the hours spent by each staff member consulting for each company department. Perhaps we would also like to see the product information. We could repeat the steps but in step (d) either drag *Dept* and *Product* in the *ROW* area or drag *Dept* and *Product* in the *COLUMN* area. However, we shall opt for modifying the existing table.

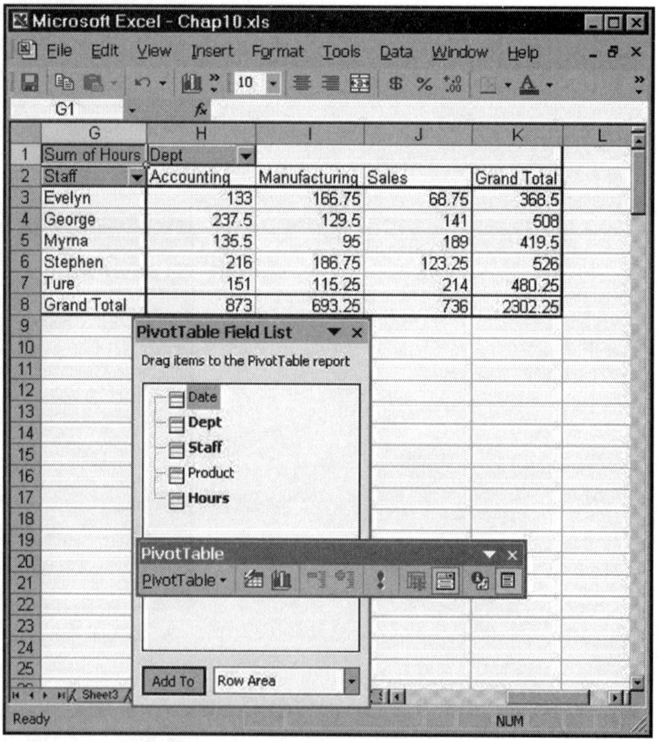

Figure 10.14

(g) Right click anywhere within the pivot table and, if the *Pivot Table Field List* (see Figure 10.14) does not appear, select the menu item *Show Field List*. Use the list to add *Product* to the column area.

(h) Experiment by dragging the *Product* button on the pivot table to the left and the right of the *Dept* button. Drag it to the left and the right of the *Staff* button. Drag it off the pivot table. Our pivot table shows remarkable flexibility.

(i) The table shows the sum of the number of hours each staff person spends in a department. Maybe we want to know the number of visits to each department. Right click on a pivot table cell, displaying numeric data and select the *Field Setting* item. Change from *Sum* to *Count*.

(j) Finally double click on George's cell under Accounting. Excel produces a mini-report on a new sheet about George's work for that department.

It is important to realize that the data in a pivot table is not live data. That is to say, if an item in the list is changed, the pivot table does not automatically reflect the change. However, we can request that the pivot table be updated, as we will see next.

(k) Note the name of the IT person in the first record in your list (cell A2) and note the total hours for this IT staff member as shown in the first pivot table.

(l) Replace the value for Hours Worked in E2 by a value exactly 10 units greater. The pivot table has not altered.

Refresh Data tool (red)

(m) Right click anywhere on your first pivot table and from the pop-up menu select and click on the *Refresh Data* item. Alternatively, with any cell in the table as the active cell, use the Refresh Data tool on the PivotTable toolbar. Your pivot table is updated. Please note that it does not matter whether you refresh the first or second pivot table, both are updated.

(n) Save the workbook.

We have just seen the tip of the iceberg! But there is not space to show more. The reader is encouraged to experiment — make notes as you go. Right click on the table and have the PivotTable toolbar displayed. Find how to make a chart of the pivot table data.

Exercise 6: Filtering Lists

Sometimes we do not want to summarize a list but wish to view or extract one or more records based on specific criteria. In this exercise we will look at the AutoFilter and the Advanced Filter features of Microsoft Excel. Problem 4 encourages you to explore the Data|Form feature on your own.

We begin with the AutoFilter tool. For this exercise, we wish to select all the records in the data of the last exercise for Evelyn relating to work on Excel which took 10 or more hours.

(a) Copy A1:E201 from Sheet6 to A4 of Sheet7.

(b) Copy row 5 to row 1. Add borders to A1:E2. We shall be using this area later in the exercise.

(c) Make one cell in the list the active cell and use the command Data|Filter|AutoFilter. Microsoft Excel adds selection buttons to the right of each cell in row 5.

(d) Click on the button in C5 and select Evelyn from the drop-down menu. Click on the button in D5 and select Excel. The list changes.

Observe the row heading. The range is no longer contiguous. Only records with *Evelyn* in column C and *Excel* in column D are shown, and these have coloured row headers to remind you the list is filtered. Buttons for fields where selections have been made have a blue arrow.

(e) Click on the button in E5 and select *Custom* ... to bring up the Custom AutoFilter dialog box — see Figure 10.15. Set the criterion to Hours greater than or equal to 10.

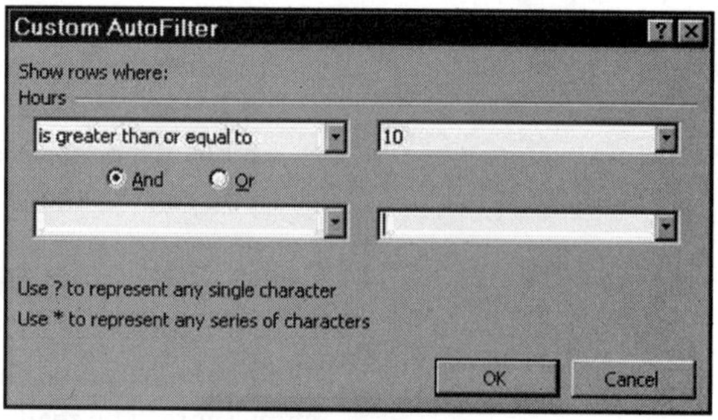

Figure 10.15

(f) Your worksheet will resemble that in Figure 10.16. Do not expect it to be identical.

(g) To return the spreadsheet to its original state, use Data|Filter|Show All. To remove the filter buttons from row 5 use Data|Filter and click on AutoFilter to remove the check mark.

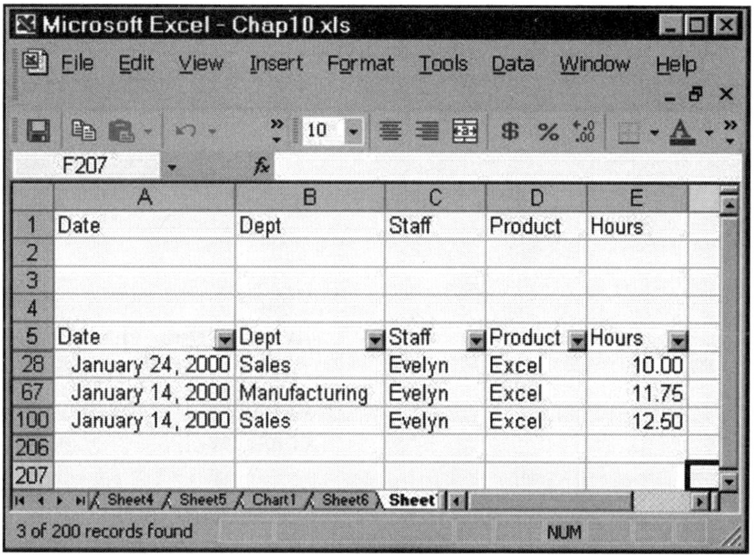

Figure 10.16

We will now use the Advance Filter Tool. For this part of the exercise we wish to find all the records relating to Evelyn's work with Excel for the Sales Dept. We need to see only records where the time spent exceeded 5 hours.

(h) We will be using A1:E2 to set the criteria for the filter. Enter these values in row 2: in B2 Sales, in C2 Evelyn, in D2 Excel and in E2 >5. These are shown in Figure 10.18

(i) Use the command Data|Filter|Advanced Filter to bring up the dialog box shown in Figure 10.17. The required action is *Filter the list in place* rather than *Copy to another location*. The list range is A4:E204 and criteria range is A1:E2.

Figure 10.17

(j) Figure 10.18 shows the result of this filter. This result is not live. If you change the data, for example by making Accounting the required Dept, it will again be necessary to use Data|Filter|Advanced Filter but the dialog box will be complete.

	A	B	C	D	E
1	Date	Dept	Staff	Product	Hours
2		Sales	Evelyn	Excel	>5
3					
4					
5	Date	Dept	Staff	Product	Hours
28	January 24, 2000	Sales	Evelyn	Excel	10.00
100	January 14, 2000	Sales	Evelyn	Excel	12.50

Figure 10.18

(k) Again, to return the data to its original state, use Data|Filter|Show All.

(l) Save the workbook.

Exercise 7: Importing and Exporting

It is common to download data from a mainframe into a 'text' file for analysis using Microsoft Excel. A text file is one without proprietary formatting. Such files can be opened with simple text editors such as Windows Notepad. In this exercise we will learn how to import such a file. We will also show how to export a file in a flat format.

(a) To simulate a file downloaded from a mainframe, open Notepad and enter data similar to that shown below. Normally you will have a file with many records but the few we have will suffice for the demonstration. Save the file as SALES.TXT.

```
Sales report from week of June 20
Mary Smith,12454,10486,9345,13847,10456
George Jones,10919,9234,13890,14500,8245
Elizabeth McDonald,12557,13456,19123,10909,9999
William Tell,10982,12430,8900,15893,10923
```

This file is an example of a *comma-delimited* file, sometimes called a CSV file. The fields in each record are separated by commas. Other formats include *tab-delimited* (the fields are separated by the tab character) and *fixed-length* (the fields have the same length in every record). While we will work with a CSV, the methods we use are applicable to all formats.

Note: If you copy and paste data from a text file to an Excel workbook, the same dialog box generally appears and may be used in the same way. Should it not appear and the text gets posted into one column, select the column of data and use the command Data|Text to Columns to parse the data.

(b) Use the command File|Open and move to the directory where you saved SALES.TXT. You will need to change the File Type to *Text* in order to see this file in the Open File dialog box. Open the file.

(c) Microsoft Excel opens the Text Import Wizard. The dialog box for Step 1 is shown in Figure 10.19. The first record in our file differs from the rest but Excel has coped with this. In other cases we might need to change the value in the Start import at row box to 2. Now click Next.

(d) In Step 2 (Figure 10.20) we specify that this is a comma-delimited file. Having done so, click Next.

(e) Step 3 (Figure 10.21) allows us to specify the format of each field. We need to make no changes here, so click Finish. The final product is shown in Figure 10.25. Note that the title bar shows *Sales.txt*. We wish to work on data, so we save it as an Excel file using File|Save As and specify Microsoft Excel format in the Save as file box of the Save dialog. The title bar should now display SALES.XLS.

The last step gives us the clue for exporting data in flat formats.

(f) With SALES.XLS open, use the command File|Save As. In the Save as file box select *Text (Tab delimited) (*.txt)* and give the new file the name SALES2.TXT. You may wish to examine SALES2.TXT in the Notepad editor.

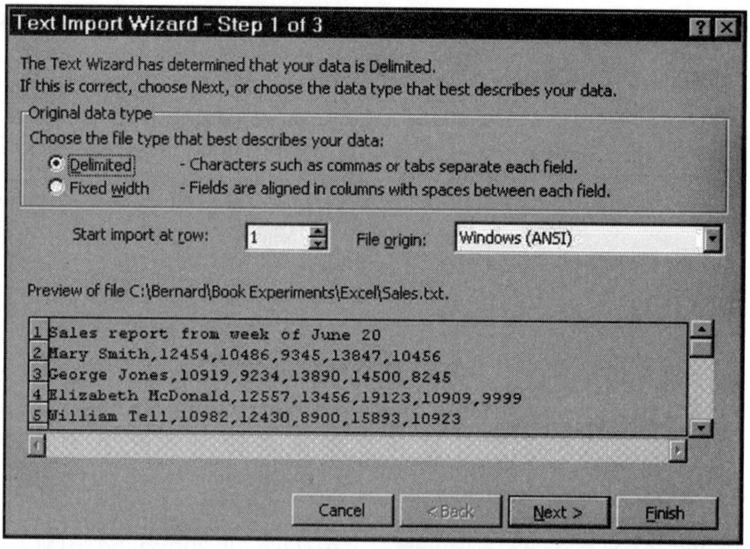

Figure 10.19

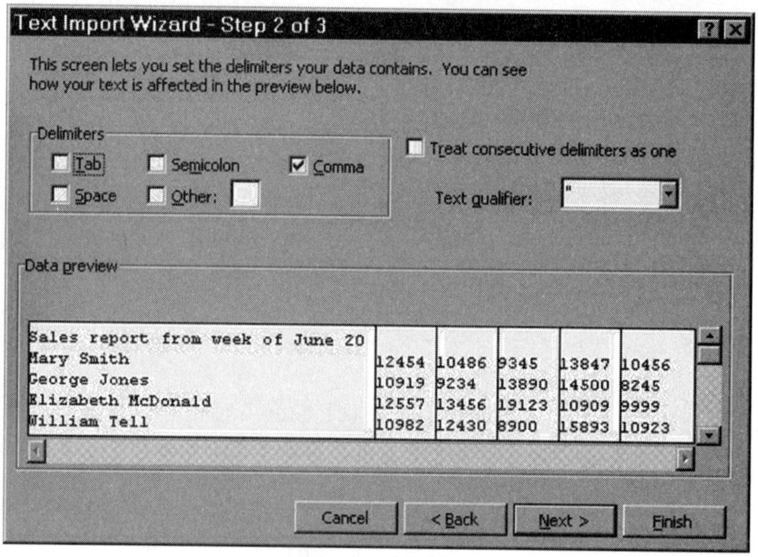

Figure 10.20

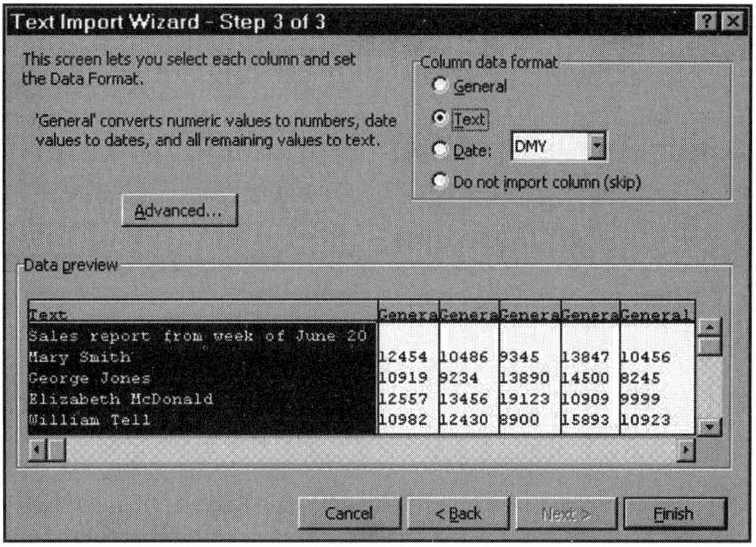

Figure 10.21

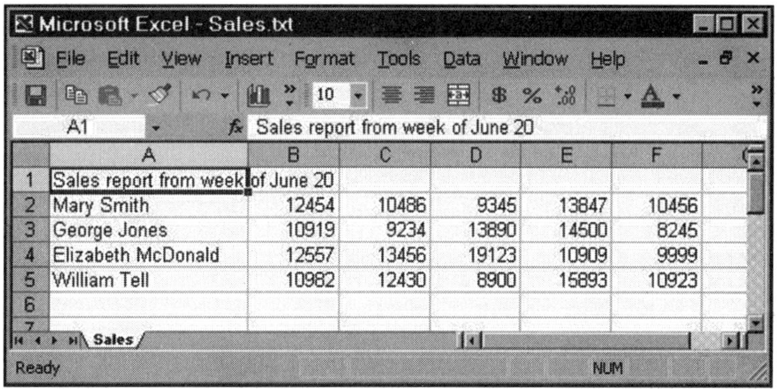

Figure 10.22

An alternative, and more powerful, method of importing data from text and other files is to use the command Data|Get External Data|Import Text File. With the latter option the dialog boxes to control the import are very similar to those shown above. However, at the very end of the process you can specify where the imported data is to go — onto the existing worksheet or a new one.

More importantly, you can now update your worksheet when the text file is changed. The Properties dialog box (opened by clicking on the Properties button in the Import Data box) allows you to specify, for example, if the worksheet is to be updated every time it is opened or at regular intervals.

Summary

The techniques you have seen in this chapter may be applied to a wide variety of problems such as summarizing sales data or reporting the results of customer satisfaction surveys.

We have learnt how to sort a table. Remember the cautionary note about what must be selected before sorting!

The RAND or RANDBETWEEN function was used to generate some test data.

We explored some ways of summarizing data. The pivot table is a very powerful tool once you have mastered it. Note that we can use the pivot table data to generate a chart. We briefly explored some data filtering features.

We have only touched upon Microsoft Excel's features for working with lists (sometimes called tables). There is a collection of worksheet functions (their names all begin with 'D') that gives you many of the features of a database application. But these are beyond the scope of this book.

Problems

1.* The first pivot table in Exercise 6 has a column total in column K. Could we have made the table without this?

2.* In step (m) of Exercise 5 we brought up the PivotTable Wizard to change the data from Sum to Count. Is there another way of doing this?

3. The Subtotals tool: copy the cells A1:E201 of Sheet6 to cell A1 of a new Sheet and sort the new list by Staff. Place the cursor anywhere within the list and use Data|Subtotals in the dialog box. You should be able to generate subtotals for each staff person. Experiment with the buttons labelled 1, 2 or 3 at the top of the work area.

4. Data Form: use the command Data|Form. Clear any existing criteria by clicking the Criteria button — do not merely erase entries from the dialog box. Set the criteria to locate records for the Sales department and the staffperson Ture. The Find Next and Find Previous buttons allow you to browse through the list.

5. Open the tab-delimited file SALES2.TXT using the method demonstrated in Exercise 7.

6. The Data Sort dialog (Figure 10.2) limits you to three keys for sorting. What if you wished to sort a table on five keys? The book web site (www.bh.com/companions/075065614X) has an Excel file (SortData.XLS) with 75 records with which you can experiment. Use the sort method twice; but in what order do you sort the keys? The same file may be used to experiment with PivotTables.

11
Dates and Times

Objectives

Upon completion of this chapter you will:

- understand how Microsoft Excel stores dates as serial numbers;
- know that dates may be entered and displayed in various formats;
- be able to use formulas involving addition and subtraction of dates;
- be familiar with the work functions NOW and TODAY;
- be able to use the functions: DATE, YEAR, MONTH, DAY and WEEKDAY;
- know how to combine DATE, WEEKDAY and CHOOSE to find, for example, the date of the first Monday in a month;
- be aware of the limitation of the WEEKNUM function;
- be familiar with the undocumented function DATEDIF;
- know how to perform calculations involving time.

Introduction

Microsoft Excel stores dates by using a serial number system. In its default setting, the Windows versions use 1-Jan-1900 as day one. The serial number of the next day is 2 and so on. To find the number of days between two dates we merely subtract one date from the other. This is explored in Exercise 2.

If 1-Jan-1900 is day 1, then 31-Dec-1900 should be day 365. Actually, Excel computes it as 366 by erroneously treating 1900 as a leap year. Microsoft states that, when Excel was introduced, it was aware that this was not the case. However, at that time Lotus 1-2-3 was the dominant spreadsheet program and it contained the leap year error. Excel was made to treat 1900 as a leap year to be consistent with Lotus 1-2-3. This will not cause errors provided we do not use a range of dates that span the last day of February 1900.

The default setting for day one is 1-Jan-1904 in the Macintosh version of Microsoft Excel. Each system can be changed using Tools|Options|Calculations and checking the appropriate box. However, this is generally not necessary since Excel automatically sets the date system when files are transferred between the two versions of the application. If you plan to make a change, it must be made before a date is entered into the workbook.

Note: Historians may visit the Web site of John Walkenbach to download his Extended Date Functions Add-In if the 1-Jan-1900 limitation is a problem.

Since day one is 1-Jan-1900, it follows that Excel cannot be used with dates prior to that time. What about in the other direction — what is the last allowable date? That depends on the version of Excel. With Excel 5 and 95, the last permitted date is 31-Dec-2078 — a limitation imposed by a 16-bit computer system. Later versions work with dates up to 31-Dec-9999.

We shall see that cells with date values may be formatted to display the result in a great variety of ways from 1/2/02 to 1 February 2002. To avoid confusion with the two systems of date formats used on the two sides of the Atlantic (*dd/mm/yy* and *mm/dd/yy*), dates in this book will generally be written in the form 1-Jan-2000. The reader is free to enter them in the numeric form that is compatible with the Regional Settings of his/her computer.

Excel represents the time of day with fractional serial numbers. The serial number of 1-July-2000 is 36708. Strictly speaking this is the serial number for midnight just as the day starts. So 36708.5 is noon on that day, while 36708.75 is 6:00 PM. Calculations involving time values that are not parts of dates are also allowed. Thus 9:00 AM is stored as 0.375 which is 9/24th of a 24-h day.

Exercise 1: Entering and Formatting Dates

We begin by showing that when a date is entered into a cell which was previously formatted General the cell takes on a specific date format.

Note: The exact format of the displayed value will depend upon your Regional Settings.

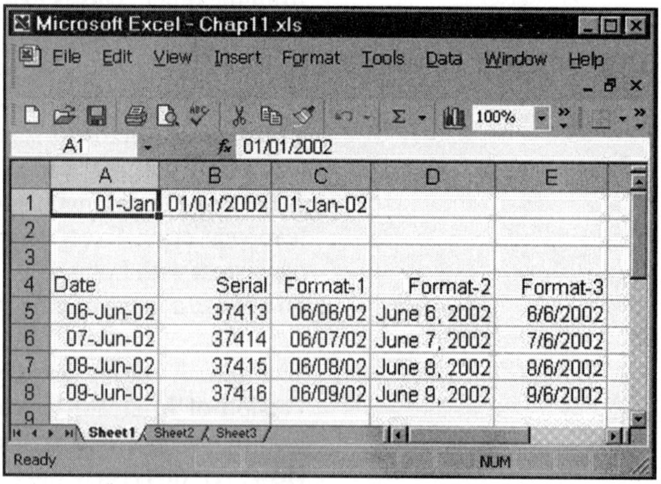

Figure 11.1

(a) On Sheet1 of a new workbook make these:
A1: 1/jan the cell displays 01-Jan.
B1: 1-1-02 the cell displays 01/01/02.
C1: 1/jan/02 the cell displays 01-Jan-02.
Note how Microsoft Excel automatically capitalizes the month and left aligns the entries in the cells.

(b) Make A1, B1 and C1 the active cell in turn and look in the formula box. In the year 2002, the reference box shows 01/01/2002 for each of them although the cells are formatted differently. Note that when the year is omitted (as in A1), Excel uses the current year.

(c) In A1 enter 6/6/99. Because the cell now has a specific format, the value will display as 06-Jun. Experiment with the cells B1 and C1 to see that they retain their formats no matter how new (valid) dates are entered.

We have seen that Excel is able to recognize a number of formats as representing dates. There is, however, one possible pitfall. If a space is typed before a date, perhaps inadvertently, then Excel will not recognize the cell as containing a date value.

(d) In D1, enter 01-jan-2002 with a space before the 01. Excel does not convert *jan* to *Jan*. The entry has not been left aligned in the cell. You may wish to widen the column to confirm this.

Next we look at the formats of the cells and experiment with some Custom formats.

(e) Using the command Format|Cells, you will see that A1 has the Custom format *dd-mmm.* The two *d*s indicate that the day is to be displayed with two digits. Hence the leading zero shows in A1. The three *m*s indicate that the month is to be displayed as a three-character abbreviation. To spell out the month in full, it is necessary to use four *m*s in the format.

(f) Move to B1 and, using Format|Cells, you will see that this cell has the Custom format *dd/mm/yy*, if you are using the UK system, or *mm/dd/yy* if you are using the US system. The two *m*s indicate that the month is to be displayed as a two digit number; likewise the two *y*s indicate the year is displayed with two digits.

(g) Moving to C1 and again using Format|Cells, you will see that this cell has the date format of the type *04-Mar-97*. If you now click on the Custom category you will see that the format is *dd-mmm-yy*. Should you wish to have a four digit year, change this to *dd-mm-yyyy*.

(h) Enter the text shown in row 4 of Figure 11.1. In A5 enter 6-Jun-02. Using the fill handle, copy this down to A8. In B5 enter =$A5 and copy down and across to E8.

(i) We will now format columns B to E to have the same value displayed in different ways. Format B5:B8 as General to display the serial number of the date. Format C5:C8 to display a date using *dd/mm/yy* (or *mm/dd/yy* if that is your Regional Setting). Format D4:D8 to display the long date format. Figure 11.1.

Note: This information is true for worksheets in Excel 97 and on. Other rules apply in Visual Basic for Applications and in older version of Excel. If in doubt, use four digits.

Under Windows 98, the default value is 29 but it can be changed in the Date tab of Regional Settings.

Finally, we look at the Y2K topic.

(j) In A8 successively enter these dates: 1-1-1, 1-1-5, 1-1-10, etc. Observe the result. Any year value up to 29 results in a 21st century date while years of 30 or more result in a 20th century date.

(k) Save the workbook as CHAP11.XLS.

Exercise 2: Simple Date Calculations

In this exercise we see some simple date calculations involving subtraction and addition of date serial values. The dates to be subtracted or added may be in any format. Figure 11.2 uses the Custom format *dd-mmm-yyyy* for all dates.

(a) On Sheet2 of CHAP11.XLS, enter the text shown in A1:C1 of Figure 11.2. In A2 enter the date 01-Jan-2002 and in B2 enter 10-Jan-2002. In C2 enter the formula =B2-A2. This will return the surprising result 09-Jan-1900. Or is it that surprising? The serial number for that date is 9. Format C2 to General to display the result as 9.

Note that the result of 9 in the step above indicates that Excel is computing the days between midnight on the first and midnight on the tenth. Recall that by midnight we mean 00:00 hours or the start of the day. Let's test this conclusion.

(b) In A3 enter the formula =A2+0.5 and format the cell to show the date and time. In the figure the custom format dd-mmm-yyyy h:mm AM/PM was used. Cell A3 now represents noon on the first. In B3 enter 10-Jan-2002; do not copy B2 to B3 since the result will be 11-Jan-2002. Copy C2 to C3 to find the difference. Note that since C2 had been formatted to General, C3 takes on this format. The result is 8.5 days as expected.

	A	B	C	D
1	Start date	End date	Interval	
2	01-Jan-2002	10-Jan-2002	9	
3	01-Jan-2002 12:00 PM	10-Jan-2002	8.5	
4				
5	Invoice date	Payment date	Current date	Note
6	01-Jan-2002	05-Jan-2002	10-Jan-2002	paid
7	01-Jan-2002		10-Jan-2002	ok
8	01-Jan-2002		13-Feb-2002	overdue
9	01-Jan-2002		01-Mar-2002	reminder
10				
11	Invoice date	Discount deadline	Due date	
12	05-Feb-2002	25-Feb-2002	07-Mar-2002	
13				
14	Birthday	Today	Age	
15	01-Jan-1999	02-Jan-2002	3	
16	05-Mar-1972	02-Jan-2002	29	
17	13-Feb-1939	02-Jan-2002	62	

Figure 11.2

In business calculations, date differences may be used to determine if a bill is overdue. Let us assume that our company gives its customers 30 days to pay an invoice. After 45 days a reminder is sent out. The next step shows the types of formulas that can be used. We will enter the current date manually (rather than using the TODAY function) otherwise the demonstration will take too long!

(c) Enter the text in A5:D5 using Alt+Enter↵ to get wrapping.

(d) Enter the dates in A6:C9. The quickest way to get the same value in A6:C6 is to enter the value in A6 and use Copy and Paste. Do not use the fill handle.

(e) The formula in D6, which is to be copied down to D9, is: =IF(B6>0, "paid", IF(C6-A6 < 30, "ok", IF(C6-A6 < 45, "overdue", "reminder")))

In the next scenario Wessex Light and Power give a discount if the bill is paid within 20 days but charge interest if it is later than 30.

(f) Enter the text in A11:C11. Enter the date in A12. The formula in B12 is =A12+20 and in C12 it is =A12+30.

Date subtraction may be used to compute ages from birth dates. The result could be out by one year occasionally because of leap years. The DATEDIF function, introduced in Exercise 7, overcomes that problem.

(g) Enter the text in row 14 and some dates in A14:A17. In B15 enter the formula =TODAY(). This returns the current date so your result will differ from that in the figure. In C15 enter =INT((B15-A15) / 365). Copy B15:C15 down to row 17.

In this exercise we have some formulas using cells containing date values. For example, C2 contains the formula =B2 - A2 and these two cells contain dates. Can we work directly with dates?

(h) In E2 enter =10/01/02 - 01/01/02 if you use the British date convention or =01/10/02 - 01/01/02 if you use the American system. Format the cell to General and it will display 4.5 (or -4.5). Microsoft Excel has not recognized the two dates. It has treated the slash symbols as division operators.

(i) Edit E2 to read ="10/01/99" - "01/01/99" (or ="01/10/99" -"01/01/99") and you are rewarded with the correct result.

Negative intervals can give a surprising result.

(j) In F1 enter 1/1/50 and in G1 enter 1/1/60. Enter the formula = G1-F1 in H1. Unless H1 has been formatted, it will display ######## and no amount of column widening will resolve the problem. Microsoft Excel thinks a date format is appropriate but the value is negative. Format the cell to General to resolve the problem.

(k) Save the workbook.

Exercise 3: What Day/Date/Time is it?

In this exercise we use the functions NOW() and TODAY() to find the current date and time. Some shortcuts are introduced to put the current date and time in cells quickly. A useful variation of the TEXT function is shown.

We often wish to date stamp our worksheets just as we date letters. Most word processors allow you to enter the current date in one of two ways. The first is dynamic: open the document tomorrow and you get tomorrow's date. The second is static: open the document next week and you get the date when you generated the document. Excel provides the same facilities. In addition, Excel enables us to put a time stamp on our worksheet.

	A	B	C	D
1	Now	Jan 4, 2002 12:30 PM	January 4, 2002	12:30 PM
2			January 4, 2002	12:30 PM
3	Today	January 4, 2002	Friday	Jan
4	Ctrl+;	January 4, 2002		
5	Ctrl+:	12:30 PM		

Figure 11.3

(a) Enter the text in column A of Figure 11.4 on Sheet3.

(b) Enter the formula =NOW() in B1 and copy it to C1:D1. This function returns the current date and time. Your values will obviously not be the same as in the figure. B1 has the custom format mmm d, yyy h:mm AM/PM. Format C1 to display a date and D1 to display a time value. Adjust the column width as needed.

(c) Recall from earlier chapters that formatting only changes what is displayed and not the cell's actual content. We may extract the date and the time values, respectively, using the formulas:
C2: =INT(NOW()) and format it to display a date.
D2: =MOD(NOW(),1) and format it to show a time.

(d) A simpler way to get just the date is to use =TODAY(). Enter this in B3.

(e) Sometimes we wish to know the day of the week and/or the name of the month corresponding to a certain date. In C3 and D3, respectively, enter the formulas =TEXT(B3, "dddd") and =TEXT(B3,"mmm"). When the last argument is entered as four characters the result is the full name, when three characters are used an abbreviation results. You can find the day of the week of your birth using something like =TEXT("12/12/1979", "dddd") in A7.

Note: If you enter a formula such as =TEXT("12/12/79", "dddd"), Excel 2002 will display a formula error tip. Open this, and Excel notes the two digit year XX and offers to convert it to 19XX or 20XX.

The values in B1:D3 are dynamic. If you save the file and re-open it tomorrow the cells will display tomorrow's date. Each recalculation of the worksheet updates these values, so the time values will change if you enter values in cells or press F9. There are times when we need static values.

(f) In B4 enter Ctrl+; (control +semicolon) and in B5 Ctrl+: (control +colon). These cells contain values not formulas. Pressing F9 has no effect on the time value in B5. Tomorrow the value in cell B4 will be the same as today.

(g) Save the workbook.

Exercise 4: The Standard Date Functions

The syntax and purpose of the standard Microsoft Excel date functions are given in the table in Figure 11.4. Very often we use these function in nested forms.

(a) Open Sheet4 of CHAP11.XLS and, referring to Figure 11.5, enter the text in column A and the numeric values in rows B1:D1. Enter the formulas in B4:B11 and copy them across to column D. Enter the formulas in column E. The result will be as in Figure 11.6.

(b) Experiment with different values in B1:D3. Using a perpetual calendar from a reference book (or the phone directory in some areas) check that you agree with the values in rows 9 to 11.

Function	**Value returned**
DATE(yy, mm, dd)	A date serial number
YEAR(date)	The year value of a date serial number
MONTH(date)	The month value of a date serial number
DAY(date)	The day value of a date serial number
WEEKDAY(date, type)	A weekday index value of a date serial number. Type = 1 (or omitted) Sunday has index 1 Type = 2 Monday has index 1 Type = 3 Monday has index 0

Figure 11.4

	A	B	C	D	E
1	yy	99	2000	2002	
2	mm	1	1	1	
3	dd	1	1	1	
4	DATE	=DATE(B1,B2,B3)	=DATE(C1,C2,C3)	=DATE(D1,D2,D3)	=DATE(2002,1,1)
5	YEAR	=YEAR(B4)	=YEAR(C4)	=YEAR(D4)	=YEAR(30000)
6	MONTH	=MONTH(B4)	=MONTH(C4)	=MONTH(D4)	=MONTH(30000)
7	DAY	=DAY(B4)	=DAY(C4)	=DAY(D4)	=DAY(30000)
8	WEEKDAY	=WEEKDAY(B4)	=WEEKDAY(C4)	=WEEKDAY(D4)	
9	WEEKDAY	=WEEKDAY(B4,1)	=WEEKDAY(C4,1)	=WEEKDAY(D4,1)	
10	WEEKDAY	=WEEKDAY(B4,2)	=WEEKDAY(C4,2)	=WEEKDAY(D4,2)	
11	WEEKDAY	=WEEKDAY(B4,3)	=WEEKDAY(C4,3)	=WEEKDAY(D4,3)	

Figure 11.5

Note: You can display the formulas in cells by using the shortcut Ctrl+~ where the second key is to the left of the 1 on the top of the so-called typewriter keys. The same shortcut returns to the normal worksheet display.

	A	B	C	D	E
1	yy	99	1999	2000	
2	mm	1	1	1	
3	dd	1	1	1	
4	DATE	01/01/99	01/01/99	01/01/00	01/01/00
5	YEAR	1999	1999	2000	1982
6	MONTH	1	1	1	2
7	DAY	1	1	1	18
8	WEEKDAY	6	6	7	
9	WEEKDAY	6	6	7	
10	WEEKDAY	5	5	6	
11	WEEKDAY	4	4	5	

Figure 11.6

Exercise 5: Date for the Next Meeting?

It is not uncommon for committees to set the dates of their meeting with rules such as 'the last Monday of each month' or 'the first Friday of each month'. The dates of many national holidays are set by similar rules. Martin Luther King Jr Day (USA) is celebrated on the third Monday in January while the May Bank Holiday (UK) is the first Monday in May. A combination of the DATE, WEEKDAY and CHOOSE functions can be used to find the dates set by such rules.

Let us see how we can find the first Monday in a month. The first day of the month is given by =DATE(y, m, 1). The formula =WEEKDAY(DATE(y, m, 1)) will return a number for the weekday with 1 meaning Sunday. Suppose WEEKDAY tells us that the first of the month is a Sunday, then we need a date with a serial number 1 greater. If it is a Monday, we need add nothing, if a Tuesday we need to add 6, etc. Rather than a complex nested IF formula, we will use =CHOOSE(WEEKDAY(DATE(y, m, 1), 1, 0, 6, 5, 4, 3, 2) to compute the days to be added to the first of the month. So the formula for the first Monday in the month is:

=DATE(y, m, 1) + CHOOSE(WEEKDAY(DATE(y, m, 1), 1, 0, 6, 5, 4, 3, 2).

The last day of a given month is found by subtracting 1 from the serial date of the following month using =DATE(y, m+1, 1) - 1. We can use a slightly simpler version of this, =DATE(y, m+1, 0), since Microsoft Excel interprets this as being one day before the first day of the month m+1. Again, we can use a combination of CHOOSE and WEEKDAY to find the last Monday or Friday, etc. Of course, we need to subtract days in this case.

(a) On Sheet5 construct the worksheet shown in Figure 11.6. Cell E1 is named *Year*. The month series is extended to 12 — only 6 months are shown in the figure. The formulas in cells displaying days of the week are used to check that the other formulas are correct. The formulas in column B are shown in Figure 11.7. Those in rows 4 to 15 should be copied to column M. It is left as an exercise for the reader to develop the formula needed in C17 which is copied down to C22.

Note: The formulas in B4:M15 will display in Excel 2002 with a green triangle in the top left corner. When one of them is selected an error tip pops up. Excel has noted the formulas down a column differ from each other. Select B4:M15, open the error tip and select the *Ignore this error* item if the green triangle bothers you.

Note: The Excel community is indebted to Norbert Hetterich for the surprisingly short formula in B19 to compute the date of Easter Sunday. No attempt will be made here to explain it.

Note: In the USA when a holiday falls on a Saturday, the preceding Friday is a holiday, when it falls on a Sunday the following Monday is a holiday. In the UK, the following Monday is a holiday if Christmas Day is Saturday or Sunday.

	A	B	C	D	E	F	G
1	**Meetings and Holidays**			Year	2002		
2							
3	Month	1	2	3	4	5	6
4	First Monday	7-Jan	4-Feb	4-Mar	1-Apr	6-May	3-Jun
5		Mon	Mon	Mon	Mon	Mon	Mon
6	Second Monday	14-Jan	11-Feb	11-Mar	8-Apr	13-May	10-Jun
7		Mon	Mon	Mon	Mon	Mon	Mon
8	Third Monday	21-Jan	18-Feb	18-Mar	15-Apr	20-May	17-Jun
9		Mon	Mon	Mon	Mon	Mon	Mon
10	Last Monday	28-Jan	25-Feb	25-Mar	29-Apr	27-May	24-Jun
11		Mon	Mon	Mon	Mon	Mon	Mon
12	First Friday	4-Jan	1-Feb	1-Mar	5-Apr	3-May	7-Jun
13		Fri	Fri	Fri	Fri	Fri	Fri
14	Last Friday	25-Jan	22-Feb	29-Mar	26-Apr	31-May	28-Jun
15		Fri	Fri	Fri	Fri	Fri	Fri
16							
17	Easter Sunday	31-Mar	Sun	Formula courtesy of N. Hetterich			
18	Good Friday	29-Mar	Fri				
19	Thanksgiving CDN	14-Oct	Mon	2nd Monday in October			
20	Thanksgiving US	24-Nov	Sun	4th Thurday in November			
21	Xmas (UK)	25-Dec	Wed	25th Dec or following Monday			
22	Xmas (US)	25-Dec	Wed	25th Dec or preceding Fri or following Mon			

Figure 11.6

	B
4	=DATE(Year, B3, 1) + CHOOSE(WEEKDAY(DATE(Year, B3, 1)), 1, 0, 6, 5, 4, 3, 2)
5	=TEXT(WEEKDAY(B4), "ddd")
6	=DATE(Year, B3, 1) + CHOOSE(WEEKDAY(DATE(Year, B3, 1)), 1, 0, 6, 5, 4, 3, 2) + 7
7	=TEXT(WEEKDAY(B6), "ddd")
8	=DATE(Year, B3, 1) + CHOOSE(WEEKDAY(DATE(Year, B3, 1)), 1, 0, 6, 5, 4, 3, 2) + 14
9	=TEXT(WEEKDAY(B8), "ddd")
10	=DATE(Year, B3+1, 0) - CHOOSE(WEEKDAY(DATE(Year, B3+1, 0)), 6, 0, 1,2,3,4,5)
11	=TEXT(WEEKDAY(B10), "ddd")
12	=DATE(Year, B3, 1) + CHOOSE(WEEKDAY(DATE(Year, B3, 1)), 5, 4, 3, 2, 1, 0, 6)
13	=TEXT(WEEKDAY(B12), "ddd")
14	=DATE(Year, B3+1, 0) - CHOOSE(WEEKDAY(DATE(Year, B3+1, 0)),2, 3, 4, 5, 6, 0, 1)
15	=TEXT(WEEKDAY(B14), "ddd")
16	
17	=DOLLAR((DAY(MINUTE(Year/38)/2+55) & "/4/" & Year)/7,)*7 - 6
18	=DOLLAR((DAY(MINUTE(Year/38)/2+55)& "/4/" &Year)/7,)*7 - 8
19	=DATE(Year, 10, 1) + CHOOSE(WEEKDAY(DATE(Year, 10, 1)), 1, 0, 6, 5, 4, 3, 2) + 7
20	=DATE(Year, 11, 1) + CHOOSE(WEEKDAY(DATE(Year, 11, 1)), 4, 5, 6, 0, 1, 2, 3) + 21
21	=DATE(Year,12,25) +CHOOSE(WEEKDAY(DATE(Year,12,25)), 1, 0,0, 0, 0, 0, 2)
22	=DATE(Year,12,25) +CHOOSE(WEEKDAY(DATE(Year,12,25)), 1, 0, 0, 0, 0, 0, -1)

Figure 11.7

Exercise 6: Other Date Functions

When the Analysis ToolPak has been loaded additional date functions are available. These include EDATE and EOMONTH which the reader is advised to look up in Help.

Note: See Appendix A for information on installing the Analysis ToolPak.

In this exercise we will explore the use of NETWORKDAYS which calculates the number of working days between two dates. The syntax for the function is *=NETWORKDAYS(date1, date2, holidays)*.

(a) On Sheet6, construct the worksheet shown in Figure 11.8. Cell B2 is named *Year* and the range E2:E11 is named *Holidays*. The dates for some of the holidays will, of course, vary with the year. It is left as an exercise for the reader to generate the correct formulas. Note that Victoria Day is the Monday on or preceding May 24. You may prefer to use your own holiday list.

(b) The formula in C4 is:
=NETWORKDAYS(DATE(Year,A4,1), (DATE(Year,A4+1,0)), Holidays).
This may be copied down to row 15. Use the AutoSum tool to find the yearly total in C16. You may wish to check this value by entering, in C17, the formula
=NETWORKDAYS(DATE(Year,1,1),DATE(Year,12,31), Holidays).

(c) Save the workbook.

	A	B	C	D	E	F	G
1	**Number of work days**				Holidays	Canadian	
2	Year	2000			1-Jan	New Year's Day	Sat
3					22-May	Victoria Day	Mon
4	1	Jan	21		1-Jul	Canada Day	Sat
5	2	Feb	21		7-Aug	First Monday in August	Mon
6	3	Mar	23		4-Sep	Labour Day	Mon
7	4	Apr	18		9-Oct	Thanksgiving	Mon
8	5	May	22		11-Nov	Remembrance	Sat
9	6	Jun	22		25-Dec	Christmas	Mon
10	7	Jul	21		21-Apr	Good Friday	Fri
11	8	Aug	22		24-Apr	Easter Monday	Mon
12	9	Sep	20				
13	10	Oct	21				
14	11	Nov	22				
15	12	Dec	20				
16		Total	253				

Figure 11.8

When in Rome ...

Microsoft Excel includes a function called WEEKNUM which computes the week number of a specified serial date. The syntax is *=WEEKNUM(date, type)*. When *type* is set to 1, or is omitted, the function uses weeks beginning on Sunday. When it is set to 2, weeks begin on Monday. Regardless of the type, January 1st is always considered to be in Week 1.

Europeans should note that this algorithm is not in accord with the International Standards Organization (ISO) Rule 8601 which states that the first week of the year is the week containing the first Thursday. Note also that in the ISO standard, weeks begin on a Monday. The following formula will correct the Excel week number to conform to the ISO rule:

=WEEKNUM(date,2) - CHOOSE(WEEKDAY(DATE (YEAR(date), 1, 1), 2), 0, 0, 0, 0, 1, 1,1)

where *date* is a cell containing a serial date value. However, this formula returns 0 rather than 52 or 53 for Jan 1, 2 and 3 when the first is a Friday; for Jan 1 and 2 when the first is a Saturday; and for Jan 1 when it is a Sunday. Visit the Web site of Laurent Longre for a Visual Basic for Applications user-defined function.

Exercise 7: The DATEDIF Function

The DATEDIF Function calculates the difference between two dates. This function is neither documented nor supported by Microsoft Excel but is implemented in Microsoft Excel to be compatible with Lotus 1-2-3. It is a very useful function as will be illustrated in the example.

The syntax is *=DATEDIF(Date1, Date2, Interval)* where *Date1* is the first date and *Date2* is the second date which must be later

Note: Actually, DATEDIF was documented in Excel 2000, Type *datedif* in the Index tab of Help to locate it — Answer Wizard will not help.

than, or equal to, *Date1*. The code used for Interval determines the format of the output. An Interval code of 'D', 'M' or 'Y' returns the difference in days, months or years, respectively. The interval code 'YD', 'YM' returns the number of days and months, respectively, *treating the two dates as if they were in the same year*. Similarly, 'MD' returns the number of days between the two dates as if they referred to the *same month and year*.

(a) On Sheet7 construct the worksheet shown in Figure 11.10. The dates in column B may be entered in any format that is compatible with your Regional Settings.

(b) The date in B13 may be for any year because the formula in C13 uses *yd* for the interval rather than *y*. Note the use of IF to avoid asking Excel to compute the DATEDIF function when *date1* is after *date2*.

	A	B	C
1	**DATEDIF function (undocumented)**		
2			
3	Today	04-Jan-2002	
4			
5	Date of birth	25-Feb-1966	
6	Age in years	35	=DATEDIF(B5, TODAY(),"y")
7			
8	Date of purchase	03-Mar-1987	
9	Days owned	5421	=DATEDIF(B8,TODAY(),"d")
10	Months owned	178	=DATEDIF(B8,TODAY(),"m")
11	Time owned	14 yrs, 10 months	=DATEDIF(B8,TODAY(),"y") & " yrs, " & DATEDIF(B8,TODAY(),"ym") & " months"
12			
13	Tax deadline	30-Apr	
14	days to file	116 days left	=IF(TODAY()<=B13, DATEDIF(TODAY(),B13,"yd") & " days left", DATEDIF(B13,TODAY(),"yd") & " days overdue")

Figure 11.9

Exercise 8: Time on Your Hands

The most important fact to remember when using time values in Microsoft Excel is that the values are stored as decimal fractions of a 24-h day. A cell that is displaying 12:00 PM contains the value 0.5.

A cell displaying 7:30, with the meaning 7 hours and 30 minutes, contains the value 0.8125. If this cell (say B4) represents an employee's time worked and he is paid £6/h it would be a mistake to use =B4*6. We would be asking Excel to compute 0.8125 * 6. We solve this by using B4*24*6 where the factor of 24 converts 0.8125 days to 7.5 hours.

Similarly, if J10 displays minutes and seconds we would use =J10*24*60 to find the actual number of minutes.

It is sometimes convenient to format cells that are to contain time values before entering the values.

For the first part of this exercise, the manager of the Volume II bookstore plans to use Excel to track the hours of her two employees. An employee is expected to work 7½ hours each day for a fixed wage. Overtime is paid at the rate of £8/h.

(a) This worksheet will be constructed on Sheet7. After entering the text values shown in Figure 11.10, format B3:E7 to use the *1:30 PM* type of the Time category — the Custom format is *h:mm AM/PM*.

(b) Experiment with entering some times in B3:E3. Begin with 9:00 am (with a space before AM). Note that a simple 9 does not give the required result but 9: does. Examples of times after noon are: 13:, 13:15, 1:00 pm and 1:0 PM. Enter the values as shown in B3:E4.

	A	B	C	D	E	F	G	H
1	Time card							
2		Start	Lunch	Return	Home	Hours	Overtime	Extra
3	Monday	8:00 AM	12:00 PM	1:00 PM	5:15 PM	8:15	0:45	£6.00
4	Tuesday	9:00 AM	1:00 PM	1:30 PM	6:00 PM	8:30	1:00	£8.00
5	Wednesday					0:00	0:00	£0.00
6	Thursday					0:00	0:00	£0.00
7	Friday					0:00	0:00	£0.00
8	Total					16:45	1:45	£14.00

Figure 11.10

(c) To compute the total hours worked in F3 use =(C3-B3)+(E3-D3). The parentheses are not essential but help to clarify the formula. Format this cell using the *13:30* type from the Time category.

(d) To compute the overtime in G3 use =F3-TIMEVALUE("7:30"). Use the same formatting as in F3. We will shortly find that this formula is unsatisfactory. To calculate the extra income in H3 use =G3*24*8 and format the cell as Currency.

(e) Copy G3:H3 down to row 7. Oh! What a mess! The problem is that the blank cells have confused Excel into trying to work with negative time values. To make things right, modify G3 to read =MAX(F3-TIMEVALUE("7:30"),0) and copy it down to row 7. Strange values will still show in column F as you enter the time values for a day but everything is fine when a day is completed.

(f) The formulas in F8:H8 obviously use the SUM function. If you enter time values for every day, you may find that F8 displays an incorrect result. It probably has the same format as F3:F7 but this cannot exceed 24. Reformat F8 with the Custom format *[h]:mm*. The brackets allow the value to exceed 24.

(g) Save the workbook.

In the next scenario your IT manager has sent an e-mail telling users that as of next Monday there will be a charge for using the network modems. The rate will be $0.50/min for calls of 5 min or less, and $0.75/min for longer ones. You wish to use yesterday's data to see what a typical day will cost your department.

(h) The worksheet will resemble that in Figure 11.11. Format A14:A20 as mm:ss and enter values in this range in the forms 0:6:15, 0:8:30, etc. Note that we must prefix the minutes by zero hours. With A14 the active cell, look in the formula box. The values are stored as minutes and seconds after midnight.

(i) Enter the formulas =IF(A14*24*60<=5,0.5,0.75) and =A14*B14*24*60, in B14 and C15, respectively. The factor 24*60 converts the time stored as a fraction of a day to a minute value.

	A	B	C
12	**Modem usage**		
13	Duration	Rate $/min	Cost
14	6:15	$0.75	$4.69
15	8:30	$0.75	$6.38
16	2:15	$0.50	$1.13
17	5:00	$0.50	$2.50
18	10:25	$0.75	$7.81
19	8:25	$0.75	$6.31
20	3:00	$0.50	$1.50
21		Total	$30.31

Figure 11.11

The formula =(EndTime − StartTime)*24 used to compute elapsed time will fail if EndTime is less than StartTime. For example, if the event began at 9:00 p.m. (StartTime) and was complete at 2:00 a.m. the next day we will get a negative value. To compensate for this we can modify the formula to read =((EndTime − StartTime) + (EndTime < StartTime)) * 24. The comparison term will evaluate to 1 or 0 so it will add the required 24 hours when needed.

Exercise 9: Time Allocation

When you work on several projects or clients in the course of a day, the times may need to be allocated different cost centres. We will learn how to do this with a pivot table. For the sake of brevity we shall use a small data set.

	A	B	C	D	E	F	G	H	I	J	K	L
1	Day	Project	Start	End	Time		Sum of Time	Project				
2	Monday	A	8:30	11:00	2:30		Day	A	B	C	D	Grand Total
3	Monday	C	11:00	11:45	0:45		Monday	3:45	3:00	0:45		7:30
4	Monday	B	13:00	16:00	3:00		Tuesday			4:00	3:30	7:30
5	Monday	A	16:00	17:15	1:15		Wednesday	1:15	0:45	1:45	3:00	6:45
6	Tuesday	D	8:30	12:00	3:30		Thursday	3:30	1:00		2:15	6:45
7	Tuesday	C	13:00	17:00	4:00		Friday	4:00			3:00	7:00
8	Wednesday	D	9:00	10:00	1:00		Grand Total	12:30	4:45	6:30	11:45	35:30
9	Wednesday	A	10:00	11:15	1:15							
10	Wednesday	B	11:15	12:00	0:45							
11	Wednesday	D	13:30	15:30	2:00							
12	Wednesday	C	15:30	17:15	1:45							
13	Thursday	D	9:00	11:15	2:15							
14	Thursday	B	11:15	12:15	1:00							
15	Thursday	A	13:30	17:00	3:30							
16	Friday	A	8:00	12:00	4:00							
17	Friday	D	13:00	16:00	3:00							

Figure 11.12

(a) On Sheet8 of CHAP11.XLS, enter the data shown in A1:E17 of Figure 11.12 after formatting C2:D17 with the Custom format *h:mm*. Times before noon may be entered as 8: or 8:30 for 8:00 AM and 8:30 AM, respectively. Times after noon must either use the PM suffix or the 24 hour clock. So, for example, 4 PM may be entered as 16:, 4:0 PM or 4:0 pm.

(b) The formula in E2 is =D2−C2. This cell should also be formatted as *h:mm* and copied down to E17.

(c) Select A1:E17. Use the command Data|PivotTable to construct the pivot table in the manner described in Chapter 10. In step 3 it will be necessary to specify that you require the Sum of Time. Use the Custom format *[h]:mm* on the results in the table. The square bracket around the 'h' allows for time summations exceeding 12 hours.

(d) Save the workbook.

The pivot table shows how much time was spent on each project during the week.

Summary

The secret to success in working with dates and times is remembering that Microsoft Excel *stores* dates and times using a serial number system, and *displays* the values in appropriate format. Midnight on the first day of the year 2000 has the serial number 36526 — the number of days since 1-Jan-1900 when allowance is made for the Excel error of treating 1900 as a leap year. We can display this date in a variety of formats (1-Jan, 1-Jan-00, January 1, 2000, etc.).

If you enter =NOW() at noon on the first day of 2010 in A1, that cell will have the value 40179.50. The fractional part of the number represents the time on a 24-h clock. Time, on its own, is stored as a value from 0 to 23.99999... representing midnight to a fraction of a second before midnight the next day. Consequently, if two cells contain time values and you need the lapsed time, the difference must be multiplied by 24.

There are a number of worksheet functions for working with dates and times. You should be familiar with NOW, TODAY, DATE, YEAR, MONTH, DAY, WEEKDAY. Take care using WEEKNUM if you wish to comply with the ISO definitions. The undocumented DATEDIF function is very useful. Many Excel experts wonder why Microsoft chose not to implement it fully. We saw one use of TIMEVALUE. You may wish to click on the Insert Functions tool and look at all the date and time functions.

The Y2K problem is now a thing of the past but if you are working with historical data, take care when displaying dates with only two digits in the year.

Problems

1.* The formula = 10/Jan/99-1/Jan/99 results in the error value #NAME?. Explain why.

2. What error results from the formula 1-Jan-99 - 10-Jan-99?

3.* Cell A1 contains a serial number for a date. (i) What formula would you use to find the date 2 years from that in A1? (ii) What formula would you use to find the last day of the year following that represented by A1?

4.* In Canada, Victoria Day is celebrated the Monday of, or preceding, 24 May. Assuming there is a cell in your worksheet named *year*, what formula will give you the date for this holiday?

5. Visit the Web site *http://www.HolidayFestival.com* to locate a list of the rules for the dates of the holidays in your country, province or state. Add these to the worksheet developed in Exercise 5.

6. Construct a worksheet similar to that in Figure 11.14. Cell E3 uses =DATE(year, month, day). Cell E2 computes the week number of that data using the simple Excel formula with weeks beginning on Monday. Cell E3 uses the formula for the week number that is in accord with the ISO definition as given in When in Rome...

   The web site of Chip Pearson (www.cpearson.com) will help you check your results.

	A	B	C	D	E
1	year	2005		date	Jan 10, 2005
2	month	1		Excel	3
3	day	10		ISO	2

Figure 11.14

12 Report Writing

Objectives

In this chapter we learn how to place Microsoft Excel workbook data and charts into word processor or presentation documents. There are two very different ways to do this: (a) using copy and paste, or (b) with Object Linking and Embedding (OLE). Alternatively, you may copy your data or chart as a picture. We will examine these methods and their respective merits in the Exercises.

Exercise 1: Copy and Paste

In this exercise we will copy some data from a Microsoft Excel workbook to a document you are writing with a word processor application such as Microsoft Word. In Exercise 2 of Chapter 5 we developed a worksheet to compare two plans for salary increases. For the current exercise let us assume that you are submitting a report on this topic and need the results from the worksheet. We will see that a simple copy in Excel and paste in Word will generate a table which is indistinguishable from a table created in Word in the first place.

Other applications: The instructions in these Exercises are for Microsoft Word. However, one can obtain very similar results in other word processors such as Corel WordPerfect and Lotus Word Pro. If an instruction fails in one of these applications, use Edit|Paste Special rather than Edit|Paste.

PowerPoint: Using the Paste tool in PowerPoint will not give you a table but an Excel OLE object as discussed in Exercise 5.

(a) Open Microsoft Word and begin a document with a heading and a few lines of text to simulate the report — see the workspace in Figure 12.1.

(b) Open CHAP5.XLS and move to Sheet2. Select A8:E17 and click on the Copy tool or use one of the shortcuts. You must leave the range selected as material sent to the Windows Clipboard from Excel remains there only while the 'ant track' is present and we do not wish to use the Office Clipboard for these exercises.

(c) Activate the Word application. Place the insertion point where you wish to insert the table and use the Paste tool. A table appears similar to the top of Figure 12.1. Note (i) how cells in the worksheet that had borders also have borders in the table, and (ii) that the characters in the table have the font that they had in the worksheet.

(d) Convince yourself that the object behaves just like a table created in Word. Add the word Totals in the bottom row. Use Table|Select Table, click on the Center Align tool and your table is centred on the page. Save the Word document as CHAP12.DOC.

(e) You may return to the workbook and deselect the range.

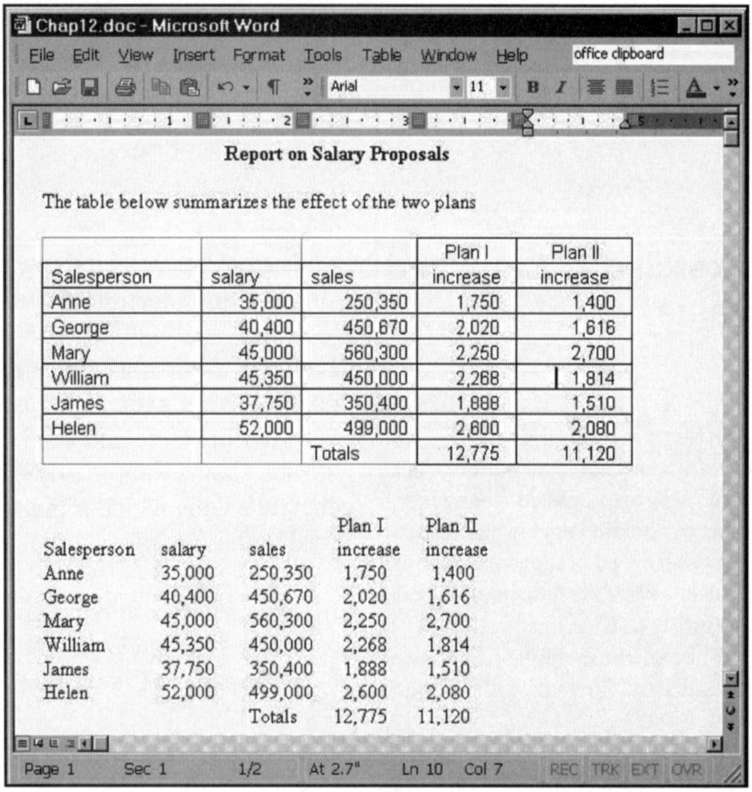

Report on Salary Proposals

The table below summarizes the effect of the two plans

			Plan I	Plan II
Salesperson	salary	sales	increase	increase
Anne	35,000	250,350	1,750	1,400
George	40,400	450,670	2,020	1,616
Mary	45,000	560,300	2,250	2,700
William	45,350	450,000	2,268	1,814
James	37,750	350,400	1,888	1,510
Helen	52,000	499,000	2,600	2,080
		Totals	12,775	11,120

			Plan I	Plan II
Salesperson	salary	sales	increase	increase
Anne	35,000	250,350	1,750	1,400
George	40,400	450,670	2,020	1,616
Mary	45,000	560,300	2,250	2,700
William	45,350	450,000	2,268	1,814
James	37,750	350,400	1,888	1,510
Helen	52,000	499,000	2,600	2,080
		Totals	12,775	11,120

Figure 12.1

Exercise 2: Copy and Paste Special

In Exercise 1 we pasted data from Excel to Word as a table. There are other options, one of which we explore in this exercise. At the end of this exercise we will have data in column form — see lower part of Figure 12.1.

(a) Open the two files CHAP12.DOC and CHAP5.XLS. Select the same worksheet range as before (A8:E16) and click on Copy.

(b) Move to the Word document. Use the command Edit|Paste Special. The resulting dialog box will be similar to Figure 12.2. The *Formatted Text* option is equivalent to a simple

Paste — the data is placed in a table and the font from Excel is preserved. We will use the *Unformatted Text* option which places the Excel material onto the Word document separating the data from each cell by a tab. You may need to tidy up the result using the [Tab] key to achieve a result similar to that in the lower part of Figure 12.1. Note that this time the font is the same whatever is current in the Word document.

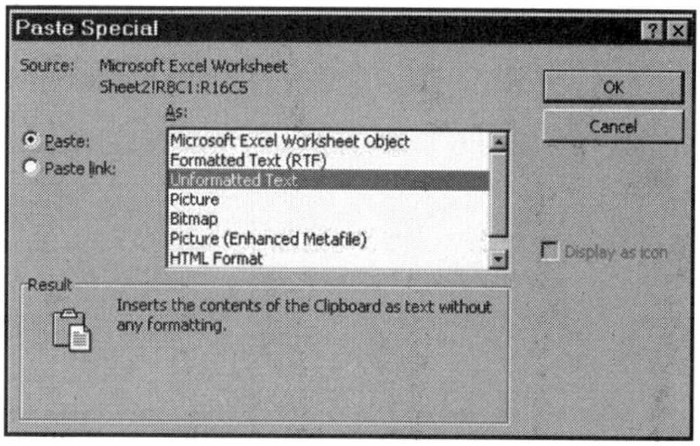

Figure 12.2

(c) For Word 2002 users only. Repeat the step needed to make the table in Exercise 1: select range in Excel and use Copy, then in Word use Paste. This time, open the Paste option smart tag and select *Keep Text Only.* The result will be to turn the table into the columnar data that we produced in step (b) in a slightly quicker way.

Exercise 3: A Picture is Worth a Thousand Words

In the first two exercises we copied data from a worksheet to a word processing document in such a way that the resulting material was in character form. In this exercise the resulting material will be in a picture form.

In Exercise 6 of Chapter 6 we found how to print a worksheet in such a way that the row and column heading would print. We saw that this could be useful for documentation. We continue the theme here and show how to get a picture of part of your worksheet into a Word document.

(a) Open CHAP5.XLS and with Sheet2 use File|Page Setup, open the Sheet tab and check *Row and Column Heading* in the *Print* area. Use Print Preview to confirm that the headers will show in a printout. Select the same worksheet range as before (A8:E16) and click on Copy.

(b) Open the CHAP12.DOC Word document. Use the command Edit|Paste Special. In the dialog box select *As Picture* or *As Picture (Enhanced Metafile)* — this can give a better result sometimes. The pasted picture will be similar to Figure 12.3. To confirm that this is indeed a picture, right click and use the item *Format Picture.* Resize the picture, add fill to the picture or change the layout. Open the Picture toolbar and put a border around the picture.

Edit | Paste Special as Picture

	A	B	C	D	E
8				Plan I	Plan II
9	Salesperson	salary	sales	increase	increase
10	Anne	35,000	250,350	1,750	1,400
11	George	40,400	450,670	2,020	1,616
12	Mary	45,000	560,300	2,250	2,700
13	William	45,350	450,000	2,268	1,814
14	James	37,750	350,400	1,888	1,510
15	Helen	52,000	499,000	2,600	2,080
16				12,775	11,120

Figure 12.3

Of course, it we had not set the Excel file to print row and column headers they would not appear in the picture. If you are documenting a worksheet recall that formulas may be displayed in Excel with Ctrl+~.

In this exercise we have placed textual material from Excel on the Clipboards and used Word to convert it to a picture. The same effect may be achieved by placing the Excel material in picture form on the Clipboard and doing a simple paste in Word. The 'secret' to this is, after selecting the range to be copied, hold down Shift before using the Edit command. If done correctly, the Edit menu will contain an item Copy Picture. The rest of the process is left for the reader to explore.

Exercise 4: Copying a Chart

As with data, when we copy an Excel chart to a Word document there are options: shall it be a picture or an object? We will make a picture. For this exercise, users of Word 2002 follow one route while users of earlier versions follow another.

(a) Open the Microsoft Excel workbook CHAP7.XLS. Select the chart on Sheet1 of the workbook and use the Copy tool.

(b) Open the Microsoft Word document CHAP12.DOC. Move to the bottom of the document.

(c) Users of Word 2002: use the simple Paste tool or command to get a picture of the chart onto your document. Open the Paste options smart tag and note the three choices: Picture, Excel chart (an embedded object) or Link (a liked object).

Other Word users: use Edit|Paste Special since a simple Paste would result in an embedded object. The dialog box will resemble that in Figure 12.2 except that, with the Paste radio button selected, only two choices appear in the list. Select the option *Picture (Enhanced Metafile)*.

Here is an alternative way that works in all Word versions.

(d) Select the chart on the worksheet. Hold down the [⇧ Shift] key and use the command Edit|Copy Picture.

(e) Move to the Word document and use the simple Paste command or the Paste tool.

Either of these methods may be used to copy a chart as a picture into a Microsoft PowerPoint presentation slide.

Exercise 5: Object Linking and Embedding

A detailed treatment of Object Linked Embedded (OLE) objects is beyond the scope of this book. However, we will briefly explain the difference between an embedded object and a linked one. We will do an exercise to get an idea of how to make an OLE object.

Within a Word document we may have an OLE Excel object. An embedded object is the easiest to think of. A simple analogy is an embassy. Within Canada's capital, Ottawa, there is an American embassy. Once you enter this property you are technically no longer in Canada but in USA territory. In the same way we may have within a Word document an area (we call it an object) that is associated with Excel and not with Word. The data in the Excel object is stored within the Word file.

Linking is similar but has an important difference. The embassy analogy breaks down. A linked Excel object in a Word document is a window into an Excel file. The data is stored in the Word file but is linked to the Excel file.

The advantage of OLE over simple copying or making a picture is that you may use all the Excel features to update the data and/or chart being displayed within the Word document.

(a) In the CHAP7.XLS workbook select the chart and click the Copy button.

(b) Move to Word, open CHAP12.DOC and with the insertion point at the end of the document, click the Paste button.

(c) Double click the chart. If you are new to OLE the result is unexpected. Although you are running a word processor, the part of the screen containing the chart now looks like Microsoft Excel. That is exactly what it is. The whole of your Excel workbook has been *embedded* in the document. If you save the document, the workbook is saved with it, not as a separate file but as part of the Word document file. You could give a copy of the file to a colleague and he/she could modify the workbook provided the file was used on a computer with Microsoft Excel installed.

(d) If you move around the sheet and then return to the document, what was a chart could now be part of the data. For this reason, if you use OLE it is better to use separate chart sheets in your workbooks.

Exercise 6: Embedding and Linking

When an object is linked as opposed to embedded, there is a separate Excel file. Suppose your Word document is a weekly report that uses data from an Excel file. Every Monday you open the Excel file and add new data. Then you open the Word document. You will be asked if you wish to update the link. When you reply positively, the Excel data in the Word document is brought up to date automatically.

Linking has certain advantages over embedding: (i) it is often easier to revise the workbook by opening it on its own, (ii) no matter what part of the workbook is active, the document displays the same data it did when the link was first established, and (iii) the document file size is not as large as with embedding.

This is a do-it-yourself exercise. We are near the end of the book and by now you do not need to be told every step. The task is to place a table and a chart from Excel (CHAP7.XLS) into Word as linked objects. You can then experiment with the results; change the Excel file and find how to update the Word document.

(a) In Excel, select the range or chart to be copied and use the Copy command, tool or shortcut.

(b) Word 2002 users: move to Word and use the Paste command, tool or shortcut. Open the Paste option smart tag and make the pasted item linked. With data you have the choice of keeping the original Excel formatting or using the Word document formatting.

Word 1997 and Word 2000 users: move to Word and use the Edit|Paste Special command. In the dialog box (Figure 12.2) there are the two radio buttons: *Paste* results in OLE embedding, *Paste Link* results in OLE linking. When copying data, in the *As* box select either *Formatted* or *Unformatted Text*.

(c) Return to the Excel file and change a value in the data. Activate the Word document and find how to update the data and chart.

Exercise 7: Creating an Equation

Notes: An applet is a small application which must be run from within another application.

The Equation Editor embeds an Equation Object in the host application file (Word, Excel, PowerPoint, etc.).

The Equation Editor is a third-party product licensed by Microsoft and other software vendors from MathType from whom you may obtain a more powerful version.

Microsoft provides an applet called Equation Editor which may be used in programs such as Word or Excel to create an equation. The author has found that more acceptable results are obtained if the equation is constructed in Word and copied to an Excel worksheet, if that is where it is needed. With a little practice and experimentation you will be able to create complex equations. In this exercise we create the expression below to get you started.

$$P = \sum_{t=1}^{N} \frac{C_t}{(1+r)^t}$$

(a) On a new page of CHAP12.DOC, use the command Insert|Object and select *Microsoft Equation 3*. The Equation Editor temporarily takes over the Word toolbars as shown in Figure 12.5. If you later edit your equation, the Equation Editor will open in its own window — Figure 12.6.

(b) Begin by typing *P*=. Note that you do not type any spaces; the applet looks after this unless you choose the *Text* style.

(c) To draw the summation symbol, click the mouse pointer over the fourth item on the bottom row of the Equation Editor toolbar. Move the pointer to the third item on the top row of the drop-down menu, since we need a symbol with two limits.

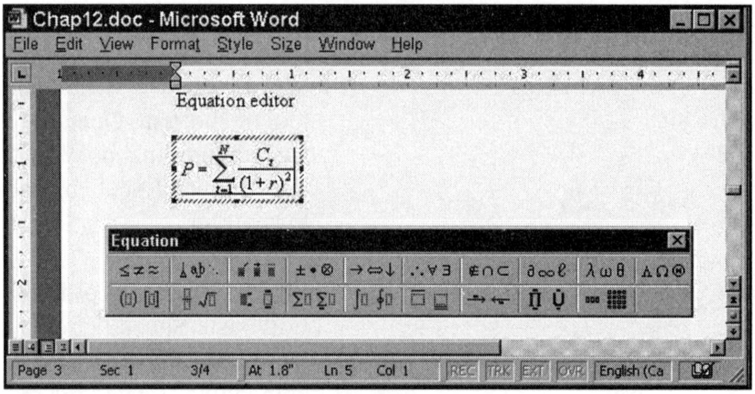

Figure 12.5

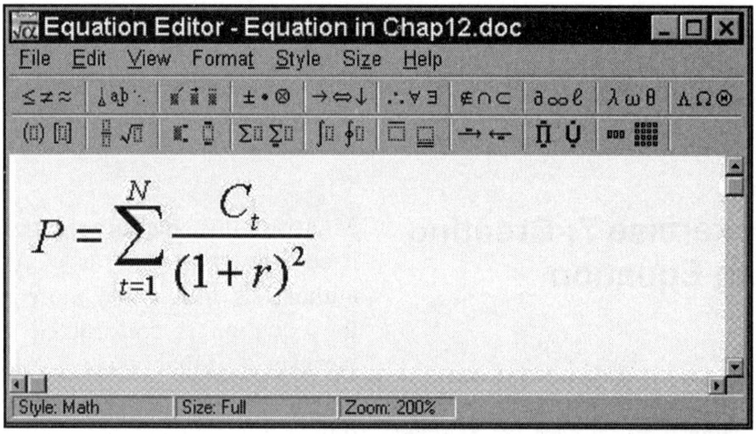

Figure 12.6

(d) Experiment by tapping the Tab key; hold down the Shift key and tap Tab. The L shape that moves around is the *insertion point*. When a box has something typed in it, the L is reversed. Now use the mouse to move the insertion point to the box which will hold the lower limit. In this box type t=1.

(e) Using either the mouse or Tab, move to the box where the upper limit will go and type N.

(f) Use Tab to move the insertion point into the box at the right of the $\sum$ symbol. Move the pointer to the second item on the bottom row of the toolbar and select the first item on the top row of the drop-down menu. This object has two open boxes stacked vertically with a bar between them. We need this for the fraction.

(g) Move the insertion point to the top box and type *C*. Now we need a subscript. Select the third item on the bottom row of the toolbar and from the drop-down menu, select the centre item of the top row. Move the insertion point to the subscript box and type *t* to give the numerator C_t.

(h) Move to the denominator (lower) box and type (1+*r*). The superscript is made in a manner similar to the subscript. Select the third item on the bottom row of the toolbar and from the drop-down menu, select the first item of the top row. Type *t* in the superscript box.

(i) Click the mouse anywhere outside the equation box to close the Equation Editor applet. Note that the equation is an embedded OLE object; it is in a Word document but is associated with the Equation Editor mini-application.

(j) Use a simple Copy and Paste to place this equation on a worksheet. This makes a new embedded OLE object. If the object looks transparent and lets the gridlines show through, you may to right click, open *Format Object*, and give the object a white fill. An alternative is to use Paste Special and generate a picture copy of the equation.

Exercise 8: Putting Microsoft Excel on a Web Page

It is possible to use the simple Copy and Paste technique to make a picture of some data or of a chart and place it on a Web page. But the result is a picture — it is static. However, with Excel 2000 and Excel 2002, we can create a Web page having a dynamic Excel worksheet. Your computer must have Microsoft Internet Explorer 4.01 or later installed to do this exercise.

We shall place part of Sheet7 of CHAP8.XLS on a Web page for this demonstration. When we make an interactive Excel area on a Web page, it is advisable to limit the cells that can be changed by the user. We do this by protecting the worksheet after unlocking the cells which the user may change.

(a) Open Sheet7 of CHAP8.XLS. Highlight B3:B5 and use the command Format|Cells|Protection and uncheck the *locked* box. Now protect the worksheet using Tools|Protection|Protect Workbook. There is no need to use a password.

A Web page is not normally kept on your desktop PC but is sent to a server. This is called *publishing*. For this demonstration we will keep the HTM document on the local PC.

(b) Use the command File|Save as Web Page. Click on the *Selection Sheet* radio button. Put a check mark in the *Add Interactivity* box. Finally, click the Save button to save the file as CHAP8.HTM. You may wish to save the HTM file in the same folder as your exercise workbooks.

(c) To view the result, open the folder where you saved the file. Click on CHAP8.HTM to open Internet Explorer. Figure 12.7 shows the Excel area within the Web page. Experiment by changing the values in B3:B5 on the Web page to see that a new payment value is computed. Since B6 was not unlocked, the user cannot tamper with the formula in it.

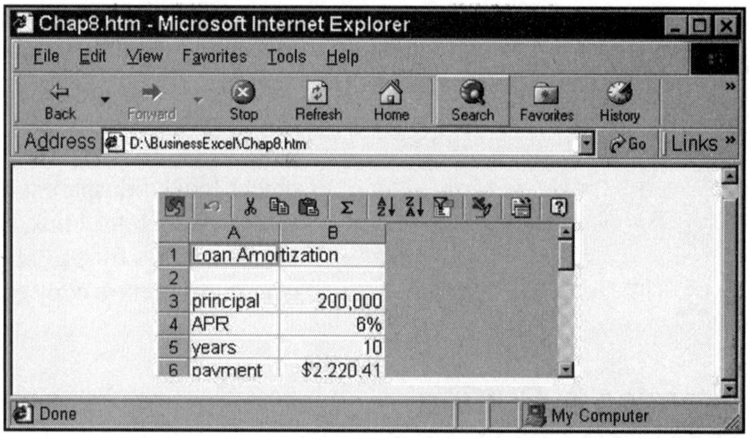

Figure 12.7

This looks a little stark. We may open the HTM file in any suitable editor (MS Word, MS FrontPage, etc.) to add our own material before and after the Excel area.

We did not get any charts into the Web page. Let us see how that is possible.

(d) Unprotect the worksheet and then protect it again, but this time in the Protect Sheet dialog box, uncheck the *Objects* box. This will let us select a chart from a protected sheet.

(e) With the top chart selected, use File|Save and indicate you want to save a chart with interactivity. Save the file as

CHAP8B.HTM. Open Internet Explorer to view the result.

There are many uses for this technique but you should be aware of the limitations. Some features are not supported. For example, formulas with nested functions are not supported. To learn more about this topic use the Content feature in Help and look under Web publishing.

Summary

Data and charts can be copied to other applications such as Word and Power Point. The simplest way is to make a picture. The Paste tool does not always make a picture, sometimes it creates an OLE object. We can use Edit|Paste Special to control what we create.

The two types of OLE objects have some important differences. When we paste a linked worksheet object on a Word document we have a gateway to Excel. An embedded worksheet object on a Word document converts an area within the Word document into Excel 'property'. The entire workbook is stored within the Word file. A linked object is stored in the Word document but what is stored may be updated when the original data is changed.

To keep a linked object up to date you need to have access to both the Word and the Excel file. With embedding you need to have access to only one file but it will be a large one!

The algorithm below will help you choose the appropriate method.

Are you sure that the workbook is complete?
- Yes: Use copy and paste.
- No: Will you always have access to workbook?
  - Yes: Use linking.
  - No: Use embedding.

When you edit an embedded Excel object it can be difficult to control the view in the Word document. If you inherit a Word document with this feature consider converting the Excel object to a workbook which can then be linked to your document. This can be done by right clicking the object and selecting the *Convert* item.

Things can go wrong when linking and embedding. Experiment with unimportant files. When working with production files, keep backup copies!

This chapter has shown how to copy from Excel to Word. We may do the converse to add textual material to a worksheet. We may also embed or link from Word to Excel. It should also be noted that, whereas the chapter discusses the Microsoft products Word and PowerPoint, these techniques can also be used with other applications such as Corel's WordPerfect and Presentation.

Excel 2000 and Excel 2002 allow us to create Web pages with areas of interactive Excel data and charts. These can be viewed only with Internet Explorer so are useful for Intranet but not Internet applications.

Appendix A
Microsoft Excel Add-Ins

When you instal Microsoft Excel, alone or as part of Microsoft Office, you may specify which of the various optional parts are to be copied to your hard drive. If you wish to use Solver and the various worksheet functions and features that require the Analysis ToolPak you should select them during the initial or subsequent installation. When you are selecting Excel components you will get a dialog box similar to that in Figure A.1.

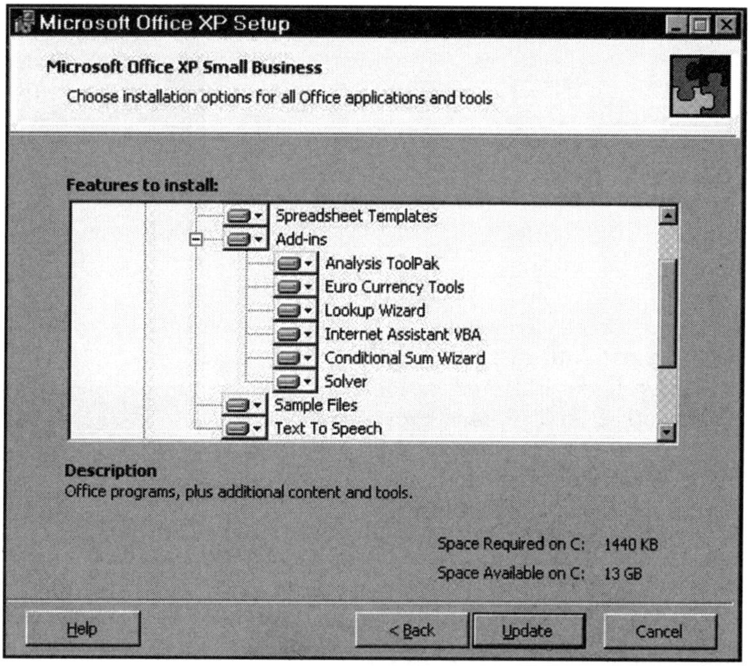

Figure A.1

When you click on an Add-In, a list of possible options (Figure A.2) appears. You can see that with the PC used to make Figure A.1, each Add-In had the icon that specifies that these items were to be installed on the computer.

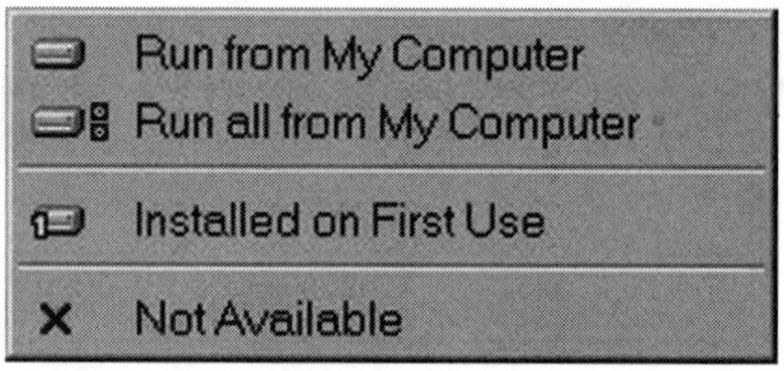

Figure A.2

The installation process copies the required files to your hard drive. When the installation is complete, you need to use the command Tools|Add-Ins to request that the features be loaded every time you start Excel. Figure A.3 shows the Add-Ins dialog box.

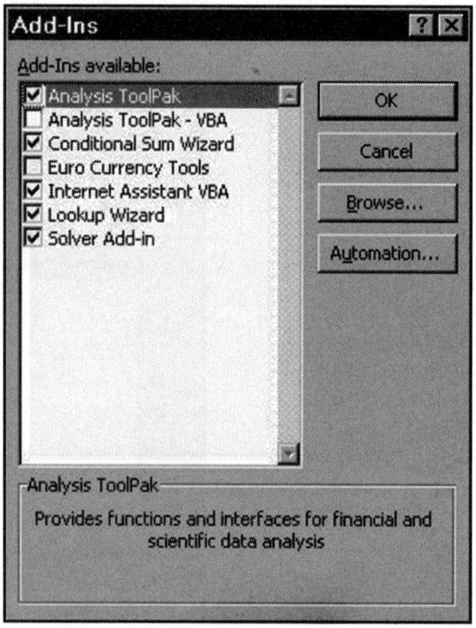

Figure A.2

Third-party Add-Ins: A number of third parties market Add-Ins for Microsoft Excel. Some Excel experts provide them free on the Web. If you receive a file with the extension XLA, place it in a folder and use Tools|Add-Ins to have the new Add-In loaded. Unless you stored the file in the same folder that Microsoft places its Add-Ins (for Office XP this is Program Files\Microsoft Office\Office10\Library), you will need to use the Browse button to locate the file. You may find that Excel takes a long time to load when you have a large number of selected Add-Ins.

So what steps should you take if you find that Solver or one of the Analysis ToolPak features is not present? The answer is to use the above process in reverse. First use Tools|Add-Ins to see if the item was installed but not selected for automatic loading. If it is present in the Add-Ins dialog box, put a check mark in the appropriate box. If it is not present, you need to reinstall Microsoft Excel from the CD-ROM using Add/Remove on the SetUp menu. Click on Excel, then on Change Options to bring up a dialog box similar to Figure A.1. Again, use Tools|Add-Ins when Excel is started.

Appendix B
Answers to Problems

Chapter 2

1. The formulas are:
   D4: =B4*C4
   F4: =D4*10%
   G4: =F4+E4
   H4: =D4-G4
   D10 =D4+D5+D6+D7+D8+D9

2. Formula in E4 is =(A4+(B4-C4)/D4)/((C4+B4)/2). All the parentheses are required. The cell E4 is formatted to display a percentage.

Chapter 3

2. The formula in B10 is =B$5 +$A10* B$6/1000. The best site depends upon the production figure.

Chapter 4

2. The function is called AVERAGE not AVG.

5. No error value will be displayed. The cell will display the value zero but the status bar will display *Circular: A10* since the function refers to its own cell. Excel 97/2000 will also display a blue dot in A10 with the Circular Reference toolbar when the formula is first entered.

6. You need to compare the two prizes at the same point in time. The easiest is the present time since the present value of the first prize is £100,000. In A1 enter =PV(8%/12, 20*12, 1000) to find the present value of the second prize.

7. =SUM(A1:A100)-(LARGE(A1:A100,1)+LARGE(A1:A100,2)+LARGE(A1:A100,3)+SMALL(A1:A100,1)+SMALL(A1:A100,2)+SMALL(A1:A100,3)).

8. George has forgotten about the order of precedence of operators. The formula should be =9000/(12000+15000).

9. Simple rounding is not enough since this could result in too few people. There are a number of possible solutions including: (i) =CEILING(SUM(A1:A100,1)), (ii) = ROUNDUP(SUM(A1:A100), 0) and (iii) =INT(SUM(A1:100) + 0.5). Note

that whereas the second argument in ROUNDUP specifies the number of decimal places, in CEILING it specifies the multiple to which you wish to round.

Chapter 5

1. One possible formula is:
=IF(A2>=5000, A, IF(A2>=4000, B, IF(A2>=3000, C, IF(A2>=2000, D, E))))

2. We could, of course, use one of: =IF(B2<=20000, B2*1.1, B2) or =IF(B2>20000, B2, B2*1.1). But do we really need the IF function? The comparison operators on their own are quite powerful. So this also works: =B2+B2*10%*(B2<=20000). The quantity in parentheses evaluates to either 1 or 0 depending on the value of B2.

4. One possible formula is:
=INDEX({E,D,C,B,A},1,MATCH(A2,{0,2000,3000,4000,5000},1))

Chapter 8

1. C8: =IF(B8=0,,B8*(1+(Rate*(Term-A8))/12)); copy this down to row 20
F9: =IF(E9>Term,0,MIN($H$8:H8)*Rate/12); copy this down to row 20

Or, to indicate entries have been made for invalid months
C8: =IF(B8=0,,IF(A8>Term,Error,B8*(1+(Rate*(Term-A8))/12)))
F9: =IF(E9>Term,IF(G9>0,Error,0),MIN($H$8:H8)*Rate/12)

3. B12: =IF(A12>Lifetime, 0, SLN(Cost, Residual, Lifetime))
B28: =IF(A28>Lifetime, 0, DDB(Cost, Residual, Lifetime, A28, 2))
The last argument (the value of 2) is optional.
B44: =IF(A44>Lifetime, 0, SYD(Cost, Residual, Lifetime, A44))

4. If the DDB and SLN functions are not used:
B11: =IF(A11>Lifetime, 0, IF(F10 - Double*F10>Residual, Double * F10, F10 - Residual))
When the residual value is zero, the DDB value will never bring the book value to zero, hence it can never make it negative. So we could simplify the formula in B11 to =IF(A11>Lifetime, 0, Double * F10)
C11: =IF(A11>Lifetime, 0, F10 / (Lifetime - A11 + 1))
D11: =IF(A11>Lifetime, , IF(B11>C11, DDB, SL))
E11: =IF(A11>Lifetime, 0, E10 + MAX(B11:C11))

F11: =IF(E11>0, Cost - E11,)

If the DDB and SLN functions are used:
B11: =IF(A43>Lifetime, 0, DDB(Cost, Residual, Lifetime, A43))
C11: =IF(A43>Lifetime,0,SLN(F42,Residual,Lifetime-A43+1))
The other formulas are as above. Note that the DDB function gives a value of 518 in the last year rather than 432 as shown in the figure. This is because the worksheet function automatically switched to the SL method in the last year.

Chapter 9

2. The formula needed in C4 is
   =Coupon*(1-1/(1+Yield)^Maturity)/Yield+Face_value/(1+Yield)^Maturity
   Both Goal Seek and Solver report a yield of 9.00% when the price is £955.14.

Chapter 10

1. There is a feature in the Options dialog that controls which totals are reported. Click on the Options button in Step 4 (see Figure 10.13) to open the Options dialog box.

2. Right click on any of the numeric data cells in the pivot table, select the Field ... item to open the PivotTable Field dialog box (see Figure 10.15) in which you can specify Count, Sum, Average, etc.

Chapter 11

1. The slash separators have been interpreted as the division operator and, hence, the words *Jan* have been mistaken for cell names. If hyphens are used as separators in the dates, Excel treats them as substation operators and the same error occurs. The workaround is to use =DATEVALUE(10-Jan-99) - DATEVALUE(1-Jan-99).

3. (i) Do not use =A1+365*2 because of a possible leap year problem but use =DATE(YEAR(A1)+2, MONTH(A1), Day(A1)).
   (ii) Use either =DATE(YEAR(A1)+2, 1,1)-1 or =DATE(YEAR(A2)+2,1,0).

4. The date of Victoria Day is given by:
   =DATE(Year,5,24) - CHOOSE(WEEKDAY(DATE(Year,5,24)),6,0,1,2,3,4,5).

Index